**What you should know
about the
Value Added Tax**

Cambridge Research Institute is a leading management consulting firm engaged in assisting management in strategic planning and decision-making . . . and in adapting to fundamental changes in economic, governmental, technological, social, and business environments.

What you should know about the
Value Added Tax

DAN THROOP SMITH
JAMES B. WEBBER
CAROL M. CERF

for

Cambridge Research Institute

 1973

DOW JONES-IRWIN, INC. Homewood, Illinois 60430

First Printing, May 1973

ISBN 0-87094-054-6
Library of Congress Catalog Card No. 73–77024
Printed in the United States of America

Contents

Chapter 3
POSSIBLE CHARACTERISTICS OF A VALUE ADDED TAX IN THE UNITED

List of exhibits

_____

* Impact on industries with various characteristics.

---

* Impact on industries with various characteristics.

Foreword

ALTHOUGH no specific proposal has been made for the imposition of a VAT in the United States, it has been mentioned with increasing frequency as a possible new source of revenue or as a substitute for other taxes considered too burdensome at present. Future tax reform must also take into account the proper balance of Federal taxes on income, capital, and consumption. The rapid spread of the tax in Europe must also be examined for its implications on the U.S. competitive position in view of the vital role of expanding world trade. It should be a matter of concern that business bears a lesser share of the cost of government abroad as a result of fiscal policies employing the use of a VAT.

There appears to be a general lack of understanding in the business community about the VAT. This is in part attributable to the fact that it is difficult to talk about the tax in the abstract because the problems arising from its adoption depend largely on what taxes, if any, are replaced. The incidence and impact of the tax would be quite different if it supplanted the employment taxes, for example, as compared with the corporate income tax. In concept, however, the VAT itself has certain advantages and deficiencies which must be properly evaluated in considering the future tax policy in the United States.

The discussions to date relating to VAT have been characterized as largely disappointing by a prominent Treasury official. Proponents frequently exaggerate the balance of payments assistance while those against the tax see it as a regressive impost on consumers. It is, of course, difficult to be enthusiastic about any form of taxation but the piper must be paid and taxpayers should at least request the tune. Accordingly, it is essential that business executives, professional tax advisors, and governmental experts interested in tax policy understand the impact of a VAT on the entire economy and its industrial and financial components.

To this end, the authors of the current study have succinctly analyzed the VAT path taken by others and its possible characteristics if introduced in the United States. No more important contribution could be made at the present time to an intelligent appraisal of future tax policy.

New York, New York   B. KENNETH SANDEN
April 1973

Preface

THIS ANALYSIS has been prepared by the Cambridge Research Institute out of a conviction that business executives and others concerned with the workings of the American economic system are increasingly concerned with understanding the future consequences of current planning and decision making in business and government. One area of concern seems to be tax policy. A much discussed potential new element of tax policy in the United States is the Value Added Tax (VAT). The VAT, common to a number of industrialized nations, has been under consideration for adoption at the national level, as well as by several of the states.

In these pages, a way of examining future consequences of a VAT for the American economy broadly, and for individual industries and business concerns, is set forth by the professional staff of the Cambridge Research Institute.

Although this analysis may be of collateral interest to economists, it is primarily oriented to the point of view of business planners and decision makers, and thus employs concepts, analytical approaches, and language consistent with a "report to management." As to whether a VAT is "good" or "bad" for the country, for business in general, or for any particular business concern is left to the reader to determine.

Appreciation is extended to the American Retail Federation for giving CRI people the opportunity to try out their ideas on them. The Federation sponsored an earlier study undertaken by Cambridge Research Institute, entitled *The Value-Added Tax in the United States—Its Implications for Retailers.*

The present analysis owes its existence principally to James B. Webber and Dan Throop Smith, directors of Cambridge Research Institute, and Carol M. Cerf, a member of the Institute's professional staff. Others at Cambridge Research Institute made key contributions as well.

April 1973

GERALD A. SIMON
Managing Director
Cambridge Research Institute

Introduction

THE Value Added Tax (VAT) has become a major form of taxation in Europe. The European Economic Community (The Common Market) requires that its members have such a tax. The Scandinavian countries have all introduced a VAT, and many other European countries are following suit. Where it has been adopted, the VAT raises substantial revenues. It is responsible for 40 percent of all tax revenues in France and Norway and for 20 to 25 percent of all tax revenues in Denmark, West Germany, and the Netherlands.

A VAT is presumed to give a country an advantage in international trade since, under GATT rules, exports can be exempt from it while they cannot be exempt from such taxes as the corporate income tax. This is one reason the United States, in view of its balance of payments deficit, has shown a growing interest in following Europe's precedent and adopting a VAT.

A VAT was first thought of in the United States as a replacement for part of the corporate income tax. Later it came to be considered as the principal source for additional revenue if expenditures ran ahead of receipts from existing taxes. In early 1972 President Nixon suggested the possibility of a VAT as a replacement for that portion of residential property taxes used to finance schools. This suggestion followed decisions in some state courts declaring the present system of school financing, with its heavy reliance on local property taxation, to be in violation of the equal protection clause of the U.S. Constitution. Use of a federal VAT for school finance would meet the combined objective of greater federal assumption of education expenses and relief of a form of local taxation which has become subject to heavy criticism.

The issue of school financing and revenue sharing, as well as the probable scale of total government spending, were controversial and unsettled at the start of 1973. No specific VAT proposal had been submitted to Congress. Prior to such a submission, there can be no great assurance about the form which a VAT would take in the United States. In view of the probable need for additional federal revenue,

1

however, it seems likely that a VAT of some sort will eventually be introduced in this country, if not in 1973 then at some time in the next decade.

In 1970 the Cambridge Research Institute conducted, on behalf of the American Retail Federation, an analysis of the possible impact of a VAT on retailing. This original analysis has now been brought up to date and broadened to consider the implications of a VAT for all segments of U.S. business. This study is designed to assist corporate management in understanding the tax and its likely impact on the U.S. economy as a whole, on their particular industries, and on their individual companies. With these data, members of corporate management can make some judgment about whether a VAT would be a better—or, more precisely, a less bad— way of raising revenues than the possible alternatives. And, if a VAT should be seriously considered by Congress, this study should help corporate management determine which of the detailed provisions of a VAT would be preferable from the point of view of their own industries and companies.

The study begins with some essential background material on the exact nature and possible variations of a VAT and on the character and effect of existing VAT's in Europe. On the basis of the theory and history of the VAT, some guesses are then made about the likely characteristics of a U.S. VAT. This background material is used to analyze the likely impact of such a U.S. VAT (versus various revenue alternatives), first on the country as a whole, and then on particular industries and companies. The final chapter indicates how the reader can use the analysis in the study to judge for himself whether he as an individual or as a representative of some business should support a VAT in the United States, whether he should only support a VAT with certain provisions, or whether he should oppose a VAT under all circumstances.

1

Characteristics of
Value Added Taxation

THE concept and characteristics of a Value Added Tax (VAT) must be understood before an analysis can be made of the issues concerning such a tax in the United States.

Definition of Value Added Taxation

The VAT is a tax on the value added by a firm to its products in the course of its operations. Value added can be viewed either as the difference between a firm's sales and its purchases during an accounting period or as the sum of its wages, profits, rent, interest, and other payments not subject to the tax during that period. In normal practice, however, the tax is calculated from sales and purchase figures, rather than by adding together wages, profits, rent, and interest. The VAT in effect becomes a tax on a firm's sales against which the firm receives a credit for the VAT paid on its purchases.

Calculation of the VAT at the retail level

The calculation of a VAT for a retailer is illustrated in Exhibit 1–1. In this simplified case, purchases are assumed to be equal to the cost of goods sold. With sales of $900 and purchases of $600, the value added is $300 (which in this case is also the gross margin). Note that the value added may also be obtained by adding the $200 in wages, rent, etc. to the $100 in pretax profit.

In Exhibit 1–1 the VAT is calculated by applying the tax rate (assumed to be 3 percent in this example) to the sales figure of $900. The total tax collected on sales is $27. From this amount a credit of $18, equal to the VAT paid on purchases, is allowed. The net tax due to the government at the retail stage is the difference between collections and credits, or $9. The crediting of the VAT paid on purchases against the VAT payable on sales is one of the basic features of this tax. It distin-

EXHIBIT 1–1
Calculation of the Value Added Tax at the retail stage

	Items without VAT		*Value Added Tax calculated at 3%*
Sales..	$900	+ $27	VAT due on sales
Less purchases (assumed equal to cost of goods sold).......................	600	− 18	VAT credit on purchases
Value added (or gross margin)..........	$300	$ 9	Net VAT due
Less labor costs, rent, etc...............	200		
Profit before tax.............................	$100		

guishes a VAT from a turnover tax in which each stage of production pays a tax without reference to taxes paid at prior stages.

Subtraction/tax credit (or invoice) method of calculating VAT

As was noted earlier, the value added by a firm can be calculated either by subtracting its purchases from its sales (subtraction method) or by adding its wages, rent, interest, and profits (addition method). In calculating the tax on value added, the subtraction method, particularly its refinement, the subtraction/tax credit method shown above, is used almost exclusively in actual practice. The addition method allows for little or no differentiation among a company's various products, and this can be a serious problem if different products are taxed at different rates or if certain products are exempt from the tax. The addition method also raises problems about what items should be included in the "value added"; for example, should a firm's charitable contributions be included and how should depreciation of capital assets be treated?

As illustrated above, the subtraction/tax credit or invoice method starts by multiplying the firm's sales by the tax rate. Deducted from this total is the amount of tax which the invoices from the firm's suppliers indicate was paid by the suppliers and presumably included in the price of goods and services purchased by the firm. The net difference between the tax on sales and the tax already paid with purchases is the tax due. The subtraction/tax credit method is the one used in European countries to compute the Value Added Tax. Among other advantages, this method assures that the VAT rate applied at the final stage becomes the effective rate for all earlier stages. This can be of concern where there is more than one VAT rate.

Another form of the subtraction technique is the subtraction/accounts or calculation method, where the tax rate is applied to the difference between sales and purchases. In our previous example, purchases ($600) would be subtracted from sales ($900) to arrive at the tax base of $300. Then the tax rate of 3 percent would be applied to find tax due of $9. While in theory this method is simple, in reality multiple rates and exemptions make its bookkeeping overly complex, because not only sales but also purchases must be classified according to the various tax rates. Furthermore, the accounts method makes it more difficult to compute the VAT rebates which are normally given on exports. However, with a single-rate VAT with almost no exemptions, the accounts method might require less paper work than the tax credit method since the VAT would not have to be listed separately on each invoice for administration of the tax. A company could simply deduct a prescribed percentage of the price paid for purchases to arrive at the VAT-exclusive purchase price. Of course, if the VAT were not indicated on the invoices, the tax would lose some of its self-policing features, for purchasers would then not know — or even care — whether their suppliers had paid the proper VAT.

Calculation of the VAT including wholesaler and manufacturer

To show further how a VAT is calculated throughout the chain of production and distribution, the simplified retail example in Exhibit 1–1 has been extended in Exhibit 1–2 to include the manufacturer and the wholesaler. First the multistage transactions are traced without a VAT. Then the exhibit shows the tax calculation (using the subtraction/tax credit method), the net VAT due at each stage, and the cumulative VAT collection by the government. The manufacturer charges an addi-

EXHIBIT 1–2
Calculation of the Value Added Tax*

	Without tax	Effect of 3% Value Added Tax		
		Tax calculation	Net VAT due at each stage	Cumulative VAT due to the government
Manufacturer:				
Sales	$500	$15		
Less purchases from other firms....................................	0†	0		
Gross margin (or value added)	$500	+ $15	$ 15	
Less labor costs, rent, etc............	400			
Profit..	$100			$15
Wholesaler:				
Sales	$600	$18		
Less cost of goods sold‡	500	− 15		
Gross margin (or value added)	$100	$ 3	$ 3	
Less labor costs, rent, etc............	50			
Profit..	$ 50			$18
Retailer:				
Sales	$900	$27		
Less cost of goods sold‡	600	− 18		
Gross margin (or value added)	$300	$ 9	$ 9	
Less labor costs, rent, etc............	200			
Profit..	$100			$27
Price to consumer:......................	$900	+ $27	=	$927
Total value added	$900			$900

*This exhibit assumes full pass forward of the tax at all levels. Therefore, in this example, the VAT does not affect profits.
†For purposes of this example, assumed to be zero.
‡In this simplified exhibit, purchases are assumed to be equal to cost of goods sold.

tional $15 (3 percent of $500) on his sales to the wholesaler to cover the VAT he owes. The wholesaler charges $18 (3 percent of $600) on his sales to the retailer who, in turn, charges $27 VAT on his sales to the consumer. The actual tax due at any one stage is the VAT on sales at that stage minus the VAT paid on purchases at the same stage. The total VAT collected by the government is the sum of the VAT collected at each stage ($15 + $3 + $9 = $27). The arrows in the first column of Exhibit 1–2 indicate how sales are made from the manufacturer to the wholesaler to the retailer. In the second column, they show how the amount of VAT paid on purchases is deducted by each firm from the VAT due on sales.

When a VAT is fully passed forward, the net effect on profits is zero at each stage because the entire tax burden falls on the consumer. In our example, the consumer paid $900 without a VAT and $927 with a VAT; the $27 difference in price equals the amount of tax collected by the government.

Different types of the VAT: Consumption, income, gross product

In our examples we have assumed that purchases for a period are equal to the cost of goods sold during that period. We have also ignored the treatment of capital assets. The alternative methods of treating purchases of capital assets distinguish the three different types of VAT—the consumption type, the income type, and the gross product type.

Under the *consumption type,* the VAT paid on all purchases in a period, including capital assets, is deductible from the VAT due on sales during that period. This is the accepted approach in Europe and is considered to be the one most likely to be adopted in the United States. It is simple because it allows all purchases to be treated alike. Of the several types of the VAT, the consumption type is the only one which avoids any tax deterrent to capital purchases. The economic base of this type of VAT is total private consumption.

Under the *income type,* the VAT paid on purchases of capital assets is amortized over the life of the assets and credited against the VAT due on sales for the successive periods. This VAT is designated the "income type" because its economic base is net national income, that is, consumption plus investment minus depreciation.

Under the *gross product type,* no deduction for the VAT on purchases of capital assets—either immediate or by amortization—is allowed. The economic base of this VAT is the gross national product, that is, consumption plus investment.

VAT and the retail sales tax

Most American businessmen are familiar with the retail sales tax. The VAT has much in common with it. Both are regarded as taxes on private domestic consumption. Generally the burden of both falls ultimately on the consumer even though the item taxed is retail sales in the one case and value added by businesses in the other. Both are indirect taxes in that they are not paid by consumers directly to the government. If exemptions and rates were the same, both tax systems would yield substantially equal revenue to the federal government.

The VAT is collected in installments at every stage in the production-distribution process, whereas the retail sales tax is collected in full at a single stage. Because of this, a VAT system involves many more tax returns than a retail sales tax. At the same time, as we shall see, collection at every stage has certain enforcement advantages.

A VAT tends to cover the service sector of the economy much more broadly than do most state retail sales taxes in the United States. This has been regarded as one of the several advantages of the VAT in Europe.

The consumption type of VAT with its crediting system provides a desirable way of avoiding a tax deterrent to capital expenditures. The experience with state retail sales taxes in this regard is mixed. Studies in Texas, California, and New York City indicated that 35 percent, 30 percent, and 28 percent respectively of sales tax revenues were derived from sales of business machines.[1]

When purchases for business purposes are exempt from retail sales taxes, the retailer has the problem of identifying commercial customers and determining whether the future use of the purchased item is such as to exempt the item from the sales tax. There is no such problem with the VAT. With this tax it is necessary only to provide customers with an invoice in which the amount added by the tax is clearly identified; then the commercial customer can simply deduct his VAT payment from the total tax he owes the government.

Self-policing features of a VAT

A VAT has unusual self-policing aspects because of its multistage and purchase credit features. The manufacturer (or wholesaler) collects the VAT on his sales and then pays the government this amount minus the VAT paid on his purchases — the VAT on both sales and purchases being based on traceable invoices. His customer, the wholesaler (or the retailer), has an interest in ensuring that the amount of VAT charged by the supplier is correct, for he, in turn, uses this amount as a credit against his taxes. The government can inspect the invoices from the manufacturer to the wholesaler and from the wholesaler to the retailer as a means of checking the manufacturer's and the wholesaler's compliance.[2] At the retail level, compliance on sales collections can be checked from the sales figures in income tax returns. However, any slippage in VAT collections is most likely to occur at the retail level. In

---

[1] Richard W. Lindholm, "Integrating a Federal Value Added Tax with State and Local Sales Levies," *National Tax Journal,* September 1971, p. 404.

[2] Some ingenious Frenchmen, however, did find a way to evade the VAT by creating false invoices, showing a VAT had been paid on nonexistent purchases. See "Value-Tax Fraud Curbed in France," *The New York Times,* January 15, 1972. In some countries businessmen also contrive to make purchases for their personal use and let the firm collect the VAT credit for the purchase.

France and Belgium particularly, retailers sometimes underreport their sales in order to reduce their VAT liability.

Adjustments to a single-rate, universally applied VAT system

Although tax authorities endorse the principle of a single-rate, universally applied VAT over other forms of the tax, we find that virtually all existing VAT systems employ at least one of the following adjustments: specified exemptions from the tax, multiple rates applicable to different categories of goods, and other devices such as a reduced tax base on certain goods. The reasons for these adjustments center around the historical pattern of taxation in the particular country, the social, political, and economic forces extant at the time of adoption, the meshing of VAT adoption with revision of other forms of taxation, and administrative factors.

Benefiting from the experience of others, countries that have lately adopted the VAT have generally tried to make their plans simpler than those of their predecessors. For example, Sweden adopted a VAT in 1969 using a single rate with few exemptions, whereas France, when it pioneered the tax in 1955, used four rates and nine categories of exemptions.

Exemptions. Exemptions can be based on classes of products, classes of services, classes of taxpayers, and stages in the production-distribution process. The following types of adjustments may be made, for all of which there are examples from the European experience:

a) Exemption of exported products at the point of export is universal in Europe.

b) Although exemption of classes of products is not widespread in countries with VAT systems, certain products, such as prescription medicines and newspapers, are often exempted for political or social reasons.

c) Exemption of classes of services, such as banking and insurance, are made throughout VAT countries and reflect the difficulty in applying the concept of "value added" to these areas. Exemption of classes of services, such as medical and dental care, is widespread for social reasons.

d) Certain classes of taxpayers are exempted from a VAT for reasons of administrative simplicity. For instance, many European countries exempt or give special treatment to the small retailer, either by deducting a certain amount of sales from his taxable base or by taxing him under special provisions.

e) Another form of exemption is the exclusion of stages in the production-distribution process. France, when it adopted the plan in 1955, excluded the retail stage. That exclusion was eliminated in 1968.

In the VAT countries, providers of exempted goods or services are not normally entitled to recover the tax invoiced to them on their purchases. In some countries, as a result, certain classes of taxpayers have chosen to be included in the VAT system when given the option. However, certain goods and services are not only exempt but also "zero-rated"; that is, not only is no VAT levied on their sale, but the business producing them is reimbursed for VAT paid on its purchases. The zero rate applies principally to exports. The significance of a zero rate, in contrast to exemption, is developed in the next chapters.

Multiple rates. Multiple rates came into being in Europe as a means of recognizing the historical, political, social, and economic realities of a particular country at the time of introduction of a VAT. Multiple rates are used primarily to lighten the tax burden on necessities, but they are also sometimes employed to impose a very heavy tax burden on luxuries. The typical rate format consists of a standard rate for most goods and services and a reduced rate for specified items regarded as necessities. France and Belgium have four different rates; Germany, the Netherlands, and Luxembourg have two rate classes. As will be demonstrated later, multiple rates can substantially increase the businessman's cost of compliance.

Other means of adjusting the VAT. One way of softening the impact of VAT on certain products is the reduced taxable base. In Sweden, new buildings have a taxable base of 60 percent of the actual value. This was done to eliminate discrimination between buildings built before and after the institution of VAT. Before VAT, Sweden imposed a sales tax on goods but not services, and it was estimated that a VAT based on 60 percent of the value of a newly constructed building would be roughly equivalent to the old tax. Sweden also reduces the taxable base to 20 percent for services in connection with water supplies, roads, streets, bridges, harbors, canals, and railways. This was done to obtain neutrality of choice when various governmental bodies are deciding whether to use direct labor or to contract out the project. (The government pays a VAT on its purchases.) Although the technique of a reduced taxable base is not in widespread use, it does allow special consideration for a product without resorting to explicit multiple rates.

To summarize, there are three ways of adjusting a VAT to accommodate special considerations and interests: exemptions, multiple rates, and reduced tax bases. We have seen that exemptions of certain small taxpayers and of certain services can help simplify administration of the tax. Multiple rates and, sometimes, reduced tax bases are employed to make the tax in some way more equitable.

If exemptions and reduced rates are excessive, the total tax base is narrowed, with the result that, to obtain a given amount of revenue, it is necessary to raise rates. Exemptions and multiple rates also pose administrative problems, particularly for such organizations as department stores and food chains, where a wide variety of goods are handled.

Difficulties in distinguishing between taxable and nontaxable goods arise under a complex VAT system, providing fuel for time-consuming court cases and greater opportunities for tax evasion. While the single-rate, no-exemption (other than exports) VAT is the most appealing from many viewpoints, economic and political realities usually have forced the countries which have adopted a VAT to introduce modifications.

Summary

The VAT is a tax on the value added by a company to its products in the course of its operations. VAT is a multistage tax applied to each level of production and distribution. The tax base for any given company is the difference between its total taxable sales and its total taxable purchases of goods and services from outside sources. Looked at another way, the tax base for a given company includes wages, interest, rent, profits, and some other payments.

The normal method of calculating the tax is to multiply the company's sales by the tax rate and subtract credits equal to the tax on all the goods and services purchased from other firms. In the consumption type of the VAT, tax credits on capital assets are deducted in full when invoiced.

Because of political, social, economic, and administrative realities, the simple concept of one tax rate is often modified by exemptions, multiple rates, and reduced tax bases. These modifications can simplify some aspects of collection of the tax, especially from small entrepreneurs, and can lighten the tax burden on consumer purchases of necessities. In other respects, however, they create additional complexities in calculating and applying the tax.

2

Value Added Tax
precedents in Europe
and the United States

THE HISTORY of the Value Added Tax began in 1918, when von Siemens of Germany originated the idea of such taxation. However, the theory was not put to an actual test until 1953, when Michigan inaugurated a modified form of the tax as a temporary fiscal expedient. The movement toward adoption of VAT's gained momentum in 1967, when the European Common Market issued a directive requiring its members to adopt a VAT. Exhibit 2–1 summarizes the key events of the last five decades in the history of the VAT.

THE VALUE ADDED TAX IN JAPAN AND MICHIGAN

In 1950 the Japanese Diet, acting on the proposal of the postwar Shoup Mission of the United States, adopted a Value Added Tax as the replacement for an existing enterprise tax which was in essence a tax on net business profits. The government reasoned that the VAT would reduce the tax burden on net profits, would thus encourage a much needed expansion in capital investment, and would be simpler to administer. The VAT, however, was repealed in 1954 without ever being implemented. Among the reasons for the repeal were confusion over its nature (a confusion compounded by the option of using either the subtraction or addition methods of computing the tax), protests from certain industries that the tax would discriminate against them, and doubt as to whether the tax itself could be shifted to the consumer.[1]

In the United States, the first important VAT-related activity had its beginnings in 1953, when the state of Michigan adopted a modified VAT called the Business Activities Tax (BAT). The BAT was not a true Value Added Tax. It was conceived in haste as a temporary political expedient, made "permanent" in 1955, and amended frequently until its repeal in 1967.

As amended, the tax severely distorted the concept of Value Added Taxation —

---

[1] Clara K. Sullivan, *The Tax on Value Added* (New York: Columbia University Press, 1965), pp. 126–46.

EXHIBIT 2–1
Sequence of VAT precedents

Foreign countries

<u>Time</u>

1918   F. von Siemens of Germany originates the idea of Value Added Taxation, to replace a newly established turnover tax there.

1950   Japanese Diet adopts a VAT on recommendation of American taxation mission. (The legislation is never implemented and is repealed in 1954.)

1954–   France adopts a limited VAT applicable primarily to industrial concerns.
55

1962   European Economic Community (EEC) Commission submits to the Council of Ministers the first draft directive concerning the harmonization of tax laws. The concept of Value Added Tax is addressed in this directive.

1965   EEC starts on second draft directive concerning the structure and method of application of a VAT.

1966   France passes a law extending its VAT system to all stages of production and distribution, including for the first time retail trade. The law becomes effective January 1, 1968.

1967   EEC adopts a directive requiring each member to establish a VAT system to include retail trade. Deadline is January 1, 1970.

       Denmark, though not an EEC member, introduces a VAT in July 1967.

       Germany passes a law introducing the VAT effective January 1, 1968.

1968   Sweden passes a law introducing the VAT on January 1, 1969.

       The Netherlands passes a law introducing VAT on January 1, 1969.

       Belgium passes a law introducing VAT on January 1, 1970.

1969   Belgium, three months prior to the VAT introduction date, postpones it for a year because of its current economic and political situation.

       Italy asks EEC to postpone until 1972 its introduction of the VAT because of a tax reform program to take effect in 1972.

1970   France introduces a significant simplification of its VAT system.

       Norway and Luxembourg introduce VAT's January 1, 1970.

1971   Belgium institutes its VAT January 1, 1971.

       United Kingdom issues a Green Paper proposing the introduction of a VAT in April 1973.

       Ireland proposes a VAT to be introduced in 1972.

       Austria proposes a VAT to be introduced January 1, 1973.

1972   Italy asks EEC for still another postponement of the introduction of its VAT.

       Ireland introduces its VAT in November.

EXHIBIT 2–1 (continued)

United States—federal, state, and local governments

<u>Time</u>

1921   T. S. Adams first suggests the incorporation of a VAT in the U.S. tax structure.

1932– Brookings Institution recommends a Value Added Tax for the states of Alabama and Iowa.
33

1941   A Value Added Tax was proposed by Wadsworth Mount at a meeting of the American Management Association.

1953   Michigan adopts a modified VAT as a temporary fiscal expedient, pending passage of a proposed reform of the state's tax structure.

1966   Committee for Economic Development recommends a VAT for the United States as a better means of raising additional revenue than raising corporate taxes and as a means of encouraging savings by taxing consumption.

1967   West Virginia legislature considers and rejects a VAT by a narrow margin. Key issue is the projected shift in inter-industry distribution of tax liabilities compared with the existing tax.

   In California the Citizen's Advisory Tax-Structure Task Force to the governor recommends adoption of a VAT to replace all local taxes on personal and business property and a portion of the state corporate income tax.

   Michigan legislature repeals the modified VAT as a part of a tax reform and replaces the VAT with personal and corporate income taxes.

1970   U.S. Bureau of the Budget internally discusses a VAT as a source of revenue to meet estimated FY 1971 and FY 1972 expenditures.

   U.S. Treasury Department study team in Europe reviews experience with the VAT there.

   President's Task Force on Business Taxation recommends against a VAT at that time but recommends the use of one if additional revenue is needed in the future.

   West Virginia again considers a VAT; the tax bill is passed by both houses of the legislature but is vetoed by the governor.

1972   President Nixon asks the Advisory Commission on Intergovernment Relations to study the VAT as a means of raising revenue to help finance local schools and thereby to reduce local property taxes.

one author has labeled it a "curious compromise of a net income, business receipts, and Value Added Tax."[2] The calculation of the unadjusted tax base (gross receipts minus purchases) and the eventual use of the income form (depreciation on real property subtracted from the tax base) were in keeping with VAT concepts. But several practices were contrary to Value Added Taxation theory:

1. All taxpayers were allowed a minimum deduction of 50 percent of gross receipts, even if their itemized deductions were less than 50 percent.
2. The tax base was further reduced by the deduction of items such as interest, dues, contributions, and taxes to arrive at "adjusted receipts."
3. For labor-intensive industries (payroll exceeding 50 percent of gross receipts), an additional deduction in adjusted receipts was allowed, further reducing the tax base.
4. Companies with losses or very low profits were allowed a credit of up to 25 percent of their tax liability.

These departures from theory limit the use of the Michigan example as a precedent for a national Value Added Tax in this country. Therefore, only a few comments will be made on it. Since the tax was enacted as a supplement to existing taxes, including a retail sales tax, the additional administrative burden was a source of complaint, particularly from small retailers. Although it was generally agreed that the tax was passed on to the consumer, the relatively low rate (7.75 mills) and the changes in its rate structure made it very difficult to confirm this point. In regard to capital investment, the Michigan tax initially was of the gross product type (no provision for capital expenditures) and was subsequently amended to the modified income type (allowing deduction of VAT on depreciation). Thus, the possible effects on capital investment of the consumption type of VAT could not be measured.

The Japanese and Michigan experiences, at best, can be thought of as isolated events with little applicability to the introduction of a VAT in the United States. The significant momentum for the current consideration of a VAT in this country is more recent and has come from Europe.[3]

HISTORY OF THE VAT IN EUROPE

Introduction of the Value Added Tax in the European Common Market

Because of a directive by the European Economic Community (EEC), the VAT has in recent years been adopted by all but one of the Common Market countries. The EEC conducted a series of studies over a five-year period to find the most satisfactory means of accomplishing the dual goal of (1) harmonizing the tax systems of the member countries and (2) allowing the member countries to raise significant

---

[2] Ibid., p. 304.

[3] In Latin America, Brazil uses the VAT concept in both federal and state taxes. Argentina and Mexico have a VAT under consideration.

revenues without adding to the cost of exports and without exempting imports from the tax carried by domestic products. On the basis of the recommendation of the Neumark Commission, the EEC issued a directive, in April 1967, obliging all EEC members to establish a system of Value Added Taxation by January 1, 1970.[4] The directive stipulated that the VAT should include the retail trade stage except where this would give rise to practical or political difficulties. Exports of each EEC country were to be exempt from the VAT, while imports were to have imposed on them the VAT of the importing country. Otherwise, exemptions from the VAT were to be kept to a minimum.

The EEC hoped that eventually the VAT's of its various member countries would be harmonized, both in the rates levied and in the provision of substantially equal tax treatment to similar transactions in all member countries. Initially, however, each country could set its own rates and determine the details of the tax in light of its own political and economic problems. The EEC directive did outline the general character of the VAT to be imposed in the member countries and made a list of some commercial services which it was compulsory to include in the VAT.[5]

In most of the EEC countries the VAT replaced a cumulative, multistage turnover tax (or "cascade tax"), which had a number of disadvantages:

1. The cumulative turnover tax, like the VAT, was imposed on many stages of the production-distribution system, but, unlike the VAT, there was no provision for deduction of the tax paid at previous stages. The cumulative tax at each stage was levied on a price which included the tax levied at the previous stage, so that the tax was, in effect, compounded. This compound effect was reduced for integrated companies which did not pay the turnover tax on internal stages of production and distribution but paid it only when their goods were finally sold. In a less-integrated production and distribution chain, the compound effect raised the effective rate of the cumulative turnover tax considerably and thus penalized less-integrated companies. The VAT, by contrast, is neutral between companies with varying degrees of integration; for the VAT does not have a compound effect, since the VAT at any stage is reduced by the amount of VAT paid at earlier stages. A well-integrated company pays a large VAT all at once; in a less-integrated production and distribution chain, the VAT is paid in smaller installments, but the total amount of the VAT is the same, if the value added or the total markup in the two situations is the same.

2. Under GATT rules, exporters may receive a rebate on either the cumulative turnover tax or the VAT that has been paid on the goods to be exported. But, whereas it is relatively easy to calculate the amount of VAT rebate to which an exporter is entitled, it is impossible to make a precise determination of the amount of cumulative turnover tax buried in the price of an exported good. Gov-

---

[4] The staff of the Neumark Commission recommended that a retail sales tax rather than a VAT be levied because it is easier to administer a single-stage tax. However, at the insistence of the French, the Belgians, and the Italians, the Neumark Commission finally recommended a VAT because of its self-policing feature.

[5] See Appendix A for the text of the EEC Directive of April 11, 1967.

ernments had to make an *estimate* of the amount of turnover tax included in the price of various types of goods and then prescribe standard amounts of turnover tax to be rebated on different categories of exports. This system generally meant that goods produced by highly integrated businesses received more rebate than they were entitled to receive. There were complaints, too, that some countries gave all their exporters bigger rebates than they really deserved.

Following the EEC directive, VAT's began to spring up all over Europe, not only in the EEC countries, but also in the Scandinavian countries. France, which had started the movement by instituting an industrial VAT in 1954–55, extended its VAT to retailers and service industries in 1968 and then simplified the tax in 1970. Because of problems with inflation, Belgium received permission from the EEC to postpone introduction of its VAT beyond the prescribed deadline, but the Belgian VAT finally went into effect in January 1971. By then every EEC country except Italy had a VAT.

Italy has been granted repeated extensions of its VAT deadline and has now scheduled the introduction of its VAT for January 1973. The Italians have been reluctant to introduce the VAT because they are worried about their rising prices. Since the VAT would replace a cumulative, multistage turnover tax with roughly the same effective rate, the VAT should not have an inflationary effect. However, since the VAT will be much less easy to evade than the turnover tax has been, the Italians expect the VAT to be collected more universally and, therefore, to have a bigger impact on the economy. The Italians have also been resisting EEC pressure to extend the VAT to the retail sector because of the administrative problems involved in collecting the tax from Italy's multiplicity of small retailers. Italian exporters have not been eager to lose the overly generous tax rebates they have been receiving under the cumulative turnover tax system. Recently the EEC insisted that these rebates to exporters be reduced as a condition for granting Italy still another extension on the imposition of its VAT.[6] However, when the Italian premier decreed still another postponement of the VAT in May 1972, he provided at the same time for exemptions from the still valid turnover tax and other fiscal relief for corporations as antirecessionary measures. The other Common Market countries complain that these "antirecessionary measures" are, in fact, hidden export subsidies.[7]

Meanwhile the EEC has been moving slowly to harmonize the VAT's of its various member countries. In 1969 the EEC issued a directive that by January 1, 1974 no country should have a VAT with more than two rates: a standard rate for most goods and services and a reduced rate for goods and services deemed "necessities." (France and Belgium currently have four rates, Italy plans to have three rates, while the remaining EEC countries have two rates.) There is at this time considerable variation in the VAT rates imposed by the different EEC members, but it is hoped that by 1975 the standard rates of each country will fall within the range of

---

[6] Alan A. Tait, *Value Added Tax* (London: McGraw Hill, 1972), pp. 146–47.
[7] "Value-Added Tax," *New York Times*, July 2, 1972, Sec. 3, p. 3.

12 to 18 percent and that by 1978 all EEC countries will have a standard VAT rate of 15 percent and a reduced VAT rate of 7.5 percent.[8] The EEC is also considering imposition of a special 1 percent VAT on top of the VAT's in existence in its member countries, and then using the revenues from this piggybacked special VAT to finance EEC activities.[9]

Current situation in Europe

Not only five of the original EEC countries but also the three Scandinavian countries have instituted a VAT: Denmark in July 1967, Sweden in January 1969, and Norway in January 1970. In Norway and Sweden the VAT replaced a single-stage, retail sales tax and was instituted because of the need to raise additional revenues. It was felt that the retail sales tax had worked satisfactorily while the rates were low, but there was some fear that evasion might begin to be a problem when the rates were raised.[10] The sales tax was, therefore, replaced with a VAT, which is considered more difficult to evade. Denmark adopted the VAT as a replacement for its single-stage wholesale tax on goods, partly because of dissatisfaction with the wholesale tax and partly because of the need to raise additional revenue.[11]

Other European countries are planning to institute a VAT, in part to harmonize their tax systems with the EEC. Ireland introduced a VAT in November 1972; Austria plans to introduce a VAT in January 1973; the United Kingdom will impose a 10 percent VAT in April 1973 to replace the purchase tax and the selective employment tax. In addition, Greece, Turkey, and Finland have introduced limited systems of Value Added Taxation; Portugal, in adopting a new, wholesale sales tax in July 1966, made allowances for a switch to a VAT; and Switzerland has indicated its preliminary plans for a VAT.

Exhibit 2-2 summarizes the situation in the eight countries which already have a VAT, in Italy, which was supposed to have its VAT by now, and in the United Kingdom, which has made quite detailed plans for its proposed VAT. As the exhibit indicates, the various countries have different VAT rates and rate categories. The three Scandinavian countries have a single VAT rate for all goods and services.[12] West Germany, the Netherlands, and Luxembourg have two rates: a standard rate for most goods and services, and a reduced rate for items deemed necessities (such as bread, sugar, meat, milk, butter, cheese, eggs, honey, prescription medicines, water, gas, electricity, coal, and petroleum). France and Belgium have four rates:

---

[8] Confederation of British Industry, "Report of the CBI Value Added Tax Working Party," September 1970, p. IV-4; and Commission des Communautés Européennes, "Conséquences bugetaires, économiques et sociales de l'harmonisation des taux de la TVA dans la CEE," *Etudes*, No. 16 (Brussels, 1970), p. 5.

[9] Hon. Edwin S. Cohen, "Foreign Experience with a Value Added Tax," *National Tax Journal*, September 1971, p. 401.

[10] Martin Norr and Nils G. Hornhammar, "The Value Added Tax in Sweden," *Columbia Law Review*, March 1970, p. 391.

[11] Carl S. Shoup, "Experience with the Value Added Tax in Denmark and Prospects for Sweden," *Finanzarchiv*, March 1969, pp. 237-41.

[12] However, as indicated in Chapter 1, p. 9, Sweden reduces the VAT base for certain items (new buildings, etc.), and this, in effect, reduces the VAT rates for these goods and services.

EXHIBIT 2–2

Summary of Value Added Taxation in Europe

Country	Date effective	Tax system replaced or to be replaced by VAT	Original EEC member?	Retailers included?	Effective VAT rates January 1, 1972[1]			
					Reduced rate	Intermediate rate	Standard rate	Increased rate
France............	1954–55; extended January 1968; simplified January 1970	In 1968, extension of earlier industrial VAT, replacement of a tax on services (T. P. S.), adjustment of local retail sales taxes and certain selected taxes	yes	yes	7.5%	17.6%	23.0%	33.33%[2]
Denmark........	July 1967	Single- stage, wholesale sales tax on goods (did not apply to services)	no	yes	......	......	15.0%[3]	......
West Germany........	January 1968	Cumulative, multistage turnover tax system and special turnover tax on transportation services	yes	yes	5.5%	......	11.0%[4]	......
Sweden..........	January 1969	Single-stage, retail sales tax	no	yes	......	......	17.65%[5]	......
Netherlands.....	January 1969	Cumulative, multistage turnover tax system	yes	yes	4.0%	......	14.0%[6]	......
Luxembourg	January 1970	Cumulative, multistage turnover tax system and special turnover tax on transportation services	yes	yes	5.0%[7]	......	10.0%[7]	......
Norway	January 1970	Single-stage, retail sales tax	no	yes	......	......	20.0%[8]	......
Belgium	January 1971	Cumulative, multistage turnover tax system (consisting of 5 major turnover taxes)	yes	yes	6.0%	15.0%[9]	20.0%[9]	25.0%
Italy...............	January 1973	Cumulative, multistage turnover tax	yes	no	6.0%	......	12.0%	18.0%
United Kingdom.........	April 1973	Purchase tax and selective employment tax	no	yes	0%	......	10.0%	......

[1] Effective rates apply to the pretax price. They are in contrast to "nominal rates," which are imposed on prices including the tax.

[2] These rates were introduced on January 1, 1970 and were set to correspond as closely as possible to former tax-inclusive rates (that is, rates applied to prices *including* the tax).

[3] Denmark's original rate was 10 percent. From April 1968–June 1970 the rate was 12.5 percent.

[4] West Germany's standard rate is likely to be raised to 15 percent. When Germany first introduced its VAT, the rates were 5 percent and 10 percent, but only six months later they were raised to the present rates.

[5] Sweden, unlike the other countries, applies the VAT on a tax-inclusive basis; that is, the rate is applied to the price *including* the tax. Sweden's tax-inclusive rate is now 15 percent and was 10 percent before January 1, 1971.

[6] Netherland's standard rate was 12 percent before January 1, 1971.

[7] Luxembourg's original rates were 4 percent and 8 percent. A 2 percent "exceptional rate" applicable to items especially important in the cost of living was introduced for the transition period and is still in force.

[8] Norway's rate can be revised annually.

[9] Belgium's intermediate rate was 14 percent, and her standard rate was 18 percent during 1971.

Sources: "The Turnover Tax on Value-Added in Europe," *European Taxation,* Vol. 3, No. 11–12, November–December 1968, pp. 23A–310; National Economic Development Office, *Value Added Tax* (London: Her Majesty's Stationery Office, 1971).

the standard rate; the reduced rate for necessities; the intermediate rate for semi-necessities such as shoe repairs, soap, wine, and passenger transportation; and an increased rate for luxury goods such as jewelry, radio and television sets, passenger cars, and furs.

The existence of more than one rate in many countries is often a practice carried over from the cumulative, multistage turnover tax replaced by the VAT. Multiple rates very much complicate administration of the tax. For this reason, the United Kingdom plans to have only a single VAT rate (10 percent) when it introduces the tax in April 1973. However, it plans to zero-rate (that is, completely exempt) certain goods and services subject to a reduced rate in other countries: food, fuel, electricity, water, local public transportation, building construction, prescription medicines, and books and newspapers.

The standard VAT rates range from 10 percent in Luxembourg to 23 percent in France. In many countries the rates have been raised at least once in the short time since the tax was instituted. Norwegian law allows the rate to be reviewed on a yearly basis.

Other changes have been made in the VAT since its introduction. For example, the French VAT was extended to the retail sector in 1968 and then was revised and simplified as of January 1, 1970. Retailers are now included in the VAT system in all countries. However, Italy—despite EEC pressure—is currently planning to extend its VAT only through the wholesale stage and to supplement this with an integrated municipal consumption tax (the initials of which, in Italian, are ICSC). The ICSC is a single-stage tax levied on the delivery of goods by wholesalers to retailers or consumers. The anticipated rate of the ICSC is about 5 percent.

The VAT has proved to be a very fruitful source of revenue for these countries. In Denmark, the Netherlands, and West Germany the VAT supplies 20 to 25 percent of the total tax revenues; in France and Norway it provides 40 percent.[13]

Exemptions currently granted in Europe

The VAT in Europe applies to the delivery of virtually all goods and the rendering of most services. Exports, however, are fully exempt from the VAT in all countries. Not only is no VAT paid on exported goods and services, but an exporter may claim a credit on the VAT paid on purchases that went into the exported item. Exports are thus zero-rated, for the VAT does not enter into their costs at all. Imports, on the other hand, have the full VAT levied on them when they enter the country; and the VAT on imports is calculated on the price including any customs duties or other taxes.

The VAT in Europe thus is levied on the destination principle rather than the origin principle: That is, the tax is levied by the state in which the income is received and spent rather than by the state in which the production or earning of income occurs. The Neumark Commission proposed that the EEC ultimately adopt a uniform rate, origin-principle VAT for trade between member nations while continuing to use the destination principle for trade with non-EEC members. The commission preferred the origin principle for intracommunity trade since the destination principle would perpetuate fiscal barriers between members. However, at least until all the EEC countries adopt uniform VAT rates, the destination principle presumably will continue to be observed.

A few goods and services other than exports are exempt from the VAT in Europe, but for the most part these are not zero-rated. No VAT is imposed on the sale

---

[13]National Economic Development Office, *Value Added Tax* (London: Her Majesty's Stationery Office, 1971), p. 43.

of exempt goods or services, but the exempt entrepreneur may not claim a refund on the VAT paid on his purchases. Exemption of a final product or service means only that the value added at the final stage is exempt from the VAT. The tax on all activities and purchases up to the point of exemption are fully taxed, and those taxes constitute part of the costs which are presumably reflected in the prices paid by consumers at the final stage. For this reason, exemption does not mean a revenue loss equal to the final sales price times the tax rate. Since only the value added at the final stage is exempt from the tax, only that amount of revenue is foregone. A zero rate, by contrast, gives the equivalent of exemption at all prior stages, with a corresponding impact on prices and revenue.

Since exempt, nonzero-rated entrepreneurs may not claim a refund of the VAT paid on purchases, they sometimes have found it preferable to join the standard VAT system where this option is available to them. This is especially true of capital-intensive businesses, for exemption deprives them of any credit for the VAT paid on investment expenditures. For example, the sale of petroleum was originally exempt from the VAT in France. But when the oil industry began to pay out substantial amounts of VAT on heavy expenditures for refineries, pipelines, and the like, the industry sought and obtained liability for the VAT on its sales in order to collect the tax from its customers against which it could credit the tax paid on its purchases.[14]

While the VAT increases the cost of purchases by the same percentage for both exempt and nonexempt firms, a firm which is allowed to waive its exemption may find it easier to pass on these extra costs to its business customers. The VAT is listed as a separate item on the sales invoice, and customers may be more likely to accept a tax than a higher price which has a tax cost hidden in it. Furthermore, a business customer may actually have an economic reason to buy from a nonexempt firm despite the fact that the total cost (price plus VAT) would presumably be higher than the cost of the same purchase from an exempt firm (whose price would include only the VAT on its purchases). The business customer may prefer to pay the higher amount in order to receive the VAT credit on its purchases, for no VAT credit is received for any VAT hidden in the cost of a purchase from an exempt firm. Loss of this credit may substantially increase the business customer's own VAT bill, particularly for a business whose purchases constitute a sizeable element of its costs and whose labor bill is a relatively less important item.

While business customers may find it to their advantage from a tax point of view to make their purchases from nonexempt firms, private customers would certainly prefer to buy from exempt firms, for private customers receive no credit for any VAT paid on their purchases whether the VAT is listed separately or buried in the sales price. The private customer would find it advantageous to buy from exempt firms, for then the price includes the VAT on the firm's purchases but no tax on the value added by the firm.

---

[14]Norr and Hornhammer, "Value Added Tax in Sweden," p. 399.

Exempting certain types of goods and services from the VAT thus reduces their cost to the private consumer even if the goods and services are not zero-rated. This is the reason every European country grants a VAT exemption to doctors, hospitals, old people's homes, educational establishments, and postal services—all services which the governments, for social reasons, feel should not be taxed too heavily. On similar grounds, the three Scandinavian countries do not impose the VAT on transportation of passengers, although the transportation of goods is subject to the VAT in every country. Likewise, for social and also political reasons five countries exempt broadcasting from the VAT, and five countries exempt newspapers. Four of the five countries even zero-rate newspapers.

Some services are exempted from the VAT because of the difficulty of applying the value added concept to them. It is on this ground that the VAT is not imposed on most of the financial services provided by banking, insurance, and stock brokerage institutions. Some countries, however, levy taxes other than the VAT on these services. The services of lawyers are also frequently exempt from the VAT.

Some goods and services are exempt from the VAT because they are taxed in some other way. This is the reason Germany exempts the leasing of immovable goods; France exempts tobacco and matches, certain second-hand goods, and entertainment; and Sweden zero-rates electric power and certain fuels.

Although some government services, such as postal services, are traditionally exempt from the VAT, the tax is generally levied on those public services which compete with private business. Thus, nationalized industries, government-owned railroads, and so forth are all subject to the regular VAT regulations.

A list of the more common VAT exemptions is provided in Exhibit 2–3. This list does not pretend to be comprehensive, nor does it cover all the nuances of the exemptions. The regulations about VAT exemptions are frequently quite complex, and even when two countries grant the same general exemption, the details of the exemption may vary considerably.

As can be seen from the exhibit, only very small segments of an economy are allowed to escape the VAT. Indeed, the EEC directive to its members specified that exemptions from the VAT should be kept to a minimum. The EEC also requires that certain services to business be subject to the VAT in every member country. For example, the transportation of goods has to be included in the VAT, although there is no such requirement for the transportation of persons. The services of engineers, architects, consultants, accountants, and so forth must be included in the VAT, but there is no such requirement for purveyors of personal services such as barbers, entertainers, travel agents, or doctors. However, many of the services on which the VAT is not compulsory are in fact included in the VAT system in most EEC countries.

The VAT burden on housing and commercial buildings

The imposition of the VAT on housing and commercial buildings has proved

EXHIBIT 2–3
Exemptions from the Value Added Tax frequently granted in Europe

Category of goods or services	Belgium	Denmark	France	Germany	Luxembourg	Netherlands	Norway	Sweden
Exports:	E⁰	E⁰	E⁰	E⁰	E⁰	E⁰	E⁰	E⁰
Services:								
Lawyers	E	E	E	T	T	T	E	E
Doctors	E	E	E	E	E	E	E	E
Hospitals	E	E	E	E	E	–	E	E
Old peoples' homes	E	E	E	E	E	E	E	E
Educational establishments	E	E	E	E	E	E	E	E
Insurance	E¹	E	E¹	E¹	E	E¹	E	E
Brokerage of all kinds	E	E	E¹	E¹	E	E	E	E
Stock exchange transactions	E	E	E¹	–	E	E¹	E	E
Banks and credit institutions	E(&T)⁷	E	E¹	E	E	E(&T)⁷	E	E
Postal services	E	E	E	E	E	E	E	E
Broadcasting	E	T	E	E	E	E²	E	E
Sports	T	T	T	T	T	E	–	T
Leasing of residences other than hotel rooms and the like	E	E	E	E	E	E	E	E
Leasing of business plant and equipment³	T	E	T	E¹	T	T	E	E
Telephone	T	T	T	T	T	E	T	–
Entertainment	T	T	E¹	T	T	T	–	E
Transportation of persons	T	E	T	T	T	T	E	E
Goods:								
Artists' work	T	E	–	T	T	T	E	E
Newspapers	E⁰	E⁰	E	T	T	E⁰	E⁰	E⁰
Certain aircraft and ships	T	E⁰	T	T	T	T	E	E
Fish (certain varieties)	T	T	E	T	T	T	T	T
Second hand goods sold by entrepreneur	T	T	T & E⁵	T	T	T⁶	T	T
Used cars sold by entrepreneur	T	T	T	T	T	T⁶	T	E
Medicines	T	T	T	T	T	T	T	E⁰
Tobacco and matches	T	T	E¹	T	T	T	T	T
Land⁴	E¹	E	E	E¹	E	E¹	E	E
Exemption provisions:								
Option of choosing exempt or taxable status under the VAT offered to certain providers of goods and services	yes	yes	yes	yes	yes	yes	no	yes
Provision made for refunding VAT paid at earlier stages on certain exempt goods and services (other than exports)	yes	yes	no	no	no	yes	yes	yes

NOTES: E = exempt from VAT on sales; E⁰ = zero-rated (no VAT on sales and a refund of VAT on purchases); T = taxable; dashes indicate information is not available. In Belgium, France, Germany, Luxembourg, and Netherlands, the law specifies what is exempt. In Denmark and Norway, the law specifies what is taxable. In Sweden, the law specifies which goods are exempt and which services are taxable. Exemptions in Italy have not yet been specified.

¹ Subject to specific taxes other than the VAT.

² Except advertising.

³ The regulations about imposing the VAT on the leasing of business plant and equipment are complex and vary from country to country.

⁴ Neither the sale nor the leasing of land is generally subject to the VAT, but work on the land – leveling, construction, etc. – is subject to the tax.

⁵ France exempts second-hand goods sold at public auction sales and second-hand goods used for business purposes. Otherwise second-hand goods are subject to the VAT.

⁶ In the Netherlands, if a used car is traded in on the purchase of a new car, the VAT on the new car is calculated not on its full price but on the difference between its selling price and the trade-in value of the old car. A similar provision is made for trade-ins of other goods.

⁷ In Belgium, the deposit and acceptance of funds, credit operations, and transfers of money or securities are not subject to the VAT, but the VAT is imposed on all other activities by banks or financial institutions. In the Netherlands, the VAT is imposed on certain activities of banks; administration activities, keeping of securities, and interest on hire-purchase transactions or payment transactions.

SOURCE: "The Turnover Tax on Value-Added in Europe," *European Taxation*, Vol. 3, Nos. 11–12, November–December 1968, pp. 23A–310; "Bill for the Introduction of a Turnover Tax on Value Added," *European Taxation*, Vol. 9, No. 6, June 1969, pp. 119–33; International Bureau of Fiscal Documentation, *Value Added Taxation in Europe* (Amsterdam, 1971).

troublesome in Europe. Each country handles it in a somewhat different way, and the EEC has not yet issued any guidance to its members on this complicated problem.

The regulations about the imposition of the VAT on housing and commercial buildings are so complex that it is difficult to generalize about them. For the most part, neither the sale nor the leasing of land is subject to the VAT, although France imposes the VAT on the transfer of building sites. On the other hand, the VAT is levied on work done to improve the land—project engineering, leveling, construction—and on alteration, repairs, or maintenance of existing buildings. Because construction work is subject to the tax, sales of newly constructed buildings and other land improvements have the VAT imposed on them.[15] Subsequent sales of buildings are normally not subject to the tax; but, in certain countries, under certain circumstances, the sale of an old building by one taxable entrepreneur to another taxable entrepreneur would be subject to the VAT. However, except for new constructions sold by the contractor, the sale of private houses is never subject to the VAT. The VAT is also not imposed on the rental of housing, except for the rental of hotel rooms and the like. The leasing of "business plant and machinery" is often subject to the VAT, but the leasing of other "immovable goods" (for example, office buildings) is generally not subject to the VAT. France, however, levies the VAT on the leasing of any building for business purposes.

Agriculture and the VAT

The regulations about the inclusion of agriculture in the VAT system are exceedingly complicated and vary from country to country. The three Scandinavian countries include agriculture in their standard VAT systems; but, to ease farmers' bookkeeping and cash flow problems, Denmark and Norway allow farmers to make less-frequent returns than other businesses, and Denmark allows farmers extra time to pay their VAT bills. Sweden does not make even these limited special provisions for farmers.

The EEC countries have much more complex regulations about the imposition of the VAT on farmers and foresters. The net effect of these regulations is generally to make farmers and foresters pay the VAT on their purchases of seed, fertilizer, and farm machinery but not to impose a VAT on farmers' (foresters') sales. The farmer or forester receives no credit for the VAT paid on his purchases and pays no VAT on his sales. However, the entrepreneur who purchases the farmer's (forester's) produce is allowed to consider a prescribed percentage of the sales price to have been a VAT and to deduct this amount from his own tax liability. In this fashion, agriculture and forestry are included in the VAT system, but the farmers and foresters themselves do not have to do the complicated bookkeeping required of most entrepreneurs. At the same time, the VAT the farmer or forester pays on his purchases is credited in an approximate fashion, and double taxation is avoided.

However, in all the EEC countries farmers (and foresters) may elect to join the standard VAT system, and large, highly mechanized farms may find it to their advantage to do so since such farms pay more VAT on their purchases than would be credited under the special system for small farmers. Farms producing goods for

---

[15] However in Denmark, if the new building is purchased for residential use by either the owner or his tenants or if the new building is an office building to be rented to other firms, the purchaser will receive a tax refund. The amount of the refund is not determined by the amount of the VAT but by the amount of floor space and tends to favor low-income housing.

export must join the standard VAT system in order to get refunds for the VAT paid on their purchases. France requires that any farm be subject to the standard VAT system if it is substantial enough to amount to an "industrial or commercial activity," although even for these farmers France makes some special administrative provisions, such as allowing them to make less-frequent returns.

The United Kingdom is planning to go further than the EEC countries in its treatment of agriculture, for under the proposed British VAT all food will be zero-rated except ice cream, sweets, and food sold in restaurants.

Special application of the VAT to small firms[16]

Every VAT country except Belgium and Luxembourg exempts very small traders from the VAT. Firms whose annual turnover or annual VAT liability is below a specified amount pay the VAT on their purchases but do not pay the VAT on their sales. Belgium has a different system for very small retailers selling goods to private consumers. Very small retailers who qualify for the special provisions do not pay a VAT on their sales, but the suppliers of these small retailers pay not only the regular VAT but also an additional tax imposed only on sales by wholesalers to such small retailers. This so-called "equalization tax" corresponds approximately to the VAT the small retailer would have paid, but it is collected before it reaches the small retailer. This tax must appear on the invoice at the time of delivery to him. The small retailer taxed through the "equalization tax" receives no credit for the VAT paid on his regular purchases since the rates of the equalization tax are designed to make allowance for these purchases. However, the small retailer receives a refund from the government for any VAT paid on capital investments.

Most of the VAT countries make special provisions for traders who are small but not small enough to qualify for exemption from the VAT. For example, France, Germany, Luxembourg, the Netherlands, Belgium, and Sweden allow such traders longer accounting periods and less-frequent payments of the VAT than is required for larger firms. France, Germany, and the Netherlands have a simplified declaration procedure for such small firms. These special provisions are not necessary in the Scandinavian countries where there is a single VAT rate and where all businesses have a longer accounting period than is customary in the EEC countries.

In West Germany, traders with sales of DM 60,000 (U.S. $18,619)* or less have the option of being left outside the VAT system and being taxed instead at 4 percent of their gross turnover, as under the former, multistage, cumulative turnover tax. These companies do not receive any credit for the VAT paid on their purchases, nor may they show the amount of the tax separately on their sales invoices. Because small companies often find these provisions to be disadvantageous, 56 percent of the small traders in West Germany have opted for the standard VAT system rather than the special procedure available to them.

---

[16] Organization for Economic Cooperation and Development, Fiscal Committee, "Report on the Taxation of Farmers and Small Traders Under Value Added Systems" (Paris, March 29, 1971), pp. 9–16.

* All conversions into dollars are based on mid 1972 exchange rates.

A different system is used for small firms in France and Belgium. Firms with sales below a specified amount may choose a system of *forfait* (literally, a negotiated settlement), in which they make a lump-sum tax payment in prescribed installments rather than computing the VAT due on their sales. This payment is calculated by the tax authorities on a somewhat different basis in each of the two countries, but in each case the *forfait* is supposed to be an approximation of the VAT the firm would have to pay if it were a regular part of the VAT system. Traders eligible for the *forfaitaire* system are thus not exempt from the VAT, but they are relieved of some of the accounting work of the standard VAT system. However, 17 percent of the small traders eligible for the *forfait* regime in France have opted instead for the standard VAT system, particularly since the simplified declaration procedure was introduced on January 1, 1971. One reason small firms sometimes opt for the standard VAT system is the feeling that the tax authorities are not always fair in calculating a firm's *forfait*.

The VAT liability of small firms is reduced in France, the Netherlands, and Luxembourg. In France, small firms whose annual VAT payment is above 1,200 francs (U.S. $235—the cut-off point for complete exemption from the VAT) but less than 4,800 francs (U.S. $938) receive a credit equal to one third the difference between 4,800 francs and the VAT due. Approximately 400,000 French traders have qualified for this reduction in their tax liability.

In Luxembourg, traders whose annual turnover, excluding taxes, does not exceed 1,000,000 francs (U.S. $22,313) are entitled to a reduction in their VAT liability. Likewise, in the Netherlands, traders whose annual net VAT liability does not exceed 3,200 Dutch florin (U.S. $986) may deduct a prescribed amount from their VAT payment.

The special provisions for small traders are summarized in Exhibit 2–4.

EXHIBIT 2–4
Special VAT provisions for small traders in Europe

Country	Freedom from VAT for very small traders with less than indicated turnover or VAT liability	Reduction in VAT for small traders with less than indicated turnover or VAT liability	Special systems for small traders with less than indicated turnover or VAT liability	Less frequent payment and declarations	
				Normal period	Period for small traders
Belgium	None[1]	None[1]	T $111,567	1 month	3 months[2]–T $111,567
Denmark	T $ 716	None	None	3 months	3 months
France	L $ 235	L $ 938	T $ 97,738[4]	1 month	3 months–L $ 1,173
Germany	T $3,721	None	T $ 18,619	1 month	3 months–L $ 372
Luxembourg	None	T $22,313	None	1 month	3 months–T $ 78,097
					12 months–T $ 5,578
Netherlands	L $ 400	L $ 986	None	1 month[3]	3 months–L $ 7,397
Norway	T $ 903	None	None	2 months	2 months
Sweden	T $2,078	None	None	2 months	4 months–T $ 20,777

Notes: T = annual taxable turnover; L = annual net VAT liability. Dollar figures are based on the exchange rates in effect in mid–1972.
[1] Belgian retailers with less than U.S. $33,470 in annual purchases do not pay a VAT on their sales, but an "equalization tax" as well as the VAT is imposed on their purchases.
[2] Declarations are required only every three months, but payments must be made every month.
[3] In practice, three months is regarded as the normal period and one month the period for exceptionally large traders or other special traders.
[4] In France service enterprises with an annual turnover of less than U.S. $29,321 are also eligible for the *forfaitaire* system.
Source: Organization for Economic Cooperation and Development, Fiscal Committee, "Report on the Taxation of Farmers and Small Traders Under Value Added Systems" (Paris, March 29, 1971), p. 16; International Bureau of Fiscal Documentation, *Value Added Taxation in Europe* (Amsterdam, 1971).

Treatment of capital purchases under the VAT

The Second Draft Directive of the EEC prescribed the consumption type of VAT as the preferable method of treating capital purchases. Under this type, a firm is given an immediate credit for the VAT paid on investment goods. (As the reader will remember from Chapter 1, the gross product type allows no deduction of the VAT paid on capital purchases, and the income type requires the VAT credit to be amortized according to the depreciation schedule of the investment good itself.) The consumption type of VAT was adopted primarily because it is simpler to apply, particularly for a business which uses its capital equipment for the production of both taxable and exempt goods. In such a case, the firm is allowed a credit, not for the total VAT paid on the capital purchase, but for the percentage of the VAT equivalent to the ratio of its taxable transactions to its total transactions. In short, a business with sales, half of which are subject to the VAT and half of which are exempt, could deduct from its VAT liability only 50 percent of the VAT paid on its capital purchases.

At the insistence of the Dutch government, the EEC Commission has also inserted in its directives the provision that member states may use the income type of VAT if they feel it is necessary for economic reasons—for example, if the consumption type threatens to distort normal patterns of capital purchases. It is not anticipated that any member state will be forced to take advantage of this option.

However, as a transition measure, all the EEC countries except France reduced the amount of credit a firm could claim for the VAT paid on capital purchases in the years immediately after the VAT was instituted. This was done for two reasons. The governments did not want to suffer a sharp drop in revenues when the VAT replaced the old, cumulative turnover taxes which had hit capital goods as well as other goods. The governments also wanted to ensure that, in the period between announcement of the VAT and its actual introduction, businesses did not postpone capital investments in order to reap the benefits of the VAT credit on capital goods purchases. By giving enterprises only limited credit for the VAT paid on capital purchases when the tax was first instituted and by then gradually increasing this credit, the EEC countries hoped to prevent any interruption in business investment.

For example, the Netherlands decreed that in 1969 and 1970 businesses could claim credit for only 30 percent of the VAT paid on their capital purchases; this was increased to 60 percent in 1971, 67 percent in 1972, and 100 percent thereafter. Belgium and Luxembourg made similar provisions, although enterprises in Belgium will not be entitled to full credit for the VAT paid on capital purchases until 1975.

West Germany took a slightly different tack. Rather than temporarily reducing the credit for the VAT paid on capital goods, Germany imposed a special, non-creditable tax on capital goods. This special tax was 8 percent in 1968 and was roughly equivalent to the cumulative turnover tax. Each year after 1968 this special tax was reduced 1 or 2 percentage points until 1973, when it was eliminated entirely.

These special provisions were not necessary in the Scandinavian countries where the VAT was a replacement, not for a cumulative, multistage turnover tax, but for a single-stage, retail or wholesale sales tax. Denmark's old wholesale tax had not affected business investment, and Denmark therefore did not need any special transitional measures for capital goods when it instituted its VAT with full credit for the VAT paid on capital goods purchases.

Under Sweden's old retail sales tax, purchases of machinery, equipment, and so forth had been subject to the tax, though usually at a reduced rate. Therefore, to prevent the postponement of business investment until after the VAT was instituted in 1969, Sweden granted a temporary allowance for purchases of machinery and equipment made in 1968. This allowance was given in the form of a deduction from the firm's taxable profits and amounted to 10 percent of the qualifying investments. Once the VAT was instituted, Sweden granted full credit for the VAT paid on capital goods purchases. However, when the VAT was introduced, Sweden simultaneously imposed a special tax of 1 percent on total annual payroll. This special tax compensated the government for the revenues lost by granting credit for the VAT paid on capital purchases, but, of course, it imposed a greater burden on labor-intensive than capital-intensive enterprises.

Norway, like the other countries, has imposed a VAT of the consumption type, but it has undone the tax's lack of deterrent to business investment by imposing an additional, special tax on purchases of fixed business assets. This special tax is imposed at a somewhat lower rate than the VAT, but, unlike the VAT, it is not deductible. The net effect, thus, is that Norway's VAT is similar to one of the gross product type.

Tax collection, payment, and refund procedures

The European practices in collecting the VAT are detailed in Exhibit 2–5. All countries except Sweden use the invoice collection method, which recognizes the VAT credit on purchases and the tax liability on sales at the time of invoicing. Sweden recognizes the tax at the point when money changes hands, but a Swedish firm may elect the option of calculating its VAT on an invoice basis. In Sweden, unlike most VAT countries, it is the *sale* of a good or service (that is, the contract to deliver a good or render a service) which attracts the VAT liability rather than the actual delivery or rendering itself.[17] In countries where the date of delivery determines the date of the VAT liability, the former must be specified on the invoice; for the VAT, the effective date of the invoice is the date of delivery.

Since the VAT is generally based on invoices rather than actual payments, problems arise when the customer pays less than the amount indicated on the invoice. This occurs when a customer is granted a discount subsequent to the sale, when the customer returns the goods, or when the customer simply never pays the bill. In such a case, a firm can generally claim a VAT refund based on the difference between the sum invoiced and the amount actually received.

---

[17] International Bureau of Fiscal Documentation, *Value Added Taxation in Europe* (Amsterdam, 1971), "Sweden," p. 17.

EXHIBIT 2–5
VAT payment and collection procedures in Europe

Country	Tax credit on purchases			Tax assessment on sales		Payment	
	At time invoiced	At time of cash payment	Excess of credits over liabilities received from government	At time invoiced	At time of cash collection	Accounting period	Time after end of accounting period in which tax payment is due
Belgium	x[3]		March, June, or September if at least Bfrs 60,000; at end of year if Bfrs 100 or more	x		Monthly	20 days
Denmark	x		On application.	x		Quarterly[1]	1 month plus 20 days.
France	x[2]		At the end of the quarter if 5,000 francs or more; at end of the year if 1,000 francs or more	x		Monthly	25 days after end of month.
Germany	x[3]		At year end if less than DM 1,000; at month-end if more than DM 1,000.	x[3]		Monthly[5]	10 days.
Luxembourg	x		Whenever refund due is more than LFR 50,000; at year end if less than LFR 50,000.	x		Monthly	Not known.
Netherlands	x		On application.	x[3]		Quarterly (monthly for exceptionally large traders and for exporters)	1 month.
Norway	x		At end of accounting period.	x		Bimonthly[1]	1 month plus 20 days.
Sweden		x[4]	At end of accounting period if more than SKR 1,000; carried to following period or year if less than SKR 1,000.		x[4]	Bimonthly[1]	1 month plus 5 days.

[1] In Denmark, Norway, and Sweden the accounting period may be reduced to one month for exporters so they may collect their VAT refunds more quickly.

[2] Although the VAT credit is recognized at the time of purchase, credit is not received until one month following for investment purchases and two months following for inventory purchases in France.

[3] Certain Dutch, German, and Belgian entrepreneurs, however, are allowed to calculate their VAT on cash actually received rather than on invoices.

[4] A Swedish entrepreneur may request that his VAT be based on invoices rather than cash payments and receipts.

[5] A German firm estimates its VAT each month, but it submits a detailed tax return only at the end of the year.

SOURCES: International Bureau of Fiscal Documentation, *Value Added Taxation in Europe* (Amsterdam, 1971); "The Turnover Tax on Value-Added in Europe," *European Taxation*, Vol. 3, Nos. 11–12, November–December 1968, pp. 23A–310; "Luxembourg and Norway: Bill for the Introduction of a Turnover Tax on Value-Added," *European Taxation*, Vol. 9, No. 6, June 1969, pp. 119–33.

The VAT accounting period is one month in most of the EEC countries, but it is two months in Norway and Sweden and three months in Denmark and the Netherlands, and it will be three months in the United Kingdom. In every country, however, exporters may elect a one-month accounting period so that they may collect their VAT refunds more rapidly. In West Germany, entrepreneurs do not have to make a precise calculation of their VAT at the end of the accounting period. VAT payments are based on estimates, and precise calculations are made only once a year. French entrepreneurs may choose between making precise VAT calculations at the end of the month or making them only at the end of the year; but, if they elect the latter option, their monthly VAT payments must be in an amount agreed upon with the tax administration.

The tax payment period is the time interval between the end of the accounting period and the date the payment to the government is due. It varies from 10 days in Germany to one month plus 20 days in Denmark and Norway.

The complexity of the forms used by businesses to report their VAT varies considerably. Exhibit 2–6 (in three pages) consists of translated copies of the Danish and French forms used to record and pay the VAT. They illustrate the extremes of simplicity and complexity in tax accounting. On the one hand, a Danish enterprise, reporting under a simple VAT system, is required to give a minimal amount of information: its total sales and purchases, with and without the VAT, and the net VAT payable. All the required information can be put on a postcard. On the other hand, a French firm fills out a longer form because of the larger number of applicable rates, the amount of detailed information required, and the necessity of calculating other taxes on the form.

Sometimes a firm's VAT credits on its purchases exceed its VAT liability on its sales because of capital expenditures, export credits, or seasonality in purchases and sales. In such a case, the firm is entitled to a refund of its excess VAT credits. In most countries, exporters may apply for their refunds from the government at the end of each month, but exporters in Belgium must wait until the end of the quarter for their refunds. Firms with only small VAT credits normally do not receive a refund but simply carry the credit forward to the following accounting period. In some cases, such firms are paid their VAT refund at the end of the year. Firms which are not exporters but which are entitled to a large VAT credit receive a refund promptly in every country except France and Belgium, which make firms wait until the end of the quarter for their VAT refunds. France originally insisted that non-exporting firms carry their VAT credit into the next accounting period and into succeeding accounting periods indefinitely until the credit was used up by VAT liabilities. This meant that in some instances, as for example in the resort hotel industry, the initial tax paid on capital expenditures could not be completely recovered for ten years, and the industry, in effect, made a forced loan of such VAT money to the government. In February 1972 French law was finally changed to provide for refunds of sizeable VAT credits. However, while allowing credit for the VAT paid on purchases of capital goods one month after the purchase is made, France does not allow companies to claim the credit on purchases of inventory goods until two months after the purchase is made.

EFFECT OF THE VAT IN EUROPE

The effect of the VAT on prices

The key question during the transition to a VAT is, "What will be its effect on prices?" Since prices are the result of many economic factors, an accurate quantita-

EXHIBIT 2–6

Danish and French forms for payment of the VAT: Danish form (a postcard)

Value Added Tax
TAX ACCOUNTING

Date	Purchases				Sales			Comments
	1 Purchase price including VAT	Tax Credit			4 Sales price	5 Tax payable	6 VAT deductible on exports	
		2 Domestic purchases	3 on own imports					

Value Added Tax
DECLARATION

Taxable Period

Kroner (rounded)	Specification
	Tax payable
	Tax deductible
	Tax liable

....
Signature

Space reserved

LETTER

To

Tax Service

Postbox 297

Copenhagen V

Official
Paid

194

EXHIBIT 2–6 (*Continued*)
French form

				No. 3310M
	DIRECTORATE OF TAXES			**CA3**
	TURNOVER TAXES			
	AND ASSIMILATED TAXES			

IDENTIFICATION NO. OF THE ENTERPRISE

IDENTIFICATION no. of establishment making the return

RETURN FOR THE MONTH OF ☐ OR THE ☐ QUARTER 19

A (I) **TAX ON VALUE ADDED:** Write on lines 01 to 10 below and in the columns corresponding to the appropriate rate of VAT the amount, including tax, attributable to transactions concluded during the tax period. **Give totals for the columns in the spaces a, b, c and d, rounded up to the nearest franc.**

■ TRANSACTIONS LIABLE TO VAT	REDUCED RATE 1	INTERMEDIATE RATE 2	STANDARD RATE 3	HIGHER RATE 4	LINE TOTALS 5
01 Sale of purchased goods without further processing					01
02 Sale of products manufactured by the enterprise...					02
03 Sale for immediate consumption.....................					03
04 Services supplied					04
05 Provision of accommodation..........................					05
06 Building work..					06
07					07
08 Transactions partially / AMOUNT liable to tax / LIABLE					Total for lines 01–08 col. 5 to be carried forward overleaf Section B line 37
09 Deliveries to self..................................					
10 Purchases from non-taxpayers.......................					
11 TOTAL (col. 5)					11

■ CALCULATION of the TAX	no	codes							F C
	12*	0100	a				6% ▶		
Apply to each of the tax bases obtained in spaces a, b, c and d the appropriate rate of VAT.	13*	0200		b			13% ▶		
The amount of VAT at the rate of 16⅔% can be obtained by dividing the tax base at c by 6, rather than multiplying by the approximate rate of 16.66%.	14*	0300			c		16⅔% ▶		
	15*	0400				d	20% ▶		
	16*								
Write the results in francs and centimes on lines 12–15 column 5.	17*	0900	Previous rates of VAT...............						
	18*	0600	VAT deducted earlier to be carried forward { in respect of capital assets..............						
	19*	0610	in respect of other goods and services.............						
	20		● GROSS VAT (total of lines 12–19) ———————▶						
■ Calculate VAT deductible overleaf, Section C	21*	0700	● VAT DEDUCTIBLE (calculated overleaf, Section C) ———▶						
	22		● NET VAT (difference line 20 — line 21) ————————▶						
■ Calculate other taxes overleaf, Section D	23	(1)	(II) OTHER TAXES (total given overleaf, Section D, line 67) ———▶						
(1) Leave this space blank	24		(Line 22 + Line 23) **TOTAL TAX** ———▶						

■ Mark with cross the box showing the method of payment:

1 CASH	2 CHEQUE	3 GIRO TRANSFER	4 STATE BOND	5

Place.................... Signature....................

Date....................

RECEIVED		PENALTY FOR ARREARS	
Sum		State.	9000.
Date		Rate ......% Others........	
No.			
No. 3853–44a.	**TOTAL TO BE PAID** ———▶		

Giro account

DEPARTMENT OF INDIRECT TAXATION

This return must be made to the department named opposite.

┌─ Date of receipt ─┐

Local Authority	Offices	Receipt	No. of file	Key	Period	Activity	S	System

ADDRESS OF THE ESTABLISHMENT
(where this differs from the addressee's) ➡

C.E.R.F.A. No. 30-0469

EXHIBIT 2–6 (Concluded)
French form

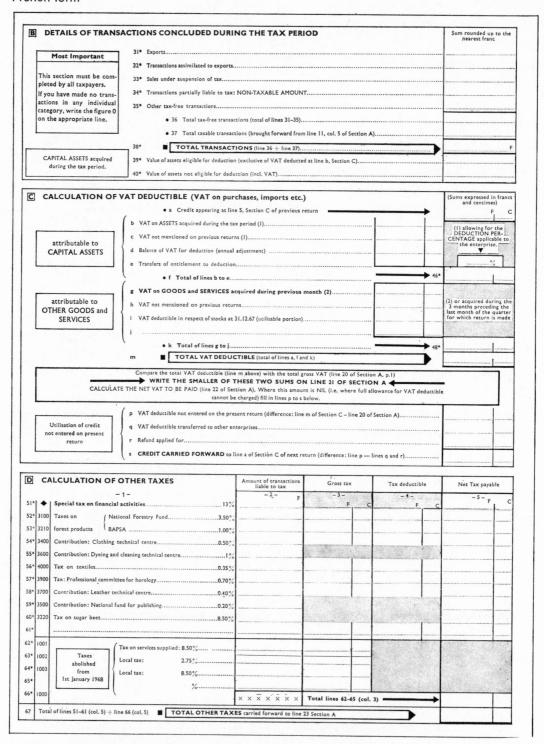

NOTE: The rates indicated on this form were those in force up to November 1968. They have since been increased.
SOURCE: National Economic Development Office, *Value Added Tax* (London: Her Majesty's Stationery Office, 1969), pp. 43–45.

tive determination of the effect of the VAT on prices in Europe is difficult, if not impossible. However, its general nature can be analyzed, and those factors that seem to encourage or discourage price changes following the introduction of a VAT can be isolated and described.

In Europe, consumer prices were affected by the VAT introduction in several ways:

1. Initially, prices usually rose because of forward shifting of the VAT. When the VAT was designed as a direct revenue replacement for another tax, the rise was often negligible, but, when the VAT was designed to raise supplementary revenues, the price rise was greater. In any case, there were differential price changes within various categories of goods and services to the extent that VAT taxed these goods and services in a different manner than the tax replaced. For instance, replacement of the turnover tax in Germany resulted in higher taxes on services and lower taxes on certain necessities.

2. At the time of introduction, certain retailers, either through ignorance of the nature of the tax or through opportunism, chose to increase prices by more than the increased burden of the VAT would warrant. The extent to which this practice was a factor in price changes was influenced by the educational and control efforts of business and government.

3. Subsequent to a VAT introduction which increased prices, wages in certain countries increased. This in turn put further pressure on prices. This tendency was accentuated by wage agreements closely tied to cost-of-living increases, for the VAT is generally included in the cost-of-living index.

Exhibit 2-7 analyzes the price and wage changes which followed the introduction of a VAT in four European countries. As measures of economic conditions the following indexes were used:

a) Industrial production index—nationwide production in units used as a very rough measure of the state of the economy;

b) Consumer price index—used as a measure of the cost of living;

c) Wage index—used as a measure of hourly earnings.

Data are provided for periods before and after the introduction of a VAT. The most significant data are the two rows under each country delineating the changes in industrial production, consumer prices, and wages six months and one year after introduction of the VAT.

To help explain why prices behaved differently in different countries, these components affecting price behavior are also shown in Exhibit 2-7:

a) The extent to which total revenue yield was changed as a result of substituting the VAT for some other tax;

b) The extent to which goods or services were taxed for the first time with the introduction of a VAT;

EXHIBIT 2-7

Price changes following VAT introduction in selected European countries

Country (VAT introduction date)	Time period	Economic conditions in a country as measured by percent of change in indexes			Extent of net revenue change through introduction of VAT	Goods or services included in VAT not previously taxed	Role of the government
		Industrial production	Consumer prices	Wages: hourly earnings			
Denmark (July 1967)	1967	−1.9%	+12.9%	+12.5%	VAT designed to raise substantially more revenues than wholesale sales tax replaced	Food items, particularly necessities Services	Government expected the price rise. Government study found that with few exceptions companies changed prices by amounts close to the VAT differential.
	1968	−3.9%	+5.4%	+13.7%			
	1969	−2.2%	+4.4%	+11.5%			
	Changes 6 months after VAT introduction	−7.9%	+7.3%	+2.0%			
	Changes 1 year after VAT introduction	−3.6%	+12.3%	+10.0%			
France (January 1968)	1967	+5.1%	+3.7%	+9.1%	Direct revenue replacement	Few, if any	Government and business cooperated in a vigorous program to monitor and minimize price increases beyond the VAT differential.
	1968	+12.1%	+6.2%	+12.9%			
	1969	+4.3%	+5.0%	+8.0%			
	Changes 6 months after VAT introduction	−12.9%	+2.6%	+5.3%			
	Changes 1 year after VAT introduction	+12.1%	+6.2%	+12.9%			
Germany (January 1968)	1967	+5.3%	+0.0%	+1.5%	Direct revenue replacement	Few, if any	Little evidence of using the VAT introduction to raise prices beyond the VAT differential. Government and industry cooperated in transitional programs.
	1968	+12.6%	+2.7%	+6.1%			
	1969	+10.4%	+2.6%	+12.2%			
	Changes 6 months after VAT introduction	+5.0%	+0.9%	+2.2%			
	Changes 1 year after VAT introduction	+12.6%	+2.7%	+6.1%			
Netherlands (January 1969)	1967	+8.1%	+4.3%	+8.5%	Direct revenue replacement	Few, if any	Prices had been expected to rise 1.3% in the 3 months after VAT was introduced, but actual rise was much greater than this. Indication that VAT introduction was used as excuse to raise prices above and beyond that needed to recoup the VAT. Government instituted a price freeze 4 months after VAT introduced.
	1968	+13.5%	+4.1%	+7.8%			
	1969	+10.6%	+7.1%	+8.5%			
	Changes 6 months after VAT introduction	+4.6%	+6.3%	+7.2%			
	Changes 1 year after VAT introduction	+10.6%	+7.1%	+8.5%			

SOURCE: International Monetary Fund, *International Financial Statistics*, Vol. 23, No. 9, September 1970; "The Turnover Tax on Value-Added in Europe," *European Taxation*, Vol. 3, Nos. 11–12, November–December 1968, p. 240; National Economic Development Office, *Value Added Tax* (London: Her Majesty's Stationery Office, 1969); Carl S. Shoup, "Experience With the Value-Added Tax in Denmark and Prospects in Sweden," *Finanzarchiv*, Vol. 28, No. 2, March 1969, pp. 236–47.

c) The government's expectations and policies regarding price changes.

In Denmark, the VAT was introduced in a period when industrial production was relatively stable and prices and wages were rising. Table 2–1 shows the changes in the consumer price index during the period of introduction:

TABLE 2–1
Denmark

Time period	Consumer price index
1966	116
1967	
First quarter	120
Second quarter	122 ⎤ Change three months
VAT introduced ⟶	after VAT: +6.6%
Third quarter	130 ⎦
Fourth quarter	131

As can be seen, the consumer price index in Denmark rose 6.6 percent during the three months following the introduction of the VAT. After six months, prices had risen 7.3 percent, and after one year 12.3 percent. The government had expected the rise because the VAT was imposed on food and services not previously taxed. In addition, the VAT had been designed to raise revenues substantially greater than the wholesale sales tax it replaced. Thus, the tax burden on each item tended to be greater than if the VAT had been a direct substitute. This higher burden was reflected in higher prices. A study conducted by the Monopoly Board of Denmark concluded that, with few exceptions, businesses changed prices by amounts close to the tax differential[18] and did not use the VAT introduction as an opportunity for unwarranted price increases.

In France, the VAT was introduced as a direct revenue replacement and included few, if any, additional goods or services not previously taxed. The price index increased 2.6 percent the first six months and 6.2 percent the first twelve months of the VAT. The general consensus is that VAT was responsible for some but not all of this increase. Economic conditions at the time of introduction were characterized by moderately rising prices and industrial production and rapidly rising wages. The decline of 12.9 percent in industrial production in the six months following the VAT reflects a nationwide strike rather than a VAT effect. Government and business cooperated in a vigorous program to monitor and minimize price increases. This program has been credited with controlling unwarranted price increases beyond the VAT differential.

The German case is cited in the literature as a model for relatively stable prices following a VAT introduction, for prices rose only 2.7 percent during the succeeding year. In 1967, the year preceding the VAT, prices and wages were virtually at a standstill, while industrial production was rising. Since the new tax was a direct replacement for a cumulative turnover tax and had many similar features, there was no need to shift additional increments of taxation forward to the consumer. Although the price index increased only slightly, the VAT did cause some price dislocations in certain segments of the economy, particularly personal services, where the new

---

[18] Shoup, "Experience with the Value Added Tax," p. 247.

tax was significantly higher than the tax replaced. Interestingly enough, it was generally small firms, not the big ones, which raised their prices by the full amount of the VAT and made no allowance for the removal of the old turnover tax.[19]

TABLE 2–2
Netherlands

Time period	Consumer price index	
1968		
First quarter	123	
Second quarter	125	
Third quarter	125	
Fourth quarter	127	
1969		Change three months after VAT: +4.7%
VAT introduced ⟶		
First quarter	133	
Second quarter	135	
Third quarter	134	
Fourth quarter	136	

The Netherlands' introduction of VAT in January 1969 took place in an atmosphere of rapidly rising industrial production, significantly rising prices, and rapidly rising hourly earnings. The immediate effect of the VAT on prices can best be seen in Table 2–2.

While the Dutch government had expected prices to increase 1.3 percent, the actual increase was 4.7 percent in the three months after the VAT was introduced. To counteract the unexpected inflation, a general price freeze was introduced on April 1, 1969 and replaced on September 4 by a "calculation rule," which allowed merchants and manufacturers to pass on certain external cost increases in their prices. These measures kept the price index from changing greatly during the second half of 1969. Therefore, the total rise in prices in the year after the introduction of the VAT was a little over 7 percent.

Learning from the Dutch experience the year before, both Norway and Luxembourg applied a price freeze when introducing the VAT. Norway's freeze straddled the introduction of the VAT on January 1, 1970. Since the VAT imposed a heavier burden than the retail sales tax it replaced, the Norwegian government expected a 5.8 percent increase in prices. However, despite the freeze, retail prices actually rose 6.25 percent between the last quarter of 1969 and the first quarter of 1970. Luxembourg expected no change in the general level of prices since its VAT exactly replaced a multistage turnover tax that had included services. However, when Luxembourg introduced its VAT January 1, 1970 a price freeze was imposed for six months. Retail prices nevertheless rose just over 2 percent.[20]

---

[19] Tait, *Value Added Tax*, p. 148.

[20] National Economic Development Office, *Value Added Tax*, pp. 44–45.

Belgium, due to introduce a VAT in January 1970, postponed its introduction because of the Dutch experience and the inflationary pressures existing in the country at that time.

Italy's decision to postpone introduction of a VAT is thought to be at least partially due to the threat of higher prices created by the self-policing features of a VAT. Many Italian firms ignore the present cumulative turnover tax. The more efficient collection features of the VAT would mean sharply higher prices, as firms increased prices to compensate for the tax.[21]

In summary, the effect of a VAT introduction on prices is determined by a combination of factors, including economic conditions, the nature of the VAT compared to the tax replaced, and the relevant policies of government and business. While there are differences according to national characteristics, in general the impact of a VAT on prices tends to be minimized by:

a) Introducing the VAT during a period of relatively stable wage and price conditions;

b) Introducing it as a direct revenue replacement for another tax rather than as a supplementary source of revenue;

c) Including only entities and categories previously taxed;

d) Cooperation between business and government to minimize unwarranted price increases.

The VAT has an impact on prices not only when it is introduced, but also when the VAT rates are increased. As was indicated earlier in the chapter, most countries with a VAT have raised their rates at least once since the tax was instituted. Whenever the rates are increased, prices tend to rise by roughly the amount of the increase. However, the increase in rates does not cause the differential price changes that occur when the VAT replaces another tax with a somewhat different impact.

Denmark provides an interesting example of the impact of VAT rate increases on prices and wages. When Denmark introduced its V.AT in July 1967, the rate was 10 percent. On April 1, 1968 the rate was raised to 12.5 percent, and on July 1, 1970 it was raised to 15 percent. Each time the rate was raised, there was a marked increase in both consumer prices and in wages in the succeeding months. While consumer prices rose only 1.5 percent in the three months before the rate increase in July 1970, they rose 2.8 percent in the three months after the increase. Similarly, while wages rose only 4.1 percent in the six months before that increase, they rose 8.4 percent in the six months afterwards. This is shown in Exhibit 2–8.

Some of the rise in prices and wages was, of course, due to normal inflationary pressures and not just the VAT rate increase. Indeed, if prices had continued to rise at the same rate, and if the increase in the VAT rate had been fully added on top of this rise, prices would have risen even more than they did. However, the increase in the VAT rate was followed by a greater increase in wages than in prices.

---

[21] "Miracle Levy Goes Awry." *The Wall Street Journal,* October 14, 1969.

EXHIBIT 2–8

Effect of VAT rate increases on the consumer price index and the wages index in Denmark

Time period		Consumer price index		Wages index (hourly earnings)	
1967					
VAT introduced ⟶					
	Third quarter	130		149 ⌐	
	Fourth quarter	131 ⌐		153	Change 6 months before rate increase: +4.7%
			Change 3 months before rate increase: +1.3%		
1968					
	First quarter	132.7		156 ⌐	
VAT rate raised from 10% to 12.5% ⟶			Change 3 months after rate increase: +2.9%		Change 6 months after rate increase: +8.3%
	Second quarter	136.6		165	
	Third quarter	137.0		169 ⌐	
	Fourth quarter	137.5		174	
1969					
	First quarter	138.2		176	
	Second quarter	139.7		184	
	Third quarter	141.2		186	
	Fourth quarter	143.6		194 ⌐	
1970					Change 6 months before rate increase: +4.1%
	First quarter	145.6 ⌐		192	
			Change 3 months before rate increase: +1.5%		
	Second quarter	147.8		202 ⌐	
VAT rate raised from 12.5% to 15%			Change 3 months after rate increase: +2.8%		Change 6 months after rate increase: +8.4%
	Third quarter	152.0		207	
Price freeze ⟶ imposed					
	Fourth quarter	154.0		219 ⌐	
1971					
	First quarter	154.3		220	

SOURCE: International Monetary Fund, *International Financial Statistics*, Vol. 25, No. 3, March 1972, pp. 102–5.

Distribution of the burden of a VAT

The principal objection to a VAT is based on the fact that it tends to impose a higher proportionate burden on people with smaller incomes. The VAT is essentially a tax on consumption rather than a tax on business, and its ultimate effect is to raise the prices consumers must pay. To the extent that consumers with low incomes spend a higher percentage of their earnings than those with high incomes, the VAT (or any consumption tax) imposes a greater tax burden on those less able to bear it. The EEC countries have sought to counteract the regressivity of the VAT by imposing multiple rates, with comparatively low rates on goods regarded as "necessities" and higher rates on other goods.

The Scandinavian countries have compensated for the regressivity of the VAT in other ways. They have a single VAT rate for all goods, but they feel that overall their fiscal structure is one of the most progressive in the world. With their extensive programs of social insurance, medical care, family benefits, and the adjustments they have made in their personal income tax, the Scandinavian governments believe they have more than offset any element of regressivity in the single-rate VAT. In short, the regressivity of the VAT can be counterbalanced by the way the VAT revenues are spent and by other taxes in the total tax system.

When the VAT was introduced, some countries increased programs of governmental benefits and assistance payments to offset increases in consumer prices caused by the VAT. The Danes, for example, introduced a system of personal grants which are inversely progressive in relation to income. They also increased the existing child grants and introduced subsidies to reduce the prices of certain dairy products.[22]

To further compensate for any regressivity of the VAT, some countries made changes in their personal income tax structure when the VAT was introduced. However, none of the countries allowed an income tax credit or a refund for the VAT paid on a minimum annual amount of consumer purchases, a system used by some states in the U.S. with sales taxes and proposed for any U.S. VAT.[23]

Transition to the VAT

When the VAT was introduced, each country made some modifications in its existing tax structure. Either a cumulative turnover tax or a single-stage sales tax was eliminated because the VAT was designed as its replacement. Some changes were made in the personal income tax structure to counteract the regressivity of the VAT, and a major restructuring of the personal income tax occurred in Denmark and Norway. In France, many excise and luxury taxes were removed, and the goods subject to these taxes had the highest VAT rate imposed on them. With other goods — such as tobacco and matches — France preserved the existing taxes and exempted the goods from the VAT. Germany retained some of its excise taxes but adjusted the rates so that the burden of the VAT and the revised excise taxes combined would equal the burden of the old excise taxes. Denmark, Norway, and Sweden generally retained their excise taxes on so-called luxury items, and the VAT was calculated on the basis of the price including the excise tax. The Netherlands retained its tax on tobacco, mineral oils, sugar, and carbonated beverages; increased the tax on alcohol by 10 percent; and imposed a "special consumption tax" of 15 percent on sales and imports of passenger cars (plus a 3 percent surcharge added January 1, 1971).[24] In the Netherlands, as in Scandinavia, these special taxes are included in the price on which the VAT is calculated.

In converting from another tax system to a VAT, the European countries developed detailed rules governing the tax status of inventories and capital purchases

---

[22] Shoup, "Experience with the Value Added Tax," p. 240.

[23] Cohen, "Foreign Experience," pp. 400–401; and B. Kenneth Sanden, "The Value Added Tax — What It Is, How It Works — Experience in Foreign Countries" (Paper delivered at Tax Institute of America Symposium, Nov. 15, 1972), p. 8.

[24] National Economic Development Office, *Value Added Tax*, pp. 42–43; and International Bureau of Fiscal Documentation, *Value Added Taxation in Europe* (Amsterdam, 1972), "Netherlands," pp. 7 and 61.

to prevent short-term distortions in business decisions. In France, for example, entrepreneurs who on December 31, 1967 had goods in stock and who in 1968 became subject to the VAT for the first time, were allowed a credit of the applicable VAT rate times the book value of their inventory. This credit, which was computed according to special rules, had to be spread over six years. The tax status of transactions taking place on the day of introduction was also clarified in each VAT country. These rules were often quite complex and caused some administrative headaches for businesses. However, these transitional difficulties usually did not last more than six to twelve months.

Once the transition was completed, businesses generally found that the accounting and reporting burden imposed by the VAT was not great compared to the burden already imposed by other taxes such as the income tax.[25] Large and medium-sized firms with computer systems or machine accounting usually found even a multirate VAT relatively easy to cope with.[26] And the Swedish experience was that the VAT lent itself to computer operations and machine accounting more easily than the retail sales tax, for virtually every sale was taxable under the VAT.[27] Worries about the possible adverse effect which the introduction of the VAT would have on business liquidity also proved to be exaggerated — such effects, if any, were of short duration.[28]

The Europeans found that education of the public during the transition to a VAT was very important. It was considered essential that business understand the nature of the new tax, the details of the regulations on its imposition, and the real impact of the tax on them. Such an educational program can reduce the administrative problems arising during the transition and can help curb the inflationary impact of the tax.

When the VAT replaced a tax which had not extended to the retail stage, the countries often carried on an elaborate campaign to inform retailers of their new tax liability. In the Netherlands, a television course was broadcast, each retailer was visited by a tax official, and information was disseminated by all the news media. West Germany, in a pioneering effort designed to try out the VAT law prior to enactment, conducted a computerized simulation in 1965. Performed by a government-industry group, it resulted in valuable suggestions to minimize the administrative problems involved in introducing the VAT.[29]

Relative ease of transition for retailers: France versus Germany

In France, the retailers complained loudly and bitterly about the VAT; in Germany, the retailers made the transition smoothly. Although there is a temptation to

---

[25] Norr and Hornhammar, "The Value Added Tax in Sweden," p. 408.

[26] National Economic Development Office, *Value Added Tax*, p. 41.

[27] Norr and Hornhammar, "Value Added Tax in Sweden," p. 408.

[28] National Economic Development Office, *Value Added Tax*, p. 41.

[29] Manfred Schirm, "The Value-Added Tax in Germany," *The Value-Added Tax: the U. K. Position and the European Experience*, T. M. Rybczynski, ed. (Oxford: Basil Blackwell, 1969), p. 32.

describe this difference in terms of stereotyped national characteristics, the facts indicate that the relative ease of transition was influenced directly by (1) the nature of the VAT introduced, (2) the structure of the tax replaced, (3) the relative size and sophistication of the retail establishments, and (4) the complexity of the transitional measures.

France introduced a VAT with four rates and nine categories of exemptions. Germany's VAT had two rates and relatively few exemptions that affected retailing. Furthermore, in Germany all items or services in any given sector (for example, food) were generally taxed at the same rate. Changing price tags to VAT-inclusive prices just prior to enactment day was a monumental job in France. The numerous changes in rates were a continuous source of aggravation there during the first year.

In Germany, the cumulative turnover tax replaced was structurally similar to the VAT system. Retailers were included in both systems. French retailers, on the other hand, had not been subjected to a national turnover tax before the VAT was extended to them.

There are about 732,000 retailers in France, or 1 for every 68 persons. West Germany has 500,000 to 600,000 retailers, 1 for every 104 persons. In addition, 48 percent of all French retailers operate very small shops in which they do all the clerical and accounting work themselves. Their relative lack of sophistication in accounting techniques created further problems.

Finally, the transitional measures set up for inventory and capital purchases were more complex and of longer duration in France. For example, French firms had to spread out over six years the tax credit on the inventory held at the time of the VAT's introduction, while German firms were reimbursed within two years for the turnover tax paid on their inventory prior to the VAT.

French experience with the VAT

To explore the problems arising with a complex, multirate VAT, let us look a little closer at the French experience with this tax.

Prior to enactment of the VAT in France, there was considerable discussion of the desirability of a retail sales tax versus a VAT. Typically, on the part of the small retailer there was sentiment, considered to be irrational by the authorities, in favor of a VAT; he believed that the retail tax singled him out for tax punishment. VAT, on the other hand, seemed to spread the tax to the wholesalers and manufacturers. At the same time, the small retailer's poor accounting practices made it difficult to establish clear-cut figures for sales. Thus, collection of a retail sales tax would have posed a severe administrative problem for both retailers and the government. With a VAT, very small retailers could be exempted from the tax without loss of revenue from the tax imposed at earlier stages.

The French VAT, although initiated for industry in 1954–55, was not extended to services and to retailers until January 1, 1968. Of the 1.9 million businesses of all types then subject to the tax, 1.6 million had sales of less than $100,000 per year and were allowed the option of a simplified *forfait* system, whereby they paid a predetermined amount calculated by the tax authorities to be roughly equal to the VAT they would otherwise have paid on their sales. The majority of those eligible, 1.4 million, exercised their option to use the *forfait*. The contribution of this large group of companies to total tax revenues has been in the range of 7 to 8 percent. The 500,-000 businesses not in the *forfait* system are faced with the problem of complying with a very complex tax.

Its greatest complexity is the multiple-rate system. We have referred before to the existence of four standard rates in France. However, nine rates can be defined.

The four statutory rates are: (1) reduced, (2) intermediate, (3) standard, and (4) increased. In addition, there are five categories that differ from the above: (5) no tax for some products, such as tobacco and matches; (6) particular rates due to a reduced tax base on certain products; (7) rate applied to works of art; (8) second-hand article rate; and (9) system applicable when another tax is added to the VAT at the retail level (for example, in the case of watches). Firms with many transactions and a diversity of goods are thus confronted with real problems in calculating their VAT.

The plight of the supermarket manager in France serves as a good example of the compliance system. Exhibit 2–9 lists the classes of goods and the percent of sales of each class in each of the four tax-rate categories. Fruit and vegetables are relatively simple, since they are taxed only at the reduced rate. However, bakery

EXHIBIT 2–9

The French supermarket: Percent of total sales revenue for various goods under each VAT rate category[1]

Type of food	Reduced rate (percent)	Intermediate rate (percent)	Standard rate (percent)	Increased rate (percent)
Food:				
Meat	97.18	2.82		
Fish	55.70	44.30		
Milk	97.60	2.40		
Fruit, vegetables	100.00			
Bakery	25.33	64.67	10.00	
Grocery[2]	27.18	72.80	0.02	
Biscuits	14.70	85.09	0.21	
Beverages		39.91	60.09	
Clothing:				
Nursery			100.00	
Children's			100.00	
Linen			100.00	
Shoes			100.00	
Other:				
Jewelry			100.00	
Camping, sports equipment		0.93	97.53	1.54
Perfumes			100.00	
Toys			99.49	0.51
Hardware			100.00	
Furniture	0.28	0.04	99.68	

[1] Prior to changes effective January 1, 1970.
[2] Includes sundries and staples such as flour, sugar, and spices.
SOURCE: Interviews with French retailers conducted for this study.

goods, groceries, and biscuits come under three different tax rates. Fortunately, from the check-out person's point of view, the tax is included in the price of the goods and is not calculated at the cash register. However, the store accountant must keep track of the VAT collected on sales in each of the categories and apply the appropriate credit on purchases to each.

The application of different rates creates what appear to be logical inconsistencies, such as taxing fruit juice at one rate and apricot nectar at a higher rate because of its method of preparation. This type of distinction may be reasonable from the tax administrator's point of view, but retailers and consumers cannot be expected to appreciate such subtle distinctions.

As has been indicated, the VAT is included in the price marked on retail goods in France. This simplifies the sales clerk's job and complicates the accountant's work. This system breaks down, however, when a sale is made to a customer who is not a final consumer and who is thus himself subject to VAT. By law, the retailer must provide such a customer with an invoice showing the price before tax and the amount of tax. This rule requires the retailer to keep a record of the two types of pricing transactions, a further complication for his accounting department.

The French firm's problems in coping with the VAT were compounded by three changes in the rate structure in the first year of the VAT. Since the tax in France is applied at date of delivery and not at the date of invoicing, these rate changes obliged many firms to reissue invoices three times during the first year of the new system.

Despite the modifications recently legislated into the system, French firms still have complaints about it.

1. The multiplicity of rates creates too much complexity.
2. Compliance cost is too high, particularly for the small firm which must retain an accountant for the first time.
3. The tax burden is too heavy on retailers. This feeling belies the economists' assurance that the burden is on the consumer and that the retailer passes the tax forward.
4. The tax administrators are too arbitrary in their calculation of the *forfait*.
5. The wording of the law is too complex for the average small firm.

The French government has modifications of the VAT under continuing study. Everyone agrees that the number of rates must be reduced, probably to two. However, the prospect of disturbing the relative positions of different products creates a substantial barrier to change. Other ideas being discussed are simplification of the form, the possibility of different rates for different types of firms, and the possibility of an average rate for small firms based on past tax paid.

SUMMARY

In 1967 the European Economic Community directed its members to adopt a VAT as a means of tax harmonization. To date, five of the original EEC countries—

France, West Germany, the Netherlands, Belgium, and Luxembourg—have enacted a VAT; but Italy has repeatedly postponed its introduction of the tax. In the meantime, Denmark, Sweden, and Norway have all adopted a VAT, mainly for reasons of tax reform, but also to bring their tax systems into harmony with the EEC. Ireland introduced a VAT in November 1972, and the United Kingdom and Austria will adopt a VAT in 1973. Other European countries with a VAT under consideration include Finland, Greece, Portugal, and Switzerland.

VAT was introduced as a replacement for multistage, cumulative turnover taxes in West Germany, Luxembourg, Belgium, and the Netherlands. It replaced single-stage sales taxes in the Scandinavian countries. The French extended what had been an industrial VAT to the retail sector and to services as a replacement for several taxes.

In each of these countries the VAT is of the consumption type, that is, a firm is given immediate credit for the VAT paid on purchases of capital goods.

Retailers are included in the VAT system of all countries except Italy. The Italians plan to have a VAT applied only through the wholesale stage and a special single-stage tax levied on the delivery of goods by wholesalers to retailers.

The effective standard VAT rates range from 10 percent to 23 percent in Europe. Denmark, Sweden, and Norway have a single rate as Britain plans to have. West Germany, the Netherlands, and Luxembourg have two rates, a standard rate and a reduced rate for necessities. The French and Belgian VAT's have four rate categories.

Most countries have special provisions for small firms and for farmers to ease the administrative burden for these enterprises as well as for the government.

Exemption practices vary in each country. Medical and educational services are exempted for social reasons in virtually all countries. Banking, insurance, and brokerage services are normally exempt because of the difficulty of applying the value added concept to these services. Housing is generally exempt from the VAT, although the tax is levied on construction and repair work and on the sales of newly constructed buildings. In contrast to the service sector, there are very few VAT exemptions for goods.

As a general rule, exempt firms pay no VAT on their sales but do pay a VAT on their purchases. In order to obtain credits for the VAT paid on purchases, some firms eligible for exemption elect instead to be included in the VAT. This option is available only to certain types of firms in certain countries.

Exports—and a few other goods—are not only exempt from the VAT on their sales, but they are also zero-rated, that is, a refund is given for the VAT paid on purchases made to produce the exports. Imports, on the other hand, have the local VAT imposed on them when they enter the country.

Three kinds of price influences occurred with the introduction of the VAT in Europe. With the adoption of the VAT, prices tended to rise for two reasons: (1) the forward shifting of the exact amount of the VAT (or the tax differential, if VAT was a direct replacement for another tax) and (2) unwarranted increases beyond the VAT amount due to ignorance of the nature of the tax and/or opportunism. The third influence on prices came subsequent to the VAT introduction. Wages tied to the cost of living increased in response to the initial increase in prices caused by the VAT. This increase in wages put further pressure on prices as businesses attempted to maintain their profitability.

One year after the introduction of the VAT, consumer prices had risen 2.7 percent in Germany, 6.2 percent in France, 7.1 percent in the Netherlands, and 12.3 percent in Denmark. For the most part, VAT was considered a significant factor in these increases. The VAT impact on prices resulted from a set of conditions peculiar to each country. However, its influence seemed to be minimized by:

1. Introducing the VAT during a period of relatively stable wage and price conditions;
2. Introducing it as a direct revenue replacement for the prior tax, rather than as a supplementary source of revenue;
3. Including only entities and categories previously taxed;
4. Close cooperation of business and government to minimize unwarranted price increases.

The VAT usually has an inflationary impact not only when it is introduced but also when its rates are increased. Most countries have increased their VAT rates at least once since the tax was introduced, and the increases always bring in their wake rising prices and ultimately rising wages.

To explore compliance problems with a complex multirate VAT, a brief survey was made of the experience of French business with the tax. France has four statutory rates plus five additional categories that affect products sold at retail. Food retailers, in particular, suffer under the multirate system. Foods such as bakery goods, groceries, and biscuits are taxed at two and sometimes three different rates. Besides the complexity of administering a multirate VAT, French firms also voice complaints about the arbitrary decisions regarding the special provisions for the small businesses.

The European experience provides very useful information as to the practical applications and implications of the Value Added Tax. As has been shown, the form of the VAT in any one country, the transition problems, the effect on prices, and the impact on business are usually peculiar to that country. Thus, in applying some of the lessons learned in Europe to consideration of the VAT in the United States, the particular needs of our country must be kept in mind.

3

Possible characteristics
of a Value Added Tax in
the United States

A Value Added Tax was first proposed for the United States in 1921. Periodically since then the proposal has been revived, but only in recent years has it been given serious consideration by the U.S. government. In 1970 the U.S. Bureau of the Budget internally discussed a VAT as a means of raising needed revenues, and a U.S. Treasury Department team visited Europe to study the experience with the VAT there. In September 1970 the President's Task Force on Business Taxation recommended that, if additional revenues were needed, some form of indirect taxation such as a VAT should be used. A majority of the task force, however, recommended that no additional revenue source be adopted at that time.[1]

In January 1972 President Nixon tentatively suggested a VAT levied by the federal government but supplying revenues to the states to help finance public primary and secondary education. The plan would give relief from property taxation since a state would be eligible for the federal funds only if schools in the state were no longer supported by either local property taxes or state residential property taxes. School expenditures would not be covered entirely by the federal government. Even with the VAT revenues, the federal government would pay only about one third of public primary and secondary education costs, but this would be a substantial increase from the 7.5 percent funded by the federal government in 1971. Under the proposed system, the states would have to finance roughly two thirds of public school expenditures rather than the 37 percent they did in 1971. In 1971 local government expenditures on elementary and secondary schools amounted to $24 billion. Under President Nixon's tentative proposal, the VAT would produce net revenues of about $13 billion to be used for schools.[2] Therefore, if local governments were allowed to make only minor contributions to school costs, financed

---

[1] President's Task Force on Business Taxation, *Business Taxation* (Washington: U.S. Government Printing Office, September 1970).

[2] A VAT with a 3 percent rate would supposedly produce $18 billion in revenues, but $5 billion of this would be lost because of proposed VAT rebates to be paid through the mechanism of the individual income tax.

from the 15 percent of their tax revenues not derived from the property taxes, the states would have to raise additional revenues of nearly $11 billion just for schools, even if school costs did not go up. The states could raise the necessary funds by increasing state sales taxes, state income taxes, state excise taxes, or by increasing state property taxes on industrial and commercial property, but they could not raise school revenues by imposing a state-wide property tax on residences, if President Nixon's suggestion should be enacted.[3]

President Nixon's proposal was only a trial balloon, submitted not to Congress but to his Advisory Commission on Intergovernmental Relations (ACIR), a national bipartisan body with members both from the general public and from the executive and legislative branches of federal, state, and local governments.

The precise form a U.S. VAT would take cannot be predicted. However, some intelligent guesses can be made about the possible characteristics it might have, and an examination can be made of some of the issues to be resolved before a VAT is enacted in this country.

Possible changes in the U.S. tax structure

If a VAT were introduced in the United States, it is quite probable that some changes in other taxes would be adopted as part of a legislative package. The extent and nature of these changes, however, is far from resolved.

Many proposals have been made for "tax reform." Substantial revisions in individual and corporation income taxation and in estate taxation have been proposed from the standpoint of both revenue yield and equity. Most of these proposals are highly controversial. Some changes which would increase revenues immediately might have a repressive impact on consumer and business activity in the long run and hence decrease revenues over time. Judgements regarding equity are always subjective. What some people regard as fair may be deemed grossly unfair by others.

Any attempt to appraise the merits of the many proposals for major tax changes would require disproportionate space in this analysis of Value Added Taxation. It is important to recognize, however, that, in the political world, tax legislation, including any adoption of a Value Added Tax, will not be made in isolation or on grounds of strict logic or objective standards of equity.

The range of possible changes in other taxes is described here briefly merely to place consideration of a VAT in a realistic perspective. Political circumstances will determine the elements of whatever package of major tax legislation, with or without a VAT, is developed in 1973–74.

Business income taxation. The most frequent proposals regarding the taxation of business income involve changes in: (1) depreciation allowances and investment

---

[3]Advisory Commission on Intergovernmental Relations, "Essential Ingredients of a Plan to Substitute a Federal Value-Added Tax for Residential Property Taxes" (Washington, D.C. February 9, 1972). The statistics on the funding of school costs were derived from: U.S. Bureau of the Census, *Statistical Abstract of the United States: 1971,* 92d ed. (Washington: U.S. Government Printing Office, 1971), p. 103.

credits; (2) the special provisions applicable to the extractive industries, including percentage depletion, intangible drilling costs, and expenditures for exploration and development in mining; and (3) the distinctive provisions regarding income earned abroad, which, in the absence of special rules, would be subject to international double taxation.

The VAT was originally proposed as a means of reducing the corporate income tax, but in 1972 the VAT was not being discussed seriously as a substitute for any part of business' income taxes or for changes in depreciation practices.

Individual income tax. Proposals for modification of the individual income tax often appear in the news. A mere listing calls to mind the traditional arguments for and against them.

Elimination of or restrictions on various deductions, including those for interest and property taxes on owner-occupied homes and those for charitable contributions, are frequently suggested. So also is repeal of the authorization for income splitting by married couples. Another proposal is replacement of the $750 personal exemption with a $150 tax credit for each member of a family, a step that, without reducing federal revenues, would reduce the tax load on those with incomes under $12,000 while increasing it for others.

Many suggestions have been made for changes in the tax treatment of capital gains, including: (1) full inclusion of capital gains in taxable income; (2) lengthening the holding period; (3) the introduction of a sliding scale of percentage inclusion of capital gains; (4) changes in the definition of capital assets; and (5) taxation of unrealized gains at periodic intervals.

If a VAT should be enacted, the individual income tax might also be modified to offset the impact of the VAT on the total tax burden of families with lower incomes. President Nixon's January 1972 proposal suggested that families with incomes up to $20,000 be given rebates on their income tax for all or part of the VAT they had paid. These rebates would be flat amounts, based on estimates of average VAT payments, and would only be partial for those with larger incomes. Persons with incomes so low they paid no income tax would be given a cash refund for their estimated VAT payments. These provisions would not actually change the individual income tax; they would just use the mechanisms of this tax to pay VAT rebates to some taxpayers.

Estate and gift taxes. Proposals for modification of estate and gift taxes recur periodically, but they are less familiar to the general public. Among the more common ones discussed by some tax specialists are: (1) a combination of estate and gift taxes to secure a unified progressive rate schedule for transfers of property during life and at death; (2) a shift from taxation of the estate of a decedent to taxation of bequests and gifts in the hands of recipients; (3) a higher rate of tax if property transfers skip intervening generations, that is, if they are made to grandchildren instead of children; (4) modification in the taxation of trusts, especially multiple trusts and those which extend beyond one generation; and (5) a presumptive realization of capital gains at death.

Proposals for such changes in estate and gift taxes have not, to date, been tied in any way to proposals for a VAT.

Payroll taxes. As social security benefits and taxes have increased, there have been some proposals to allocate some general revenues to the social security trust funds. Any move of this sort would be a break with the contributory principle on which the social security system was founded, but both this principle and the traditional practices in funding the system have now been challenged. If social security benefits were to be financed in part from general funds, the need for additional revenues would be increased, strengthening the likelihood of adoption of a VAT. The VAT, thus, might possibly be used as an alternative to increasing payroll taxes, but it is not likely to be enacted as a substitute for existing payroll taxes.

Property taxes. Some of the impetus for a VAT has developed as a result of decisions in state courts limiting the use of local property taxes for school finance. President Nixon's suggestion in January 1972 that a VAT might provide revenue which would simultaneously let the federal government increase its share of education finance and relieve residential property taxes indicated a possible tie between a federal VAT and state and local property taxes. Some comments on property taxes are thus appropriate in a current discussion of a VAT.

In 1971 local property taxes produced revenues of $36.7 billion, which accounted for 85 percent of all local tax collections. State property taxes raised about $1.1 billion.[4] A little over half of all local property taxes paid by both businesses and residences were used to finance schools. Local residential property taxes alone were estimated to have provided $10.2 billion for education in 1970.[5]

As was mentioned earlier, the White House proposal envisions a federal VAT designed to yield approximately $18 billion annually. However, some $5 billion of this would be lost through VAT rebates paid through the mechanism of the individual income tax to counteract the regressivity of the VAT. Therefore, only $12 to $13 billion of the VAT revenues could be distributed to the states for the support of public elementary and secondary schools. This would be sufficient to replace the school funds now derived from local *residential* property taxes but would not make any real dent in the need for school funds derived from *business* property taxes.

Under Mr. Nixon's tentative proposal, however, a state would be eligible for federal VAT revenues only if its schools were no longer financed by local taxes on either business or residential property. In addition, no state-level tax on residential property to support schools would be permitted. However, there would be no prohibition against higher *state* property taxes on *business* plant, equipment, and inventories. Therefore, that portion of local business property taxes now used to

---

[4]U.S. Bureau of the Census, *Governmental Finances in 1970–71* (Washington: U.S. Government Printing Office, 1971), p. 20.

[5]Charles Schultze et al., *Setting National Priorities: The 1973 Budget* (Washington: Brookings Institution, 1972), p. 343. Note that these figures are for a different year than the preceding figures.

support schools might be replaced by state business property taxes. Unless a state elected to raise the necessary funds by some other type of taxation, business generally would enjoy no net reduction in its total property tax.

The use of property taxes of any kind to finance education varies considerably from state to state at present. Hawaii, for example, does not use residential property taxes at all to finance education. If VAT revenues were distributed to help states finance their schools, some states could reduce – or at least not increase – certain taxes other than property taxes. Other states, under any reasonable distribution formula, would not receive enough VAT revenues to replace fully even the school funds now derived from residential property taxes, not to mention the school funds derived from local business property taxes. A VAT thus might possibly reduce, but it is not likely to replace *all* residential property taxes used for schools even if the President's scheme is actually enacted.[6] And it should be remembered that school costs may rise so rapidly that any new tax designed to pay these costs might end up covering largely the increase in the costs and not really replacing existing sources of revenues for schools. Indeed, school costs may escalate rapidly in the next few years because of the growing pressure for equalization of expenditures among various school districts. While this pressure may stimulate "leveling up" of spending in low-expenditure school districts, it is not likely to cause much "leveling down" of spending in high expenditure districts.[7]

Even if President Nixon's suggestions are not adopted, recent court rulings may push the states into assuming a larger share of school costs in order to reduce the variation in school expenditures among school districts within the state.[8] If these court decrees are upheld by the Supreme Court, local property taxes may eventually have to finance a lower proportion of school costs. In this case, local property taxes could be reduced or stabilized even without the introduction of a VAT. On the other hand, state property taxes are likely to increase, and, even if the states should impose residential property taxes to finance the schools, the growing reliance on state rather than local property taxes may increase the total property tax burden of business. Local governments tend to underassess commercial and industrial property, partly because of a desire to keep tax-paying businesses within their jurisdictions. State governments, though eager to keep businesses in the state, are not likely to be as concerned about keeping business within any one part of the state. State assessors tend to have more expertise than local assessors, and they are less likely to let big companies assess themselves. The growing importance of state property taxes, therefore, may result in higher assessments and stiffer total property tax bills for many businesses.[9] This increasing

[6] Schultze et al., p. 343.
[7] New York State Commission on the Quality, Cost and Financing of Elementary and Secondary Education, *Report* (New York, 1972), p. 25.
[8] Courts in five states have ruled that the present system of financing schools with revenues from local property taxes cheats poor children of their constitutional rights. See, for example, "Courts Say Property Levy Must Go," *Washington Post*, February 22, 1972.
[9] "Tax 'Revolution'," *Wall Street Journal*, March 13, 1972, p. 1.

emphasis on state rather than local property taxes is likely to occur whether or not a VAT is introduced, but state property tax rates would presumably be lower with a VAT that produced revenues for the states directly or indirectly.

In summary, it seems likely that, even if the VAT is introduced in the form suggested by President Nixon, business might not receive any net reduction in its total property taxes, although some homeowners might have smaller property tax bills. If the VAT is not introduced, business' total property tax bill may well increase. A VAT should thus be regarded not as a means of reducing business' property taxes but as an alternative to increasing those taxes.

Excise taxes. The Excise Tax Reduction Act of 1965 and the Revenue Act of 1971 eliminated most federal excise taxes. Most of those that remain—such as those on tobacco, alcoholic beverages, and gasoline—are accepted on special grounds. They are not likely to be reduced if a VAT is introduced in the United States. The question arises, however, whether the United States should follow the lead of the Scandinavian countries and the Netherlands and impose its VAT on the basis of the price including any excise taxes. This would have the effect of putting a greater VAT burden on goods subject to excise taxes.

State sales taxes. In addition to possible modification of the existing federal tax structure, enactment of a VAT might affect some state taxation. Coordination of a federal VAT with state and local sales taxes could pose some problems. It is perfectly possible for a sales tax to piggyback on a VAT. The federal government could collect both taxes and remit the sales tax revenues to the appropriate state. The problem arises because of the lack of uniformity in state sales tax laws—not only in the rates of the sales taxes, but also in the methods of collection, accounting periods, and so forth. Considerable negotiation between the state and federal governments would be required to iron out the problems involved and certainly could not be accomplished before the VAT is enacted. A VAT imposed simultaneously with state sales taxes would pose an administrative burden on retail businesses until the two taxes were coordinated.

The states may resist the VAT because it is, in a sense, a sales tax, an impingement on a revenue source which they have heretofore preempted. The existence of state and local sales taxes will probably prevent the federal government from levying as high a VAT rate as is customary in Europe.

One possible way of coping with these problems would be to impose a VAT with a higher rate than currently proposed and automatically turn over to each state part of the VAT revenues collected within the state as compensation for eliminating the state's sales tax. However, the revenues generated by a federal VAT and rebated to the states might differ from the revenues previously generated by a state retail tax even if the rates were equivalent. Some states, for example, have relatively little production but high retail sales; these states would collect less revenue from a VAT collected in installments along the production-distribution chain than from a sales tax collected in full at the retail stage.

In any case, initially at least, a U.S. VAT is likely to be a supplement to, and not a replacement for, state and local sales taxes. The question then arises as to whether the VAT should be levied on prices including or excluding state and local sales taxes. If the VAT base were prices including sales taxes, citizens in areas with high sales taxes would have a higher VAT burden than those in low-sales-tax areas.

Probable VAT rate

In 1972 the VAT rate mentioned most often was 3 percent. By the time a VAT is actually enacted, the need for revenues may be so great that a higher rate, up to 5 percent, may be necessary. On the other hand, the existence of state and local sales taxes and objections of the states to the imposition of a VAT may make it impossible for the federal government to levy more than a 3 percent VAT initially. There will also be pressure to keep the VAT rate low because the VAT will not be replacing either a cumulative turnover tax or a sales tax as it did in Europe, and the imposition of the VAT will, therefore, have an inflationary effect. It should be kept in mind, however, that the standard VAT rate in Europe ranges from 10 percent to 23 percent and that most European countries have raised their VAT rate at least once since the tax was inaugurated.

The Internal Revenue Service would find it much easier to administer a VAT with a single rate, as is the custom in the Scandinavian countries and as is planned for the United Kingdom. Having more than a single VAT rate has been estimated to increase a government's administrative costs by 50 to 80 percent.[10] It also increases business' compliance costs considerably, since more itemization and definition would be required on invoices to distinguish goods subject to different rates. Furthermore, disputes often arise over the classification of various sales. From the points of view of the tax administrator and the businessman, it would be preferable to counteract any regressivity of the VAT by making adjustments in personal income tax rather than by reducing the VAT rate on necessities. In any case, with a VAT rate as low as 3 percent, there would be less need to have a reduced VAT rate for necessities. It is conceivable, however, that Congress would provide a reduced rate for such items as medicine, food, household utilities, local public transportation, and possibly clothing. If so, the reduced rate might be half the standard rate, or 1.5 percent.

Possible exemptions from the VAT

The exemptions to be granted under any U.S. VAT are major issues to be resolved. Economists argue that exemptions should be kept to a minimum in order to keep the VAT base broad and to minimize distortions in the economy. Every exemption granted increases the VAT rate that must be levied on other goods and

---

[10]National Economic Development Office, *Value Added Tax* (London: Her Majesty's Stationery Office, 1971), p. 41.

services to produce a prescribed amount of revenue. Exemptions also tend to make the administration of the tax more difficult. Congress, however, would undoubtedly be subject to considerable pressure to grant a variety of VAT exemptions.

As was indicated in Chapter 2, there are two types of exemptions: zero rating and the normal exemption. Zero-rated goods are exempt from the VAT when sold, *and* producers of such goods are entitled to a refund of any VAT paid on purchases to produce such goods. Zero rating thus removes any VAT paid on a good at any stage. Exempt goods have no VAT levied on their sale, but the exempt entrepreneur may not claim a refund of the VAT paid on his purchases, which thus becomes part of his costs and is reflected in higher prices to his customers or lower profits.

It is a clear advantage to a producer to have his goods zero-rated: His purchases cost him less than they cost other producers since he, in effect, pays no VAT on his purchases. The zero-rated producer can also sell his goods for less since no VAT has to be added to the price. The only minor disadvantage of a VAT to zero-rated producers is that they actually have to pay the VAT on their purchases and then wait for a refund of this VAT. But this affects the zero-rated company's cash flow position only temporarily since soon rebates of VAT paid on past purchases come in as the VAT is paid out on new purchases.

Having a regular VAT exemption gives a company no such clear-cut advantage as does a zero rating.

1. Both the exempt and the nonexempt firm pay a VAT on their purchases. However, the nonexempt firm has the VAT due on its sales reduced by the VAT paid on its purchases. In a certain sense, then, the firm with no exemption pays no VAT on its purchases, and the exempt firm pays more for its purchases than the nonexempt firm.

2. Exempt companies receive no credit for the VAT paid on capital expenditures. Thus exempt companies are deterred from capital investments more than companies which are *not* exempt. Being exempt can be costly to capital-intensive companies.

3. The VAT paid on purchases increases the costs of exempt companies. They must, therefore, either suffer reduced profits or increase their prices. In many cases, therefore, the VAT paid on purchases is passed on by the exempt firm in higher prices charged its customers. However, the business customers of the exempt company receive no credit for the VAT cost hidden in the sales price. If a VAT had been imposed on the company's sales, the VAT would have been indicated separately on the sales invoices, and the business customer could deduct from his own VAT liability the VAT paid on the purchases. Of course, a VAT generally increases the prices of both exempt and nonexempt companies. It tends to increase the prices of exempt firms *less* since their prices include the VAT paid on their purchases but no tax paid on the firm's value added. However, business customers might prefer to pay more for goods from companies without an exemption in order to receive the VAT credit, which exempt companies cannot give.

4. Exemption of a company in the middle of a production-distribution chain transforms the VAT into a cascade turnover tax, for all subsequent purchasers of the exempt company's products never receive any credit for the VAT the exempt company paid on its purchases. The VAT paid on the exempt firm's purchases is a hidden cost in the price at each subsequent stage, and, if markups are a fixed percentage of purchase costs, the final price to the consumer may be considerably higher than the lost VAT credit would warrant. (In the normal VAT system, companies tend to apply their markup to their purchase prices exclusive of the VAT.)

5. Exemption of a company which sells its products primarily to final consumers eliminates the cascading effect. Final customers do not in any case receive credit for the VAT paid on their purchases, whether the VAT is listed separately or hidden in the sales price. Final consumers, therefore, would certainly find it to their advantage to buy from exempt companies, whose prices presumably would be lower since they included the VAT paid in earlier stages but not the VAT on the value added by the exempt companies.

Exhibit 3–1 illustrates the effect of granting VAT exemptions to firms at various stages in a production-distribution chain. The exhibit assumes that VAT costs are always passed forward fully and that markups are a fixed amount, not a fixed percentage of purchase costs. Obviously the figures used in the exhibit are arbitrary ones, chosen simply for purposes of illustration.

As can be seen in the exhibit, if no firms in the production-distribution chain are granted a VAT exemption, a $100 item would cost the final consumer $105, if the VAT rate were 5 percent. If a company in the middle of the chain were exempt, the final cost to the consumer would be $107.10, $2.10 higher than the cost to the consumer with no VAT exemptions. However, if the company selling to the final consumer were the only one exempt, the final cost would be $103, $2 less than the cost to the consumer if no VAT exemptions were allowed. Obviously then, granting exemptions to those who sell goods or services to final consumers reduces the cost of the exempt products. On this ground, it can be argued that providers of medical or educational or legal services to consumers should be exempt from the VAT in the interest of reducing the cost of these socially necessary services. On the other hand, granting VAT exemptions to companies which sell to business customers rather than final consumers distorts the impact of the VAT and increases the final cost to consumers if the VAT is shifted forward, as it normally is.[11]

If these are the effects of exemptions, what exemptions should be granted with the U.S. VAT? And should companies eligible for exemption be allowed to waive their exemption as certain companies in some European countries are allowed to do?

---

[11]Exemptions would not distort the impact of the VAT, however, if the subtraction/accounts method of calculation was used instead of the customary subtraction/tax credit method. (See Chapter 1, pp. 4–5.) With the accounts method, credit is not given for VAT paid at earlier stages, for the VAT is based, not on sales, but on the difference between sales and purchases. Therefore, the impact of the VAT is not affected by the loss of credit for the VAT levied on purchases of exempt firms.

EXHIBIT 3–1
Effect of exempting a firm from VAT

	No companies in production-distribution chain are exempt	Company in middle of chain is exempt	Company selling to consumer is exempt
1. Cost of middleman's purchases exclusive of VAT	$ 40.00	$ 40.00	$ 40.00
2. Five-percent VAT on these purchases..	+ 2.00	+ 2.00	+ 2.00
3. Total cost of middleman's purchases	$ 42.00	$ 42.00	$ 42.00
4. Middleman's markup or value added (assuming the markup is *not* a fixed percent of purchase costs)............................	+ 20.00	+ 20.00	+ 20.00
5. Middleman's sale price including VAT paid on purchases..................	$ 62.00	$ 62.00	$ 62.00
6. Five-percent VAT on middleman's value added (if middleman is not exempt)...	+ 1.00	+ 0.00	+ 1.00
7. Price to purchaser of middleman's product	$ 63.00	$ 62.00	$ 63.00
8. VAT credit earned if purchaser is a nonexempt business (sum of #2 and #6)..	− 3.00	− 0.00	− 0.00
9. Effective cost to purchaser...	$ 60.00	$ 62.00	$ 63.00
10. Business purchaser's markup or value added (assuming the markup is not a fixed percent of purchase costs).........................	+ 40.00	+ 40.00	+ 40.00
11. VAT-exclusive price paid by private consumer	$100.00	$102.00	$103.00
12. Five-percent VAT on price charged private consumer (if seller is not exempt)..	+ 5.00	+ 5.10	+ 0.00
13. Total cost to private consumer	$105.00	$107.10	$103.00

Exports. Exports will almost certainly be zero-rated so that the VAT will not increase export prices and thus not handicap the United States in its efforts to sell more abroad. Imports, on the other hand, will certainly have the VAT levied on them when they enter the country.

Companies which produce goods both for export and for domestic sale will undoubtedly receive a VAT rebate only for those purchases directly related to producing the export goods. With capital purchases, the percentage of the VAT rebated will presumably correspond to the percentage of the company's products that are sold abroad.

Various services relating directly to exports or performed entirely for use abroad will undoubtedly be zero-rated as they are in Europe. There will, however, be some allocation problems for American professional services performed here for use, in part, abroad or performed, in part, abroad for use here. For example, with an accounting firm auditing the international operations of a worldwide operation, what part of its charges would be zero-rated? Or what about a management consulting service intended to benefit, at least in part, a corporation's foreign branches and divisions? Or, in reverse, what about research and development done by a foreign subsidiary of an American company but then used in a product manufactured here? Should such research expenses be taxed as imports?

Zero-rating other products. Should anything besides exports be zero-rated under the U.S. VAT? In some countries newspapers are zero-rated, but, except in the United Kingdom, very little other than exports is zero-rated in Europe.

Financial services. In Europe a VAT exemption is granted to the providers of financial services, such as banks, insurance companies, and stock brokers. These exemptions are traditionally granted on the grounds that it is difficult to apply the "value added" concept to such services. Interest paid on deposits and accrued on policy reserves do not constitute "value added" by financial institutions, which are, for purposes of calculating the source of income, merely intermediaries between lenders and borrowers. The net returns on capital constitute income and are taxed as such under the income tax. Likewise, stockbrokers and insurance companies are essentially intermediaries. Stockbrokers are intermediaries between buyers and sellers of stock, and insurance companies are intermediaries between those paying insurance premiums and those receiving insurance payments. The VAT could not reasonably be applied to all the funds that pass through the hands of such institutions. The "sales" of such institutions are generally quite different in character from the sales of other goods and services. Furthermore, the interest and insurance premiums paid by businesses are considered factor costs, like wages, which contribute to the firm's value-added and are therefore included in the VAT base of nonexempt businesses. In this fashion, many financial services are taxed, at least indirectly, under any VAT.

Some countries do impose a VAT directly on a limited number of financial services. For example, the Netherlands imposes a VAT on certain activities of banks: administration activities, keeping of securities, and interest on hire-purchase transactions. And, when a VAT is not imposed on financial services, sometimes these services are subject to some other kind of tax.

If the United States should elect to impose a VAT on certain types of financial services, it is probable that the subtraction method of computation (sales minus purchases) would not be feasible, and calculation would have to be made by adding together wages, profits, rent paid for premises, and other items. This would exclude from the VAT that portion of the interest collected from borrowers which was subsequently paid out to the bank's depositors. It would exclude from the VAT that portion of an insurance company's revenues which was subsequently paid out to holders of insurance policies. And it would exclude from the VAT that part of the money collected by stockbrokers which was paid over to those from whom they were buying stock. In any case, careful thought would have to be given to which financial services, if any, it would be desirable and practical to subject to a VAT in the United States.

Legal services. Some European countries exempt the services of lawyers on somewhat the same ground that financial services are exempted from the VAT. However, the exemption of lawyers is by no means universal, and, even when exemption is permitted, lawyers serving primarily business clients often find it advantageous to be included in the VAT. However, if legal services to business are subject to the VAT while those to private clients are not, lawyers may have some problems determining which purchases should be considered to have been made for business clients and therefore to be eligible for a VAT credit.

Should all lawyers be exempt from the U.S. VAT? Or should the exemption be given only to legal services for individual rather than business clients? Or should no lawyers be exempt?

Medical and educational services. Medical and educational services are universally exempt from the VAT in Europe. Should the United States also exempt the services of doctors, dentists, hospitals, and educational institutions? Should the United States go even farther and zero-rate these services?

Prescription medicines. Prescription medicines are usually exempt from sales taxes in the United States. Should they also be exempt from the VAT? Most European countries exempt medicines delivered by a doctor or a hospital but not medicines sold commercially. Sweden, however, not only exempts but even zero-rates all prescription medicines, and Britain plans to do the same.

Newspapers and broadcasting. Newspapers are subject to the VAT in some European countries, exempted in some, and zero-rated in others. Should the United States exempt (or even zero-rate) newspapers? Broadcasting is often exempt from the VAT in Europe, but broadcasting is much more likely to be a government-owned operation in Europe than in the United States. It seems unlikely that the United States will exempt radio and television stations when so many of them are privately owned.

Second-hand goods. Second-hand goods sold by an entrepreneur are usually subject to the VAT in Europe. However, the auto industry there complains about the double taxation of used cars, which have a VAT imposed on them when they are sold new and another VAT when they are later resold by a used car dealer. In the Netherlands, however, the purchaser of a new car pays the VAT, not on the full price of his new car, but only on the difference between the selling price of the new car and the trade-in value of his old car. The Netherlands makes similar provisions for the trade-in of other goods. Should the United States follow the precedent of the Netherlands or the precedent of the other European countries?

Or should the United States handle this problem by exempting all second-hand goods from the VAT? This would eliminate discrimination between second-hand goods sold by dealers (subject to the VAT in Europe) and second-hand goods sold privately (not subject to the VAT and, for administrative reasons, impossible to include in the VAT system). If this were done, of course, no tax allowance on new items would be given for trade-ins, and this might seem harsh to consumers, who feel that the best measure of value added for them is the "boot" which they pay for the new over the old item. However, it is fairly clear that taxation on the full price of new cars would increase the market price of used cars and of trade-in allowances, if sales of used cars were not taxable. Market forces, in effect, would tend to bring about a new set of equilibria in prices between new and used cars in which only the equivalent of the boot was taxed. Successive owners of a used car would pay prices which reflected proportionate shares of the original tax on the new car, and those who sell or trade in used cars would benefit from the higher prices for them.

Housing. Imposing the VAT on housing presents perplexing problems. The Europeans generally do not levy the VAT on either the sale or the leasing of land,

and the United States presumably will follow this precedent, particularly since land is already subject to property taxes.

The Europeans do impose the VAT on work done to improve the land: construction work, levelling, project engineering, and so forth. And since the VAT is imposed on construction work, the VAT is imposed on the first sale of a new building but generally not on subsequent sales of the building.

To follow the European precedent in this would pose some problems in the United States, for the VAT in the United States is not designed as a replacement for another tax with a reasonably similar impact. In the United States a pre-VAT building would have no VAT included in its cost and would therefore have a price advantage over a post-VAT building.[12] Owners of pre-VAT buildings could rent or sell them at a lower price or a higher profit than owners of post-VAT buildings. Actually the owner of a pre-VAT building would not have an unduly large advantage if the initial rate of the U.S. VAT were as low as 3 percent. The European countries have sometimes raised their VAT rates by 3 percent or more without throwing their housing industries into disarray. However, the problems posed by levying the VAT on housing have caused the British to zero-rate housing: No VAT will be levied on the first sale of a residential building, and the VAT paid on the construction of the building will be rebated. Sweden resolved the problem of discrimination between pre- and post-VAT buildings by establishing the VAT base for newly constructed buildings at only 60 percent of the actual value of the building. This was designed to make the VAT roughly equivalent to the retail sales tax levied on construction materials (but not on labor) before the VAT was introduced.

If, unlike most of Europe, the United States should exempt the housing industry from the VAT, this would cause the VAT to lose much of the economic neutrality that is one of its great virtues. Exempting any such important segment of the economy from the VAT seriously erodes the VAT base, necessitates a higher VAT rate to raise the needed revenues, and distorts the economy. It seems likely that, despite the inherent problems, the U.S. VAT will be imposed on construction, repair, and maintenance work and on the first sale of new buildings. Subsequent sales of old buildings might well be exempt unless the building is sold by one taxable entrepreneur to another. In such a case, the purchaser would be content to pay the VAT, for he could then deduct this VAT from the tax liability on his sales.

Like the Europeans, the United States will probably not impose a VAT on the rental of housing (other than the rental of hotel rooms and the like). If a VAT should be imposed on rents, then, to be fair, it should also be imposed on the imputed rents of owner-occupied housing. The British found that calculating imputed rents was a mare's nest, and, after one hundred years of anguish over including imputed rents as part of taxable income, the British abandoned this inclusion. The United States will probably decide not to get involved in that quagmire.

---

[12] Any pre-VAT good would, of course, also enjoy a price advantage, but this generally would be of only short duration since most goods do not have the long life a building has.

However, some European countries do impose a VAT on the leasing of certain "business plant and equipment," although only France imposes the VAT on the leasing of any building for business purposes. Since the precedents in this area are so varied, it is difficult to guess how much the U.S. VAT will be imposed on the leasing of commercial and industrial buildings. The United States might decide to impose the VAT on such leases so that the owner of such a building would be treated like other taxable entrepreneurs. The owner would charge his tenants a VAT on their rents but could claim a credit for the VAT paid on the purchase or construction of the building. Any company renting space in the building from the owner would not be hurt, since the company—unless it were an exempt firm—could deduct from its own VAT liability the VAT paid with its rent. If the leasing of commercial and industrial buildings were exempt from the VAT, the VAT included in the cost of constructing these buildings would push up rents, but the renters would be unable to deduct this VAT from their VAT bills.

In summary then, many issues must be resolved in determining how the U.S. VAT should be imposed on real estate and construction. Should the sale or leasing of land be exempt? Should the VAT be levied on construction and repair work and on the first sale of the new building? Should no VAT be imposed on the sale of older buildings? Should a VAT exemption be granted on the rental of residental and/or commercial property?

Agriculture. If the United States' VAT has a single rate, there may be some pressure to exempt food from the VAT or possibly even to zero-rate it, as the United Kingdom is planning to do. However, if food were exempt, this would reduce the VAT base by nearly one fifth and would certainly distort the economic neutrality of the tax. For these reasons, economists would prefer to have food subject to the VAT and then compensate low income consumers for the VAT paid on food purchases through income tax refunds and cash rebates.

Accordingly, it seems likely that the United States will follow the precedent of most of Europe and include agriculture in the VAT system. However, to simplify administration of the tax and to ease the bookkeeping and cash flow problems of farmers, small farmers will probably be exempt from the VAT, and special provisions—such as longer accounting periods and slower VAT payments—may also be made for larger farmers.

Retailers. The existence of state and local sales taxes may cause the United States to consider excluding the retailing sector of the economy from the VAT. In such a case, retailers would owe no VAT on their sales, but they would not be able to get credit for the VAT paid on purchases. The retailer could then be expected to apply his normal markup to his purchase price including the VAT. If the retailer were included in the VAT system and received credit for the VAT paid on his purchases, he would be more likely to apply his markup to the purchase price exclusive of the tax.

Exclusion of retailers from the VAT would have two advantages: It would avoid possible confusion at the retail level between the federal VAT and state and local sales taxes, and it would reduce the number of taxpayers and thus lower the administrative costs of collecting the VAT. The price paid for these advantages, however, would be high. To begin with, the tax base would be reduced by the value added in the retailing sector of the economy. An additional reduction of the tax base would result from the elimination of services, most of which would be difficult, if not impossible, to tax at the wholesale level. A severely diminished tax base would require significantly higher VAT rates to raise a given amount of revenue.

The higher rates of such a VAT would, in turn, affect the collectibility of the tax. Higher rates on wholesalers and manufacturers would provide greater incentive, if not for tax evasion, at least for manipulation of normal business practices. Retailers, for example, would be tempted to deal directly with manufacturers to avoid the VAT added on at the wholesale level. Traders would be artificially encouraged to add as much value as possible at the retail stage; for example, advertising might be done increasingly at the retail stage rather than earlier.

Retailers themselves would not necessarily benefit from exclusion from the VAT. Exclusion would save them the cost of complying with the tax. But the retailer would undoubtedly pay a higher VAT rate on his purchases, and this tax would be included in, and thus would increase, his inventory costs. The increased inventory costs would mean increased carrying costs and property tax liability. Retailers would be unable to get credit for the VAT paid on capital expenditures, a complaint frequently voiced by retailers in France prior to their inclusion in the VAT. This inability would make capital expenditures more expensive for retailers than for other entrepreneurs.

One of the key concerns with the introduction of a VAT is to be able to identify and control inflationary tendencies, particularly those due to unwarranted increases in prices. With retailers excluded and the wholesale VAT included in the base of the retailer's markup, the inflationary impact would be more difficult to identify and thus less susceptible to control. Exempting retailers from the VAT is, overall, not likely to reduce consumer prices.

Small businesses. Special provisions will undoubtedly be made for small businesses, particularly small retailers. Very small firms may well be exempt from the VAT. They may pay the VAT on their purchases and charge the VAT on their sales, but they may not have to keep VAT records or to pay their small VAT liability to the government. Special provisions may also be made for slightly larger firms not eligible for exemption from the VAT. Such firms might have their VAT liability reduced somewhat. To simplify their accounting problems, they might also be allowed longer accounting periods, and/or they might be permitted to remit VAT payments on the basis of estimates of their average VAT liability made by tax authorities rather than on the basis of their actual sales and purchases. Such provisions would be designed to reduce the administrative burden for both the government and the small businessman, but they should not significantly erode the VAT base.

The special VAT provisions for small businesses might be designed to give a slight competitive advantage to the small businessman to compensate him for his comparatively high compliance costs. Compliance with the VAT (like compliance with any tax) may pose more problems for small firms than for large concerns with automated accounting. On the other hand, the special VAT regulations might impose a slightly heavier tax burden on small businessmen in order to encourage them to join the regular VAT system.

In any case, the exact nature and the slant of the special provisions for small businesses are issues yet to be resolved with any VAT introduced in the United States.

Revenues likely to be generated by the U.S. VAT

The claim has been made that the VAT proposed by President Nixon would produce $18 billion in revenues with a 3 percent rate.[13] This claim, which is based on the fact that total personal consumption expenditures in 1970 were $615.8 billion, does not make allowance for the fact that a good many consumption expenditures may not be subject to the VAT. As can be seen in Exhibit 3–2 (pp. 64–65), a 3 percent VAT is not likely to produce more than $12.8 billion revenues from personal consumption expenditures ($7.1 billion from expenditures likely to be subject to the full VAT, plus $5.7 billion from expenditures that might be subject to a reduced rate). If the VAT rate is reduced to 1.5 percent for certain "necessities," then the total revenues from personal consumption expenditures would be only about $10 billion.

However, additional revenues would be generated by imposing the VAT on the construction of private housing, of private hospitals, and of buildings for religious and private educational institutions. The government could also collect VAT revenues on the purchases made by VAT-exempt institutions such as banks, insurance companies, private schools and universities, hospitals, and so forth. To simplify the administration of the tax for construction companies, the VAT might be imposed on the construction of public buildings as well as on private construction, but this would not produce any net revenues for the government. Such a VAT would increase the government's costs by the amount of the VAT collected on public construction projects. Thus the total net revenues likely to be generated by a 3 percent VAT collected on construction projects and on purchases by VAT-exempt organizations would be roughly $1.7 billion. Accordingly, the maximum total revenues a 3 percent VAT is likely to generate is $14.5 billion ($1.7 billion plus $12.8 billion from the VAT imposed on personal consumption expenditures). The total revenues from a dual-rate VAT (3 percent and 1.5 percent) would be around $11.7 billion. These figures, of course, are based on the 1970 GNP; as the GNP grows, so too would the VAT revenues.

If Congress should insist on a dual-rate VAT but wanted to design the tax so it

---

[13] Advisory Commission on Intergovernmental Relations, "Essential Ingredients of a Plan to Substitute a Federal Value-Added Tax for Residential School Property Taxes" (Washington, D.C.: February 9, 1972).

would raise as much revenue as a 3 percent single-rate VAT, this could be accomplished by raising the standard VAT rate to 3.7 percent and the reduced rate to 1.9 percent. However, both business and tax administrators could make VAT calculations much more easily if the rates were round numbers, for example, 4 percent and 2 percent.

Treatment of capital expenditures

Any VAT imposed in the United States will undoubtedly be of the consumption type; that is, it will give firms immediate credit for the VAT paid on capital equipment as well as the VAT paid on purchases of inventory goods or raw materials. The consumption type is used in all European countries which have adopted the VAT system. It has two advantages: First, it prevents the VAT from becoming a deterrent to investment by permitting a firm to deduct the tax paid on its capital purchases from its total VAT liability; second, by allowing the same tax credit on all purchases, it eliminates the need for separate accounting for capital and inventory purchases.

Unlike many European countries, the United States will presumably grant full credit from the beginning for VAT paid on capital purchases. There would be no need for special transition measures since there is presently no equivalent of the VAT imposed on capital purchases and, under a consumption type VAT, there would in effect still be no tax on capital purchases.

Refunds of excess VAT credits

Normally the credits a company receives for the VAT paid on purchases would be less than the VAT owed on its sales. In certain cases, however, a company's VAT credits might exceed its VAT liability. This could happen especially with exporters, who incur no VAT liability on their sales and are entitled to a refund of the VAT paid on their purchases; but it could also occur with companies making substantial capital investments or companies with considerable seasonality in sales and purchases. Companies with substantial excess VAT credits would presumably receive cash refunds from the government not too long after the end of the VAT accounting period, but companies with small or irregular credits would probably be required to carry the credit forward into the next accounting period.

Probable tax accounting and payment procedures

The United States will probably use the subtraction/tax credit method of calculating the VAT; that is, a company will multiply its total sales by the VAT rate and then deduct from this VAT liability the total VAT paid on all its purchases. The VAT rate will presumably be applied to prices excluding the VAT itself and any sales taxes but including any excise taxes or import duties. The price on which

EXHIBIT 3-2

Revenues likely to be generated by a 3 percent VAT (figures are in millions of dollars)

	1970 Expenditures	Revenues from expenditures likely to be subject to 3% VAT	Expenditures possibly subject to a reduced VAT rate		Expenditures possibly exempted and so producing no revenues
			Revenues if subject to 3% VAT	Revenues if subject to 1.5% VAT	
1. Tobacco	$ 11,188	$ 336	$	$	$
2. Alcoholic beverages	17,714	531			
3. Food (except food in 4 and 5)[1]	92,062		2,762	1,381	
4. Food produced and consumed on farms	748				748
5. Food purchased in restaurants[1]	21,233	637			
6. Shoes and other footwear	8,063		242	121	
7. Shoe repair, etc.	420		13	6	
8. Clothing and accessories other than footwear	44,333		1,330	665	
9. Clothing issued to military personnel	158				158
10. Laundering, cleaning, altering, etc., garments	4,507		135	68	
11. Jewelry, watches, and miscellany	4,797	144			
12. Personal care (toilet articles, barbers beauty parlors, bath, etc.)	10,101	303			
13. Housing: rentals and inputed rentals for owner-occupied dwellings	91,224				91,224
14. Household equipment, (furniture, appliances, china and utensils, cleaning supplies, stationery, etc.)	47,347	1,420			
15. Household utilities	23,715		711	356	
16. Telephone and telegraph	9,841	295			
17. Domestic service	4,715				4,715
18. Services of doctors, dentists, hospitals, etc. plus health insurance	38,684				38,684
19. Drug preparations, ophthalmic products, orthopedic appliances, etc.[2]	8,584		257	129	(2)
20. Services of brokers, banks, other financial intermediaries, and of life insurance companies	27,303				27,303
21. Legal services	3,876				3,876
22. Funeral and burial services	2,188		66	33	
23. Personal business other than items 20–22	2,130	64			
24. Local public transportation	1,557		47	23	
25. All other transportation	76,314	2,289			
26. Magazines, newspapers, sheetmusic[3]	4,097		123	61	(3)
27. All other recreation	34,952	1,049			
28. Private education and research	10,353				10,353
29. Religious and welfare activities	8,826				8,826
30. Expenditure in the U.S. by foreigners	2,417	73			
Totals for personal consumption expenditures:	$613,447[4]	$7,141	$5,686	$2,843	$185,887

[1]The figures given by the source for the food expenditures in Items 3 and 5 were actually $102,562 and $28,447 million, but those figures included expenditures for alcoholic beverages (Item 2), which were listed in a footnote in the source. Only a very rough estimate could be made of how much of the total expenditures for alcoholic beverages should be deducted from the figure given for Item 3 and how much from Item 5.

[2]Prescription medicines might be exempt from the VAT, but the source does not indicate how much of the expenditures for "drug preparations and sundries" ($6,742 million) was for prescription medicines. It is conceivable that some of the other expenditures listed in Item 19 might also be exempt. If so, expenditures subject to the VAT might be reduced by about $5,000 million.

[3]Conceivably newspapers might be exempt from the VAT, but the source does not indicate the size of consumer expenditures for newspapers alone.

[4]This figure for personal consumption expenditures does not include expenditures abroad by U.S. residents. It therefore differs somewhat from the figure in the text.

EXHIBIT 3–2 (*Continued*)

	1970 Expenditures	Revenues from expenditures likely to be subject to 3% VAT	Expenditures possibly subject to a reduced VAT rate		Expenditures possibly exempted and so producing no revenues
			Revenues if subject to 3% VAT	Revenues if subject to 1.5% VAT	
31. Private housing construction including additions and alterations	$ 29,881	$ 896	$	$	$
32. Public housing construction	1,105	[33][5]			(5)
33. New construction for private hospitals and religious and educational institutions	4,257	128			
34. New construction of public buildings and military facilities	11,448	[343][5]			(5)
35. Other public construction (highways, sewer systems, etc.)	16,739	[502][5]			(5)
36. Purchases (other than real estate) by purveyors of medical and educational services and by non-profit organizations	9,736[6]	292			
37. Purchases by financial and insurance enterprises	12,904[6]	387			
Totals exclusive of personal consumption expenditures:					
With bracketed figures	$ 86,070	$2,581	$ 0	$ 0	$ 0
Without bracketed figures	$ 56,778	$1,703	$ 0	$ 0	$ 0
Grand totals:					
With bracketed figures	$699,517	$9,722	$5,686	$2,843	$185,887
Without bracketed figures	$670,225	$8,844	$5,686	$2,843	$185,877

[5] Construction of public housing or public buildings of any sort might be exempt from VAT. However, there would be administrative problems if the VAT distinguished between public and private construction, and in Europe public construction seems generally to be subject to the VAT if performed by a private contractor. Imposing a VAT on public construction would, however, not produce any net revenues for the government since it would increase government costs by the amount of the VAT collected on such construction.

[6] These figures are only rough estimates, calculated from *Scientific American*'s "Input/Output Structure of the United States Economy," 1970.

SOURCE: Statistics on 1970 consumption and construction expenditures were obtained from U.S. Department of Commerce, *Survey of Current Business*, vol. 51, no. 7 (July 1971), pp. 24 and 33. The figures in the remaining columns were calculated from these statistics.

the VAT is calculated will probably be the actual cost to the customer, including not only the cost of the good itself but also shipping, installation, insurance, interest, and other such charges. A company calculating the tax credit on its purchases may possibly not be allowed to count the VAT paid on purchases of gifts, entertainment, and the like, if the precedents of some European countries are followed.

Following Europe's example, the United States will probably require that a company's VAT be calculated on an invoice rather than a cash basis; that is, the VAT credit on purchases and the tax liability on sales would be recognized at the time of invoicing rather than at the time money changes hands. Presumably the effective date of invoices will in most cases be the date the goods or services are delivered rather than the date the invoice is prepared. Special provisions will undoubtedly be made for services rendered over a period of time and for payments received before the goods or services are delivered.

Should the U.S. VAT have some flexibility in these regulations, to permit certain companies to calculate their VAT on a cash basis rather than an invoice basis? The cash basis is advantageous for companies which sell more on credit than they buy on credit.[14] If companies were given a choice, they undoubtedly would have to be consistent about using a cash or invoice basis and could only change from one system to the other with the permission of the tax authorities.

Companies calculating their VAT on an invoice basis would hopefully be allowed credit for excess VAT paid on invoices which the customer subsequently did not pay in full (for example, because a discount was later granted, because the goods were returned, or because the customer went bankrupt).

The VAT accounting period might be as short as one month, as it is in most of the EEC countries. If, in the interest of simplifying administration of the tax, the accounting period should be somewhat longer, say two or three months, exporters would probably be allowed to use a one-month accounting period anyway so they could get their VAT refunds more rapidly. If the accounting period were only one month, companies might be allowed to make just an estimate of the VAT they owed and postpone a detailed accounting until the end of the year or at least until the end of the quarter. Farms and small firms might be allowed longer accounting periods than other enterprises.

Companies may be given perhaps one month after the end of the accounting period to pay their VAT bill. In Europe companies are given from 10 days (in Germany) to one month plus 20 days (in Denmark and Norway). Longer accounting and payment periods would help businesses' cash flow situation[15] but would slow down the flow of revenues to the government. Conceivably the government could be persuaded to accept a slower revenue flow in order to help businesses' cash flow and thus to compensate them, in part, for the cost of complying with the VAT.

In Europe, when goods are sold to commercial customers, the invoice must indicate both the price of the goods without the VAT and the amount of the VAT. This is necessary to enable commercial customers to claim credit for the VAT paid on their purchases, and it certainly will be a requirement under the U.S. VAT. However, the Europeans do not require that the VAT be indicated separately on retail goods and services sold to consumers. This poses a problem when a retailer sells to a commercial customer who is eligible to claim credit for the VAT paid on his purchases. In most countries the retailer must prepare a special invoice for his commercial customers. In Denmark, however, which has a single VAT rate, the commercial customer simply saves his sales slip and calculates for himself what the VAT must have been. Should the United States require that retailers indicate the VAT separately on their sales slips? This is the usual procedure with state and local sales taxes, and it makes it unnecessary for a retailer to distinguish between his private customers and his commercial customers. Listing the VAT separately on retail sales slips would make customers more aware of the tax, would help them understand its effect on prices, would make it easier to stop companies which used the tax as an excuse for unwarranted price hikes, and might facilitate analysis of the inflationary impact of the VAT.

---

[14]Calculating the VAT on an invoice basis versus a cash basis is discussed at greater length in Chapter 6.

[15]The effect of longer VAT accounting and payment periods on a business' cash flow is analyzed in Chapter 6.

Summary

Many issues have to be resolved before a VAT is enacted in the United States. The first problem concerns the relationship of the VAT to other taxes. Should special provisions be written into the individual income tax to reduce the VAT burden on low- and even middle-income consumers? Should VAT revenues be used to reduce residential property taxes? Should any other tax changes be made along with, or instead of, a VAT?

Then there is the question of the VAT rate. Should the rate be the 3 percent talked of in 1972? Should there be a reduced rated of, say, 1.5 percent for certain necessities? This would reduce the VAT's burden on the poor but would very much complicate administration of the tax.

Presumably exports will be zero-rated, that is, exempt from the VAT on their sales and entitled to a refund of the VAT paid on purchases to produce them. Should anything else be zero-rated under a U.S. VAT? Should certain items not be zero-rated, but exempt from the VAT on their sales? The question of exemption occurs principally with the following: the services of banks, insurance companies, and stock brokerage firms; the services of lawyers or at least of lawyers serving primarily private rather than business customers; the services of doctors, dentists, hospitals, and educational institutions; prescription medicines; possibly newspapers; the sale and leasing of land; the construction and sale of new buildings; the sale of older buildings; the leasing of commercial property; the leasing of any residences except hotel rooms and the like; very small farms and firms.

A 3 percent VAT with a limited number of exemptions would not have been likely to generate more than $14.5 billion in revenues at the 1970 level of GNP. Revenues from a VAT would increase in proportion to increases in the GNP.

Companies will almost certainly be given full credit for the VAT paid on their purchases of capital goods as well as for the VAT paid on their purchases of raw materials and inventory goods. Companies whose credits exceed their VAT liability will presumably be given a refund.

4

Economic Impacts of a
Value Added Tax in the
United States

THE INTRODUCTION of a Value Added Tax in the United States would affect, among other things, the growth of private consumption, business investment, wages and prices, the equity and neutrality of the tax structure, the country's balance of payments, and the government's cost of tax administration. There would be direct impacts in these areas as well as indirect effects reflecting subsequent adjustments to the direct impacts of the tax.

Before discussing these effects, it is necessary to state the limitations placed on the examination of such broad issues.

First, this chapter attempts to present a brief and simplified analysis of a highly complex subject—the economic aspects of taxation. In addition, factual knowledge about this topic is limited, particularly for a relatively new tax such as the VAT. Given these limitations, only the broad outlines of the impact of a VAT on the United States are presented. The focus is "the big picture," those macroeconomic issues of national importance, such as public and private consumption, investment, and the balance of payments.

Second, the analysis concerns the impact of a VAT as a revenue supplement rather than as a partial substitute for existing taxes.[1] Although some tax changes might be made when the VAT is introduced, the principal purpose of the VAT will presumably be to raise additional revenues rather than to replace other taxes.

Finally, the analysis rests on a comparison of the various effects of a VAT with the effects of increasing existing taxes, because the impact of a VAT cannot be evaluated in isolation from the alternatives to it. No attempt has been made to compare a VAT with taxes which are not currently a part of the tax structure, such as a national retail sales tax.[2] In comparing the impacts of the various taxes, it should be

---

[1] For readers interested in the impact of a VAT as a revenue substitute, we suggest *The Role of Direct and Indirect Taxes in the Federal Revenue System* (Princeton: Princeton University Press, 1964).

[2] For some comparison of a VAT with a retail sales tax, see Chapter 1, pp. 6–7.

remembered that no tax is positively desirable in and of itself. The question is, if additional revenues are needed, what is the least undesirable way to raise them.

General effect of any tax

The purpose of any tax is to divert income from private hands to the government to pay for public expenditures. In any economy with substantially full employment of resources, an increase in government expenditures may be inflationary unless it is balanced by a corresponding decrease in private expenditures.

Taxation may reduce private expenditures in various ways. Income taxation diverts funds directly from private hands to the government. A sales tax or Value Added Tax diverts funds to the government in a more indirect way. Such taxes increase prices, with the result that a given dollar amount of private expenditures from personal incomes buys fewer goods for personal consumption. Thus, real personal income is reduced by both direct and indirect taxes, but the increased government expenditures provide society with desired services and goods which the private economy is either unwilling or unable to supply. If the political process is working effectively, the additional government services and goods will provide greater satisfactions to people generally than the private expenditures foregone.

Whatever the method of taxation, in most situations the expansion in government activities is small enough to absorb only part of the normal growth of the gross national product. Thus, total private consumption is not actually reduced in most cases. A larger government command over resources merely curtails the expansion in private consumption which would otherwise take place. Only if the increase in government expenditures is very rapid or very large, as during a war or as a result of a drastic change in policies regarding welfare or other activities, may there have to be an actual curtailment of total private consumption.

In the absence of adequate taxation, government expenditures will be paid for by deficit financing. Such financing will be inflationary if there is no substantial slack in the economy. Price increases produced by the inflation arising from deficit spending should be distinguished from price increases caused by taxation. Deficit spending involves an artificial injection of newly created purchasing power into the stream of spending. The government command over resources is satisfied, and in the process the general level of prices is pulled up. The private command over resources is reduced because private incomes do not buy as many goods and services as they otherwise would. The impact of such an inflation is capricious. Some prices advance faster than others. Some increases in costs lag behind price increases; others lead. Cost-price relationships become distorted. Those with fixed incomes—that is, those on pensions and annuities or those holding savings or other bonds—especially suffer. The government can always secure the products and services which it desires. But, with deficit financing, the diversion from private consumption and investment tends to be arbitrary and, in most respects, extremely unjust. Inflation is indeed the "cruelest tax of all."

Price increases caused by sales, value-added, or other indirect taxes are different from price increases triggered by deficit financing, although the distinction between the two types of price increases has not been adequately recognized in economic analysis. Price increases caused by indirect taxes are usually predictable. The impact on private consumption is at least contemplated. A given amount of revenue is sought by the government. Specific taxes are enacted which will, through price increases, reduce the goods and services which can be purchased by various identifiable groups of the population. A tax may be selective – as on liquor, gasoline, or jewelry – or it may be general. The effect on consumption and the actual redirection of spending depends on the elasticity of demand for the taxed product. A tax on salt for household use, as an extreme example, would have little effect on its consumption. The immediate impact of the tax could be predicted, based on the consumption of salt, although the larger repercussions throughout the economy would depend on the elasticity of demand for all other purchases by families whose freely available funds for general use had been decreased by the higher price of salt. The ramifications of any indirect tax are, therefore, sometimes unpredictable since they depend on elasticities of demand, the availability of substitute products, and the composite preferences of people in the use of their incomes and capital.

An analysis of the effect of a broad-based sales tax or a Value Added Tax on the general level of prices becomes exceedingly complex. The immediate impact of the tax is to raise the price of all goods and services subject to it, but this general price increase may affect different segments of the economy in different ways. The overall result of the higher prices, however, is to divert some purchasing power to the government to use in its purchases of goods and services. There is still the same total purchasing power in the economy and the same aggregate amount of goods and services produced, but the composition and distribution of these aggregates are different.

In terms of a shift of purchasing power from the private to the public sector, the effect of sales and other indirect taxes is similar to that which occurs if the government diverts private income into its hands directly by income taxation; but the indirect method operates through a price increase, which does not take place under direct taxation.

Because additional government expenditures inevitably divert consumption from the private to the public sector, it is impossible for the total private use of resources to be maintained at the level that would have been attained otherwise, assuming substantially full use of resources. And, since the objective of taxation is to divert resources in a rational rather than a capricious manner, as with deficit financing, it is incompatible with that objective for any group to attempt to offset higher prices attributable to indirect taxes by increasing their income. It is, of course, equally incompatible with the objective of increases in direct taxation for any group to attempt to offset reductions in after-tax income by pay increases. Attempts of particular groups to avoid the impact of a tax merely shift the burden to others and produce unintended, and sometimes disruptive, repercussions in the economy.

Incompatability or inconsistency with public policy is no reason to expect restraint in private actions, and on practical grounds it must be recognized that both tax-induced price increases and tax-caused decreases in take-home pay are likely to stimulate attempts to offset them. This is particularly true with indirect taxes, such as sales taxes and value-added taxes. Since, unlike higher income taxes, tax-induced price increases are customarily reflected in the cost-of-living index, increases in direct taxes are more likely than higher income taxes to trigger demands for wage increases.

If cost-of-living indexes excluded the effects of indirect taxation, indirect taxes might have a less inflationary impact on the economy. Exclusion of indirect taxes would be consistent with the present policy of making allowances in the cost-of-living index for improvements in the quality of products. Taxation, after all, pays for additional government expenditures which are supposed to improve the quality of life in a general way. Price increases caused by taxes should be distinguished in this respect from price increases arising from cost/push inflation. Furthermore, if those with lower incomes were given rebates for some or all of their VAT payments, the VAT would not raise the cost of living for such groups as much as the VAT-induced price increases would indicate. Separate identification, if not exclusion, of the tax component in the cost-of-living indexes would add clarity and provide a better basis for public policy in many respects.

Price increases due to a value-added or broad-based sales tax have implications for monetary policy even though, as indicated above, the new taxes merely involve a shift in the command over resources from the private to the public sector and do not change total income or total output in the economy. The change in the composition of the total output of goods and services would not, of itself, call for a change in the money supply over what it should otherwise have been. However, because such indirect taxes in the ordinary course of collection are added to existing prices, expansion in the money supply over what otherwise would be appropriate is necessary to accommodate the price increases initiated by such taxes. Without such an expansion in the money supply, there would be numerous disruptions in the relations among costs, incomes, and prices; the supply of money would be inadequate to keep the monetary economy operating smoothly in the face of the tax-induced price increases.

In contrast to the need for expansion of the monetary supply to minimize cost-price disruptions under indirect taxation, a shift of spending power due to higher *direct* taxation of individuals is made with a minimum of disruptions in cost-price relations if there is *no* expansion in the money supply. Indeed, an increase in the money supply under these circumstances would be inflationary. If the increase in direct taxes sets off successful attempts to increase wages and salaries to maintain after-tax incomes, a different problem arises for monetary policy; but this is the familiar one of whether the money supply should be expanded to accommodate a cost/push inflation.

An increase in the corporation income tax raises a very special case in the analysis of tax and monetary policy because of uncertainty about the incidence of the tax.

For those who argue that the tax is not shifted, the tax merely transfers income from dividends and corporate retained earnings to the government. No change in the money supply is appropriate. For those who believe the corporate income tax is shifted forward, the higher prices stimulated by this tax would necessitate a larger money supply than would otherwise be required. An appraisal of the monetary implications of a major increase in the corporate income tax is beyond the proper scope of this book. It is sufficient to note the problem and to distinguish it from the implications for monetary policy arising from a broad-based indirect tax.

VAT as a source of government revenue

In comparison with other federal taxes, a VAT would yield high revenues at a low rate. This advantage of a VAT is due to its large base, which, in a VAT applied to all goods and services, would equal total personal consumption. As was shown in Chapter 3, a 3 percent VAT with a limited number of exemptions might raise $14.5 billion in revenues at the 1970 GNP level. If a reduced rate of 1.5 percent were granted certain necessities, the VAT revenues would be only $11.7 billion.

If, as President Nixon suggested, some VAT rebates were paid through the mechanism of the individual income tax to counteract the regressivity of the VAT, several billion of VAT revenues might be lost. When the possibility of exemptions was not considered and a 3 percent VAT was calculated to produce $18 billion in revenues, it was estimated in early 1972 that compensating adjustments in the individual income tax would absorb $5 billion of the VAT revenues. If actual VAT revenues were less than $18 billion because of exemptions, presumably smaller adjustments would have to be made in the individual income tax. With a 3 percent single-rate VAT that raised $14.5 billion, perhaps only $4 billion would be lost in rebates paid through the individual income tax and the net increase in government revenues might be around $10.5 billion. With a dual-rate VAT (3 percent and 1.5 percent) that raised $11.7 billion, perhaps only $3 billion would be lost in rebates paid through the individual income tax, and the net increase in government revenues might be around $8.7 billion.

Steep increases in existing taxes would be required to raise revenues equal to those the government would net from a 3 percent VAT with income tax adjustments. For example, to raise $10.5 billion, corporate income taxes would have to be increased 32 percent (based on 1970 data).[3] This could be done by raising the normal rate from 48 percent to around 63 percent; or, roughly $10 billion could be raised by eliminating the 7 percent investment credit (which would raise revenues of over $3 billion), withdrawing the recently enacted provision for accelerated depreciation allowances (which would raise another $3 billion or more), *and* changing the cor-

[3] 1970 corporate income tax revenues were $32.8 billion. See U.S. Bureau of the Census, *Statistical Abstract of the United States: 1971*, 92d ed. (Washington: U.S. Government Printing Office, 1971), p. 374.

porate income tax's special provisions for the extractive industries and other special provisions.[4]

Another way of raising $10.5 billion in new revenues would be to increase individual income taxes in some fashion. A surcharge of approximately 12 percent would raise such revenues.[5] Alternatively, nearly $10 billion could be raised by making three changes in the individual income tax: (1) taxing interest paid on state and local government bonds ($1.2 billion); (2) eliminating the deductions allowed for mortgage interest and property taxes (over $4 billion); and (3) allowing deductions only for charitable contributions and medical expenses that exceeded 3 percent and 5 percent respectively of income ($4.1 billion).[6] If the individual income tax were revised to tax capital gains fully, the government would collect an additional $9.3 billion in revenues if gains developed and were realized as they would have been under existing taxes. If accrued, unrealized capital gains were taxed on death, still another $4.4 billion would flow into the government's coffers.

Instead of collecting net revenues of $10.5 billion from a 3 percent VAT, the government could raise the same amount by increasing payroll taxes 27 percent (based on 1970 figures).[7] Such an increase could be accomplished either by raising social security tax rates or by increasing the amount of salary subject to the tax or by a combination of the two.

Another means of collecting an additional $10.5 billion in revenues would be to raise property taxes by about 28 percent. (As was indicated in Chapter 3, total 1971 revenues from state and local property taxes were $37.8 billion.) Of course, increasing property taxes would raise additional money only for state and local governments and would, in fact, *reduce* federal revenues unless the deduction for property taxes were eliminated from the federal income tax. To compensate for such a loss in federal income tax revenues, property taxes would need to be increased by perhaps 30 percent if total revenues of governments at all levels were to swell $10.5 billion.

In summary, then, to raise revenues equal to those the government would net from a 3 percent VAT with income tax adjustments, corporate income tax revenues would have to be increased by something like 32 percent, individual income tax revenues would have to go up around 12 percent, payroll taxes would have to go up approximately 27 percent, *or* property taxes would have to be increased perhaps 30 percent. This is illustrated in Exhibit 4-1.

---

[4] "Tax Reform, or Slamming a Revolving Door," *Monthly Economic Letter* (First National City Bank), May 1972, pp. 9–12; "Nixonomics versus Taxes: The Campaign against Reform," *Boston Sunday Globe,* April 30, 1972, p. 72.

[5] 1970 revenues from the individual income tax were $90.4 billion, according to the U.S. Bureau of the Census, *Statistical Abstract,* p. 374.

[6] These figures were calculated by economists Benjamin Okner and Joseph Pechman at the Brookings Institution, Washington, D.C. Unfortunately the Brookings figures were calculated on the basis of 1972 income levels, while the other calculations in this section of the report are based on 1970 figures.

[7] 1970 revenues from employment taxes and contributions were $39.133 billion, according to the U.S. Bureau of the Census, *Statistical Abstract,* p. 374. In 1970 the effective rate of the social security tax was 9.6 percent (4.8 percent from employees plus 4.8 percent from employers). A 27 percent increase in this tax then would have raised the effective rate of the tax to 12 percent. By 1973, however, the effective rate of the tax had already gone up to 11.7 percent, and the maximum salary subject to the tax had been raised from $7,800 to $10,800.

EXHIBIT 4–1
Yield of various federal taxes in 1970 figures

	Value Added Tax (minus revenues lost through compensating adjustments in individual income tax)		Income taxes		Payroll tax	State and local property taxes (1971)
	3% single rate	Dual rate of 3% and 1.5%	Corporate	Individual		
Yield ($ billion)	$10.5	$8.7	$32.8	$90.4	$39.1	$37.8
Percent increase required to equal net revenues of 3% VAT	—	21%	32%	12%	27%	30%[1]
1970 rate	3.0%	3.0% standard rate 1.5% reduced rate	48%	14–70%	9.6%[2]	Various
Rate required to yield $10.5 billion additional revenue equal to yield of a 3% VAT minus revenues lost through adjustments in individual income tax[4]	3.0%	3.7% standard rate[3] 1.9% reduced rate	63%	12% surcharge	12%	Increase of 30%

SOURCE: Statistics on the yield of all taxes except the VAT are from: U.S. Bureau of the Census, *Statistical Abstract of the United States*, 1971, 92d ed. (Washington: U.S. Government Printing Office, 1971), p. 374. Reasoning in calculating VAT revenues is explained in the text.

[1] Although property taxes would only have to be increased about 28 percent to raise an additional $10.5 billion in revenues, a greater increase would have to be made if there were to be compensation for the reduction in federal income tax revenues caused by higher property taxes.

[2] The 1970 legal rate of 4.8 percent is applied twice to wages since both employers and employees are taxed by this amount. Thus the 1970 effective rate was 9.6 percent. Since 1970 the effective rate has been raised to 11.7 percent.

[3] See Chapter 3, pp. 62–63.

[4] Additional revenues could, of course, be raised by making changes in the various taxes rather than increasing the rates.

Impact of VAT on total spending

The VAT will have differential impacts on the three elements of total spending: consumption, investment, and government spending. If the revenues generated by the VAT are promptly spent, total spending should not change; only the division of total spending among the different types would change.

Effect of a VAT on private consumption. The introduction of a VAT in the United States would have two immediate effects: (1) a rise in consumer prices as companies passed the tax forward to the consumer and (2) a reduction in unit sales below the level they would otherwise attain (to the extent that consumers did not dip into savings to maintain their pre-VAT level of consumption).[8]

The consumer with a fixed disposable income and no savings to cushion the effect of the price rise would be forced either to buy less-expensive goods or to buy fewer items. In the latter case, the purchases he would forego first would most likely be luxury goods. There would be an overall decrease in consumer demand and a greater demand for low-priced goods relative to high-priced items and for necessities relative to luxuries.

If the VAT were not passed forward in full, those companies which chose to absorb all or a portion of the tax would gain a temporary price advantage. However, for a number of reasons it is reasonable to assume that companies generally would

[8] It must always be remembered that in a dynamic economy a "reduction" or a "decline" means only that the level would be lower than would otherwise occur. In absolute terms, there may still be an increase.

pass the VAT forward fully. In the first place, companies would find an immediate increase in the cost of purchases as their suppliers passed the tax forward. Secondly, companies with low profit margins simply could not afford to absorb a tax of 3 percent on their sales. Of course, competitive forces could affect the ability of individual companies to shift the tax forward. If the demand for a company's products were elastic, the company might be compelled to absorb at least part of the VAT in order to protect its sales. However, if the VAT is listed separately on sales slips, buyer resistance to the higher prices directly attributable to the tax might be minimized.

For these reasons, it appears safe to assume that the vast majority of companies would be able to pass the VAT forward. A full pass forward of the VAT, as already noted, would tend to decrease consumption in the form of lower unit sales than would have occurred otherwise.

Other taxes also affect consumption. An increase in the excise tax would reduce consumption in the same manner as a VAT, except that excise taxes are normally imposed on, and therefore reduce the consumption of, only a limited number of goods and services. An increase in the individual income tax would reduce disposable income which, in turn, would decrease consumption. But the decrease in consumption would be less than with the imposition of a VAT because of the progressive nature of the income tax. Higher income taxes would make the biggest dent in the disposable income of wealthier taxpayers, who usually spend a lower proportion of their income than families with smaller earnings. The VAT, by contrast, may reduce the purchasing power of some lower income families as much as, or more than, that of some higher income families. The decrease in consumption caused by higher income taxes would be less if individual income taxes were not increased across the board but were changed in some way that principally increased the tax burden on those with high incomes. For example, increasing the tax on capital gains would mainly affect those with high incomes, and, therefore, such a tax change should have less of an impact on consumer spending than a general income tax hike.

An increase in the corporate income tax can be thought of as increasing prices if full shifting of the tax to the consumer occurs. If no shifting occurs, shareholder dividends and thus income of shareholders might be reduced.[9] Again, however, any potential reduction in dividends caused by an increase in the corporate income tax would tend to affect high-income groups more than the low-income groups and therefore have less of an impact on personal consumption. Increasing the payroll tax would reduce the take-home pay of the worker and, to the extent the employer's share of the increase is passed forward, would raise prices. This would have a pronounced effect upon consumer demand since, unlike the individual income tax, payroll taxes hit those with low incomes harder than those with high incomes. Increases in business property taxes, if shifted, would raise prices. Increases in residential property taxes would reduce homeowners' disposable income and raise rents for

---

[9]The question of shifting the corporate income tax is unresolved in tax circles. In this report, the distinction between the two assumptions of shifting is noted where applicable.

others. In short, any tax in some way diminishes private consumption from the level it would otherwise attain; but a VAT, higher payroll taxes, or higher residential property taxes would have the most immediate effect on private consumption.

Effect of a VAT on savings and investment. It has already been noted that the introduction of a VAT might cause a temporary reduction in savings as consumers tried to maintain spending levels. The VAT could have a longer-term, positive effect on savings because the tax provides an incentive for individuals to save. Unlike the personal income tax, the VAT taxes only that part of an individual's income which is spent. If the VAT, in fact, stimulated saving, the resulting increase in funds available for loans would encourage investment.

A VAT of the consumption type would not create any tax deterrent to business investment. However, by dampening consumer demand, the VAT might discourage businesses from expanding unless the decline in consumer spending were fully compensated for by a rise in government spending.

A rise in the individual income tax would discourage investment, since the reduction in disposable income would lead to decreased savings. The income tax provides an additional disincentive to save in that all income is taxed, whether saved or spent, and any money earned by savings is subject to further tax. Any reduction in savings caused by higher individual income taxes would, in turn, decrease the supply of funds available for investment and increase the cost of capital, resulting in a negative impact on investment. The decrease in investment would be particularly pronounced if, instead of imposing a surcharge, the individual income tax were increased by eliminating the special provisions for capital gains; for such a tax change would hit hardest those most likely to have funds to invest.

An increase in the corporate income tax, to the extent it was not shifted, would reduce retained earnings and dividend income. Lower retained earnings would mean fewer internal funds for investment. Lower dividend income would reduce the savings of the shareholders and thus reduce investment funds available from outside sources. Both of these effects would raise the cost of capital, thereby discouraging investment.

If the corporate income tax is not fully shifted, a further result of raising the tax would be to decrease the number of worthwhile new investments. Normally, new investments are undertaken by corporations if they promise to yield a satisfactory rate of return after taxes. An increase in the tax rate would mean that the pretax return on an investment must be greater to meet a company's required rate of return. To the extent that the number of projects that would meet the higher criterion is limited, an increase in the corporate income tax would reduce investment.

If the corporate income tax is fully shifted, an increase in this tax would have a mixed effect on savings and investment. Prices would go up, and, as with the VAT, this *might,* in theory, encourage consumers to spend less of their income and to save more. On the other hand, a company's uncertainty about its ability to fully shift the higher corporate income tax could discourage investment.

If the corporate income tax were increased not by raising the rates but by eliminating the investment credit and the speeded up depreciation allowances, business would not only have fewer funds to invest but also less incentive to invest the funds it had.

Higher payroll taxes might induce a business to invest in labor-saving equipment in order to reduce its tax load. Payroll taxes thus provide an indirect incentive for investment. Payroll taxes imposed on employees would reduce disposable income and therefore the amount employees could save without reducing their standard of living. However, since payroll taxes hurt low-income people more than those with high incomes, higher payroll taxes should cause less of a decline in savings than higher individual income taxes.

Higher property taxes would discourage investment in real estate and any other assets subject to such taxes. Higher property taxes would also reduce the funds available for savings.

In summary, an increase in the corporate income tax (if not fully shifted) would probably be the greatest deterrent to savings and investment. Imposing a VAT or increasing payroll taxes might provide the least deterrent.

Effect of increased government expenditures following a VAT introduction. The resources transferred by a VAT from the private to the public sector would presumably be redeployed as expenditures by the public sector. If the VAT revenues were spent and not used to reduce the federal deficit, the decrease in consumer spending would be compensated for by an increase in public spending, and overall economic activity would remain about the same. But the regional pattern and composition of public expenditures is considerably different from the pattern and composition of private consumption. Public expenditures occur with some uniformity over the country in such categories as education, welfare payments, veteran benefits, or highway construction; but other important categories of public expenditures are concentrated in certain parts of the country. Defense spending, for example, would tend to be concentrated more in California than in Florida, and funds for relief of central cities would flow to urban areas, as opposed to suburban and rural areas. This difference in impact would be to the advantage of companies in the areas of increased government expenditures, and sales of such companies might actually increase over what they would have been in the absence of a VAT. For other companies, however, in areas less affected by increased government expenditures, recovery in the growth rate of sales or profits might be postponed or not occur at all.

Public funds may not only be spent in different areas but also on different goods and services than consumers' funds. Reducing the money available for private consumption, for example, might dampen housing sales while the new tax revenues might increase expenditures for school construction. Thus, the effect of a VAT (or any tax) on different types of businesses will be greatly influenced by how the revenues are spent.

Impact of a VAT on prices

Inflation can be thought of in two dimensions: demand/pull and cost/push. Demand/pull inflation is characterized by an overheated economy: high employment, with an inadequate labor supply to fill demand, high investment, and consumer demands that outpace supplies. During periods of demand/pull inflation, additional taxation reduces disposable income, which in turn cuts demand and helps stabilize prices (assuming that the revenues from the additional taxation are not spent by the government). The imposition of a VAT as a supplement without a corresponding increase in government expenditures would have a dampening effect in a period of demand/pull inflation.

In contrast, there is a cost/push inflationary potential with the introduction or increase of a tax that raises prices (such as a VAT) or that reduces disposable income (such as the personal income tax). In either case, the consumer may try to recapture his purchasing power by pressing for wage increases. Such gains in wages may lead to higher prices and set the inflationary spiral in motion. Cost/push inflation does not necessarily occur at a time when the economy is booming and employment is high, as does demand/pull inflation; it may also appear in a time of rising unemployment.

A VAT would have a clear cost/push inflationary potential because its introduction most likely would cause an immediate increase in prices by at least the full amount of the tax. It could also have a direct impact on wages, since the VAT (unlike income and payroll taxes) may be included in the cost-of-living index to which many wages are tied. If the VAT is not included in this index, then it would exert less upward pressure on wages. Also, a VAT with rebates for some taxpayers ought to have less impact on wages than a VAT without such rebates, for a VAT with rebates should not increase the cost of living for those with low wages and would raise it only moderately for middle-income groups. If there were VAT rebates for some taxpayers, this would strengthen the argument for excluding the tax from the cost-of-living index.

In addition to price increases directly attributable to the tax, the VAT may fan inflationary fires already existing in the economy. In Europe, the Netherlands experienced price increases beyond the amount of the VAT rate because certain businesses took advantage of the strong inflationary trend existing at the time of the tax's introduction. The extent to which excessive price increases would occur in this country would depend, among other factors, on the economic conditions at the time of introduction, the extent to which the VAT would be a supplementary tax, and the role of the government in its introduction.

The role of the government would be felt through the education of businessmen and consumers and through monetary and fiscal measures. An education and publicity campaign would (1) ensure that the tax was correctly levied, (2) alert customers to excessive price increases above the amount of the tax, and (3) explain the price increases in relation to the tax increase, in hopes of avoiding unduly high wage demands. Without exception, European governments carried out such programs at the time the VAT was introduced. Although they would undoubtedly be helpful in the United States, such programs, of course, would be less important in controlling the effects of the VAT than the fiscal and monetary measures open to the government.

The government, however, may not be able to take sufficiently restrictive fiscal and monetary measures to dampen fully the inflationary pressures exerted by a new VAT. As was noted earlier, the government might find it advisable to increase the money supply after the VAT is introduced. An overly restrictive monetary policy designed to curb inflation might disrupt the economy in view of the VAT-induced price increases. From a fiscal standpoint, the VAT revenue would presumably be used to finance additional expenditures. The federal government could, of course, adopt a restrictive fiscal policy, spending little of its increased revenues or using them to reduce an existing deficit. However, the relentless pressure for higher public expenditures would make it exceedingly difficult to adopt such a policy. In addition, restrictive monetary and fiscal policies might aggravate our existing unemployment problems and encourage any recessionary tendencies extant in the economy at the time of the VAT's introduction. Another measure the government could take would be to reinstate or reinforce controls on wages and prices if inflation arising from the VAT could not be abated by any other means. (Price controls were adopted in the Netherlands, Norway, and Luxembourg at the time of, or shortly after, the introduction of the VAT.)

Increases in other taxes could also affect cost/push inflation. Exhibit 4–2 outlines the inflationary potential of various taxes. Of these taxes, the VAT has the most immediate impact on prices, for businessmen normally add the VAT on to their prices as soon as the tax is introduced. Corporate income taxes, payroll taxes, and business property taxes all increase business costs, and businesses may shift these higher costs to consumers by increasing prices. However, these increases are likely to occur more slowly and more subtly than with the VAT. Any price increases triggered by these various taxes feed demands for higher wages, and higher wages in turn push prices up.

Taxes paid by individuals rather than businesses (personal income taxes, homeowners' property taxes, and that part of payroll taxes paid by employees) do not have an immediate effect on prices. However, because they reduce take-home pay, they stimulate demands for higher wages, and higher wages eventually push prices up. In short, any tax has some cost/push inflationary potential, but no other tax (except a sales tax) has quite the inflationary impact of the VAT.

Impact of a Value Added Tax on the neutrality of the U.S. tax structure

Two features of the VAT make it a neutral tax on business: its incidence and its scope.

A VAT is a tax on consumption. In principle, it is passed along the chain of

EXHIBIT 4-2
Potential for cost/push inflation of various forms of taxation

Form of taxation	Increase in rate to match 3% VAT (from Exhibit 4-1)	Immediate effect on prices and wages	Possible cost/push developments in the short term	Possible cost/push developments in the longer term
VAT	......	Prices of goods and services rise by 3%. Possible unwarranted increases above 3%.	Price increases feed demand for wage adjustments.	Wage increases create pressure for additional price increases.
Corporate profits tax	From 48% to 63%	None.	If increased tax shifted forward, prices begin to increase. If not shifted, shareholders begin to feel the pinch of reduced dividends.	If shifted forward, price increases may lead to demands for wage increases.
Individual income tax	Surcharge of 12%	Take-home pay reduced by higher withholding tax.	Reduction in take-home pay builds pressure for increased wages.	Wage increases create pressure for higher prices.
Payroll tax	From 9.6% to 12%[1]	Take-home pay reduced by higher tax on employees. Labor cost increased by higher tax on employers.	Reduced take-home pay provides impetus for higher wage demands. Increased labor cost gives impetus to price increases.	Pressure on both wages and prices.
Property taxes	An increase of 30%	Disposable income is reduced because of higher residential property taxes.	Reduced disposable income provides impetus for higher wage demands. Businesses hit by higher property taxes may increase prices.	Higher wages increase pressure for higher prices. Higher prices put pressure on wages.

[1] Payroll tax figures are based on 1970 rates, which have since gone up.

production and distribution and finally paid by the consumer. As a result, the tax is not paid by businesses except when competitive pressures do not allow complete forward shifting of the tax.

Furthermore, a VAT is neutral in its impact on business because of its scope. Although a few services may be exempted, almost all businesses share the burden of collecting the tax. A VAT is levied equally on the sales of all kinds of businesses: unincorporated firms and partnerships as well as corporations, profitable and unprofitable companies, and companies relying primarily on debt financing as well as those using mainly equity financing. Since the tax is, for the most part, imposed evenhandedly throughout the economy, the tax should not distort business decisions; that is, it should not cause a business to change its structure or investment policies simply for tax reasons. Of course, granting significant exemptions to the tax or using more than a single VAT rate diminishes the neutrality which is one of the major advantages of a VAT.

This neutrality is a quality lacking in the corporate income tax which is levied only on incorporated businesses and companies with a profit and thereby favors unincorporated firms and unprofitable companies.[10] In addition, it favors debt financing over equity financing, in that the interest on debt financing is deductible as a business expense while the return to equity investors is taxed. Furthermore,

---

[10] To the extent that the tax on corporate profits is passed forward to consumers, it does not place a tax burden on a company or its stockholders but is capricious in its effect on prices of different products and services.

the tax increases in proportion to the efficiency with which capital is used, that is, in proportion to profits. The tax is considered to encourage wasteful spending since expenses reduce profits and thereby reduce a corporation's tax bill. With a 48 percent corporate income tax, it can be argued that the federal government pays nearly half of a business's unnecessary expenses (for example, lavish entertaining of customers).

A payroll tax is also not neutral in that it imposes a heavier burden on labor-intensive companies than on capital-intensive ones. A property tax lacks neutrality in two respects: 1) It taxes only companies with certain types of assets, usually land and buildings; and 2) property tax rates and assessments vary dramatically from district to district.

The individual income tax is generally a tax on people as persons, not a tax on businesses. However, unincorporated businesses are taxed through the individual income tax, and any differences in the provisions of the individual income tax and the corporate income tax may give advantages or disadvantages to unincorporated firms versus corporations.

Thus, no other presently imposed tax has the theoretical neutrality toward differing types of businesses as does the VAT. No tax other than the VAT is designed to avoid distorting business decisions. However, as will be seen in Chapter 5, some of the economic neutrality of the VAT may be lost because of the inflationary effects of the tax.

Distribution of the burden of a VAT

The relative regressivity, proportionality, or progressivity of various taxes is a point of controversy in tax literature.[11] The generally accepted theory on this issue is that a widespread tax on consumption bears more heavily on individuals and families in lower-income brackets than on persons in higher-income brackets. The former spend a larger portion of their incomes on taxable items than do the latter, who put relatively larger amounts of their incomes into savings and investments not subject to a consumption tax. As a result, consumption taxes absorb a larger percentage of the income of low-income groups than of their wealthier compatriots. For example, people with yearly incomes under $6,000 receive 12 percent of all income in the United States, but pay 16 percent of the sales taxes.[12] In a similar fashion, a VAT, as a tax on consumption, is regressive. To counteract this negative aspect, five out of the eight European countries which have introduced a VAT have included in its structure concessionary rates for certain necessities.

As with its other features, the relative regressivity of a VAT can be properly

---

[11] For a fuller discussion of different theories of tax regressivity as well as a statistical calculation of the relative regressivity of selected taxes, see Daniel C. Morgan, Jr., *Retail Sales Tax. An Appraisal of New Issues* (Madison and Milwaukee: University of Wisconsin Press, 1964); and Dan Throop Smith, "High Progressive Tax Rates: Inequity and Immorality?," *University of Flordia Law Review*, Spring 1968, pp. 451–63.

[12] "Whose Tax Burden Is Heaviest?" *Wall Street Journal*, May 9, 1972, p. 24.

evaluated only in comparison with the distribution of the burden of other taxes. Federal excise taxes have a mixture of regressive and progressive elements. Levied on luxury goods, these taxes are designed to be progressive, that is, taking a larger percentage of their collections from higher-income groups than from lower-income groups. However, to the extent that they are levied on items such as tobacco, alcoholic beverages, and automobiles, which are purchased by people with all levels of income, these taxes are more severe on lower-income groups than they are on higher-income groups. Individual income taxes are progressive; the rate of the tax increases as personal income rises. Estate and gift taxes are notably progressive, both in rates and because of substantial exemptions.

The burden of the corporate income tax depends on its incidence. As noted before, this issue is in dispute among tax experts. To the extent that it is shifted forward and reflected in higher consumer prices, this tax has a somewhat regressive effect. However, corporate income taxes, if shifted, would not raise prices evenly throughout the economy. They would have a comparatively small impact on the prices of goods and services produced in largely unincorporated, labor-intensive industries such as food, housing, and medical care, which absorb 57 percent of the expenditures of those in the lowest income group. Therefore, corporate income taxes, even if shifted, are less regressive than a VAT would be. To the extent the corporate income tax is borne by the corporation and its stockholders, it is relatively progressive, since the proportion of stockholders in this country who are in lower-income brackets is small. It should be noted, however, that retired persons often depend on dividends for their limited income.

The payroll tax is levied on wages and salaries up to $10,800 annually (as of 1973) and, therefore, that portion paid by employees creates a heavier burden on persons with incomes below this amount than on those with incomes above it. Furthermore, unlike the income tax, payroll tax rates do not go up with income. It should be kept in mind, however, that contributors to social security receive benefits from the program that may exceed payments. Some portion of the payroll tax paid by employers is probably shifted to consumers through higher prices; this shift would increase the regressivity of the tax.

Property taxes are considered to be proportional in the middle-income range into which the great majority of Americans fall. However, property taxes tend to take an unduly large bite out of low incomes and an unduly small bite out of large incomes. For example, people with yearly incomes under $6,000 receive 12 percent of all income in the United States but pay 17 percent of the property taxes.[13] This regressivity is vastly increased by the deduction of property taxes allowed on the individual income tax, a deduction of greater benefit to those paying a high rate of income tax. *Local* property taxes, as presently administered, are also considered inequitable in that rates vary so much from district to district and assessment practices often leave much to be desired.

---

[13] Ibid., p. 24.

In summary, the individual income tax and estate tax are clearly progressive. Excise taxes have a mixture of regressive and progressive elements. Property taxes, though proportional for middle-income groups, are regressive for those with either high or low incomes. Payroll taxes are distinctly regressive. Corporate income taxes can be thought of as having different burdens depending on the incidence of the tax. A VAT would tend to bear more heavily on individuals in the lower-income brackets than on persons in higher-income brackets.

Proponents of a VAT argue that the tax's regressivity can be offset. The most obvious way to do this is to adopt a multiple-rate structure, with lower rates levied on the necessities that comprise the bulk of the poor's purchases. Multiple rates, however, would reduce the economic neutrality of the tax and would greatly magnify the cost of administering it. A more effective and less costly way to reduce the regressivity of a VAT would be to make counterbalancing changes in the structure of current welfare programs and the individual income tax.

These changes could take three forms. Increasing welfare payments could provide relief for the persons in the lowest income groups, but this would not help middle-income groups who would bear the burden of the VAT and perhaps also the burden of increased individual income taxes needed to pay for increased welfare benefits. Larger deductions on individual income taxes would help middle-income groups but would not help those whose income was too small to pay any income tax anyway. The only way to compensate for VAT outlays made by those with income too high to qualify for welfare and too low to pay an income tax would be cash rebates paid by the government. Such cash rebates could also be used for those on welfare as an alternative to increasing the size of welfare checks. And, if the rebates were paid through the mechanism of the income tax and were extended, at least in part, to middle-income groups, as President Nixon has suggested, the need for compensatory changes in the actual income tax structure would be reduced. Higher welfare payments, higher deductions on the individual income tax, or cash rebates paid either directly or through the mechanism of the income tax would all cost the government money and would, therefore, considerably reduce the net revenues from the VAT.

Even these revenue-consuming compensatory measures would not entirely counteract the regressivity of the VAT. The Brookings Institution has calculated that a broad-based 3.25 percent VAT with income tax credits or rebates for those with low incomes would consume a higher percent of income for families with incomes from $15,000 to $50,000 than for those with larger incomes. The percent of income such a VAT would consume in different income classes is indicated in Exhibit 4–3. This exhibit does show that, although a VAT with credits taxes only lightly very high income groups, it is at least progressive for those with incomes up to $25,000. On the other hand, a VAT with no credits but with exemptions for food, medical care, and rent, would be regressive throughout the income scale.

Proponents of a VAT as a means of raising needed additional revenues argue that our present tax structure is so progressive that a substantial increase in the

EXHIBIT 4–3
VAT Impact on different income classes

1972 Income class	Present effective individual income tax rate as % of income	Effective tax rate as % of income with a VAT	
		3.25% Broad-based VAT with credits	3% VAT with no credits but with exemptions for food, medical care, and rent
$ 0– 3,000 .... 0.5		0.1	1.8
3– 5,000 .... 1.7		0.6	1.5
5– 10,000 .... 5.1		0.8	1.5
10– 15,000 .... 8.6		1.1	1.4
15– 20,000 ....10.5		1.7	1.4
20– 25,000 ....11.8		1.9	1.3
25– 50,000 ....13.9		1.7	1.2
50– 100,000 ....22.2		1.1	0.7
100– 500,000 ....31.0		0.8	0.5
500–1,000,000 ....32.8		0.4	0.2
$1,000,000 and over..................34.2		0.2	0.2

SOURCE: Charles Schultze et al., *Setting National Priorities: 1973 Budget* (Washington: Brookings Institution, 1972), p. 441. In this table, income (given at 1972 levels) is equal to sum of adjusted gross income, transfer payments, state and local government bond interest, and excluded realised, long-term capital gains. Effective income tax rate takes into account deductions, exemptions, etc. written into present income tax law. With the VAT with credits, it is assumed that full VAT credits would be given to four-person families with income up to $5,000, while VAT credits would be phased out completely at $20,000.

tax burden on those with high incomes would be counterproductive; it would reduce the incentive for high-income people to increase their earnings either by working harder or by saving and investing. On the other hand, those concerned about the regressivity of the VAT point to the fact that, while our tax system overall is generally progressive, in recent years an increasingly higher proportion of government revenues has been derived from payroll taxes and sales taxes, which tend to be regressive. As a consequence, the top 20 percent of families (in terms of income) paid only 49.6 percent of all taxes in 1968, whereas they had paid 51.7 percent in 1962.[14]

In any case, it should be remembered that for a tax system to be equitable, it is not necessary for *every* tax to be progressive. What is important is that the overall fiscal design, taking into account both the total tax structure and the beneficiaries of government spending, is such that all segments of the population are treated fairly.

An analysis of the distribution of taxes by income classes gives only half the picture. The benefits of government expenditures also are unevenly distributed over income classes. If a group receives a much higher distribution of benefits than it pays in taxes, the combined effect is a redistribution of income even if the entire tax system is only proportional or even mildly regressive.

---

[14] These figures are from two articles: Roger A. Herriot and Herman P. Miller, "Tax Changes and Income Groups – 1962–1968," and J. Fred Bateman, "Taxes: Who Benefits and Who Pays?" Both articles are in the February 1972 issue of *Business Horizons,* published by the Indiana University Graduate School of Business.

There has been inadequate attention to the distribution of benefits of government expenditures by income classes. A recent tentative analysis shows a clear distribution in favor of those with incomes below $8,000–$10,000, while those with incomes above this level pay more in taxes than they receive in benefits.[15] Other studies will doubtless be made and may modify the conclusions somewhat; but a basis has been laid for an analysis of both sides, instead of only one side, of the fairness of government taxation and expenditures.

Impact of a VAT on the balance of payments

A VAT has been advocated as a means of improving the U.S. balance of payments. However, a VAT in and of itself may not benefit our trade balance. Any benefits that occur would simply be in comparison with the effects of the alternative taxes.

The VAT in international trade. The General Agreement on Tariffs and Trade (GATT) regulates the taxation of goods in international trade. One of GATT's purposes is to eliminate from international trade the price distortions created by indirect taxes. GATT provides that indirect taxes—including sales taxes, the VAT, excise taxes, etc.—may be rebated in full at the point of export. Exporters are entitled to refunds of all indirect taxes paid at any stage up to that point. The country importing these goods may levy its own indirect taxes on goods as they are imported. For example, when a French company exports to Germany, it does not pay the VAT on those exported goods; when the goods enter the German market, they are taxed under the German system of VAT, just as are domestic German goods. Thus, exports from one country are not burdened with two taxes, one as they are exported and one as they are imported. In this way, international trade is encouraged.

The Value Added Tax, in contrast to the cumulative (cascade-type) turnover taxes used by many European countries before adoption of the VAT, is particularly adaptable to this mechanism of tax rebates on exports. A characteristic of a cascading tax is that it is levied on the price of an item at each stage of production; as a result, the tax base at later stages of production includes the tax itself, and the tax is compounded every time the item changes hands. When the item reaches the export stage, the amount of tax included in the price depends on how many times the product has changed hands. Since this can vary considerably, even with a given product, it is difficult to determine how much tax is included in a product's price. Governments must issue rules prescribing how much tax can be considered to be buried in the price of each type of product, and the prescribed amount is normally less than the actual tax in some cases and more in others. Therefore, the tax rebate received by the exporter on any item may be either less or greater than the actual tax paid. As a result, the exported item may in fact include some of the indirect taxes, which is contrary to the aim of GATT; or the rebate may be greater

---

[15] Ibid.

than the actual turnover tax paid and may thus be an export subsidy, which is specifically forbidden by GATT.

In contrast, the VAT is always invoiced at each stage of production, and credit is given for VAT paid at earlier stages. An exporter is thus able to recover the exact amount of tax paid on the item. Consequently, goods entering international trade are certain to be free of indirect taxes, and hidden export subsidies are not feasible. This advantage of the VAT over other indirect taxes is part of the reason for its adoption within the EEC.

From the point of view of international trade, a VAT is also better than a retail sales tax. Although a sales tax is not supposed to be levied on exports, some sales tax often gets buried in the cost of producing export goods (that is, sales tax paid on purchases made to produce the export goods). Since the sales tax in this case is hidden in the price, it cannot readily be rebated on exports even though rebates of sales taxes are permissible under GATT rules.

While GATT permits indirect taxes to be rebated when goods cross an international border, rebates of direct taxes are specifically forbidden. Thus, the export price of goods includes any corporate income tax, payroll taxes, and property taxes that are shifted to the customer.

Effect of a VAT on U.S. trade. If a VAT were levied in the United States, exports should not be affected one way or the other. At present no such tax is levied on exports; after the tax was introduced, rebates would prevent any VAT from entering into the cost of producing export goods. In short, both before and after the introduction of a VAT, the tax burden on exports would be the same. Other things being equal, U.S. export prices should not change, and no stimulation would be provided to the sale of U.S. goods abroad.

A VAT would be imposed on imports for the first time; but, since the same VAT would be applied to domestic goods, the competitive position of imports vis-à-vis domestic goods should not change. However, since a VAT would reduce private consumer demand generally, fewer goods might be imported into this country, and our balance of trade might improve somewhat. This effect of the VAT would, of course, depend on whether the government spent its VAT revenues on purchases that stimulated imports.

In the long run, a VAT might hurt the U.S. balance of trade. If a VAT should trigger a cost/push inflation, then wages would go up, and the cost of producing goods would increase. In such a situation, export prices are likely to go up, and sales of exported goods might decrease. At the same time, the price of domestic goods would rise, while import prices would not increase; imports would thus become comparatively cheaper (if, of course, the country producing the goods were not suffering a similar inflation).

While the inflationary effect of a VAT might in the long run hurt the U.S. balance of trade, our balance of payments would be much more adversely affected if, instead of imposing a VAT, certain existing taxes were increased. Increasing corporate income taxes would have a deleterious effect whether or not the higher tax were shifted. If the tax were shifted, prices would go up. The price of U.S. exports would rise, and, under the present GATT rules, any corporate income tax hidden in export prices cannot be rebated. Higher export prices would generally reduce export sales, though this would be partially compensated for by the fact that the higher the price, the more dollars an export sale earns for the country. The price of domestic goods would also rise, and domestic products would be less able to compete with imports, which would not be subject to the higher corporate income tax. If the higher corporate income tax were *not* shifted, profits would decline, and overseas money would find investment in the U.S. less attractive. Less capital would flow to this country to help our overall balance of payments. In addition, lower profits for U.S. companies would reduce the money available for investment in cost-cutting equipment or in research on product improvement. Ultimately, U.S. goods might become less attractive than the goods of other countries.

Increasing payroll taxes would have somewhat the same effect as increasing corporate income taxes, but the impact would be focused primarily on labor-intensive companies. Since, apart from agriculture, labor-intensive companies are less likely to be big exporters than capital-intensive companies, the higher payroll taxes should have less effect on U.S. export prices than an increase in the corporate income tax. On the other hand, labor-intensive companies already suffering from import competition would be in a worse position if payroll taxes rose. It should be remembered, however, that half of any increase in payroll taxes would be imposed on wage earners, not business.

Any tax levied on individuals—whether payroll taxes or the personal income tax—should have no immediate effect on prices. However, such taxes, by reducing disposable income, reduce consumer demand. With lower consumer demand, imports into the U.S. might shrink, if higher government expenditures did not stimulate compensating increases in imports. Of course, in the long run, higher taxes on individuals may stimulate demands for higher wages, and this, in time, would push up prices both for U.S. exports and for domestic goods competing with imports.

If individual income taxes were increased by taxing capital gains fully, this would not dampen consumer demand seriously, but it would make less money available for investment. This, in turn, might make it more difficult for businesses to increase their productivity or improve their products. Ultimately American goods might become less attractive to foreign customers, and our balance of trade might be hurt.

Increasing business property taxes would probably not greatly affect the U.S. balance of payments, for property taxes are not considered to be a significant element in most of our export prices.[16] Increasing the taxes paid by homeowners would, of course, reduce disposable income; this, in turn, would diminish consumer demand generally and perhaps reduce imports.

---

[16]John F. Due, "Statement Regarding the Proposal for a Federal Value Added Tax to Substitute for Local Property Taxes in Financing Education," *The Value Added Tax* (Arlington, Va.: Taxation with Representation, 1972), p. 72–45.

In summary then, a VAT, unlike the corporate income tax or payroll taxes, is neutral initially in its effect on a country's balance of payments. Over the longer run, like any tax that reduces consumer demand (for example, the individual income tax), the VAT may slow down imports into the United States if the higher government revenues derived from the new tax are not spent in such a way as to encourage imports. However, like any tax that leads ultimately to higher prices, the VAT may in time reduce our ability to compete on the international market.

In theory, changes in a nation's tax structure should not have any permanent effect on its balance of trade if exchange rates are allowed to fluctuate. Any tax change that causes export prices to rise should ultimately be compensated for by a devaluation of the currency. Any tax change that caused a prolonged depression in the demand for imports should ultimately be counterbalanced by an upward valuation of the currency. Of course, in the United States, which until recently refused to allow the exchange rate of its currency to change, modifications in the tax structure can affect the balance of trade. And, even when exchange rates are flexible, tax changes can affect foreign trade until the necessary adjustments have been made in exchange rates. Furthermore, even flexible exchange rates are not determined solely by a country's balance of trade but are also affected by its capital accounts, its currency held by other countries, and so forth.

Fluctuations in exchange rates also cannot compensate for changes in taxes which are not general taxes but taxes on certain kinds of goods or certain kinds of companies. Such taxes distort international trade since they impose a disadvantage on particular types of goods or firms and interfere with the pressure exerted by the international market for efficient use of resources. From the point of view of the international market, a VAT is a better tax than the corporate income tax, payroll taxes, or business property taxes since the latter taxes impose a heavier burden on certain types of companies than on others, while a single-rate VAT with few exemptions is levied evenhandedly over most of the economy.

A VAT also offers a government a useful tool in regulating waverings in its balance of trade. VAT exemptions for exports or the VAT rate on imports can be temporarily reduced; this would have the effect of an exchange rate adjustment on the trade account, but it would not stimulate the inflow and outflow of international hot money or change the relative value of deposits or securities quoted in a definite number of monetary units.[17] West Germany, when troubled with a sizeable trade surplus, made such changes in its VAT in November 1968 and then rescinded these changes in the border tax adjustment when the mark was revalued in October 1969.

The VAT and economic cycles

Unlike the revenues from the corporate income tax or the individual income tax, revenues from the VAT are not likely to fluctuate a great deal when the econ-

---

[17] See, for example, Harry Johnson and Mel Krauss, "Border Taxes, Border Tax Adjustments, Comparative Advantages, and the Balance of Payments," *Canadian Journal of Economics,* November 1970, pp. 595–602.

omy alternates between recessions and boom periods. Consumer purchases, of course, rise and fall with the economy but not so sharply as corporate profits or personal incomes. Property taxes vary very little with swings in the business cycle. Revenues from payroll taxes decline as unemployment grows, but, as with the VAT, these fluctuations are likely to be smaller than those that occur with the individual income tax and especially with the corporate income tax.

While the VAT supplies the government with a reliable, relatively stable source of revenues, it does not provide the government with an automatic device for promoting cyclical stability. When the economy declines, so too do revenues from the individual and corporate income taxes; normally this produces a federal deficit, which can stimulate a revival of economic activity. In boom periods income tax revenues rise, and the higher revenues may be used by the government to reduce its deficit and thereby the economy-stimulating effects of the deficit. In a seriously overheated economy, the government can impose a surcharge on income taxes in hopes of dampening the boom.

Since revenues from a VAT fluctuate less, the VAT has a less stabilizing effect on economic cycles. VAT rates can be increased to discourage buying in a boom period, but, to be effective in this respect, changes in VAT rates have to be made quickly and not after prolonged debate in Congress. If a VAT rate increase is debated at length, consumers may rush to buy goods before the rate goes up, and an existing boom will be heated up, not cooled off. For this reason, *if* a VAT were to be used as a fiscal tool, it would be advisable for Congress to give the President some discretion in altering VAT rates within certain limits. In any case, great caution would have to be used in increasing VAT rates because of the impact of the VAT on prices. A tax increase which led to an immediate price increase is obviously not desirable when an economy is already suffering from inflation.

A consumption type VAT does provide a government with a fiscal tool that could be useful in a boom period: The government could reduce or eliminate the credit given for the VAT paid on capital purchases and thus discourage excessive business investment.

Cost of administering a VAT

A VAT would necessarily increase the operating costs of the Internal Revenue Service. Various factors would determine the level of these costs.

Factors affecting the government's administrative costs. The first determinant of governmental administrative costs would be the characteristics of the tax itself. In this country, a VAT would probably be levied as a supplementary tax, covering previously untaxed goods and services. Because it is costlier to initiate a tax than to increase the rate of an existing one, a VAT would require some new services and additional manpower within the IRS. If state and local sales taxes were piggybacked on the federal VAT, this would create additional headaches for the tax administrators. If state and local sales taxes were not piggybacked, there would be administrative problems for retailers who had to pay both types of taxes. In short, problems would arise both because the VAT would be a new tax and because it would overlap to some extent with existing taxes. Furthermore, some exemptions or reduced rates are likely to be included in the structure of the VAT, and this would certainly increase administrative costs. British sources estimate that having more than a single VAT rate would increase the government's administrative costs by 50 to 80 percent.[18]

The second determinant of administrative costs would be the complexity of collection and enforcement procedures. Quarterly returns with monthly tax deposits would demand more of the IRS than annual returns with quarterly payments. Detailed tax forms would complicate administration of the tax. Strict enforcement of the tax, including extensive field audits and spot checks, would raise the cost to the government, though this additional expense might be offset by higher tax collections due to the reduction of error and evasion. However, the self-policing features of a VAT would tend to increase the likelihood of voluntary compliance and reduce the need for enforcement.

Finally, administrative costs would depend on the efficiency of the government and business as tax collectors. Administrative costs due to lack of efficiency would probably be minimal since virtually all U.S. businesses have had experience with federal or state taxes of some kind, and the IRS is certainly a modern and efficient organization.

Level of administrative costs. Professor John Due has estimated that administrative costs of state sales taxes, at varying rates, range from 0.63 percent to 1.9 percent of tax receipts.[19] Due also estimates that administrative costs of a federal sales tax would be 1.75 percent of collections for a 3 percent tax and 0.7 percent of collections for a 10 percent tax, compared with 0.47 percent of collections for other federal taxes.[20] The VAT, in contrast to a national sales tax, would require tax returns from all segments of the economy, not just retailers. This would tend to create somewhat higher administrative costs. Given this consideration and using Due's estimate as a base, a reasonable guess of the government's administrative cost of a 3 percent VAT might be 2 to 3 percent of collections. However, in 1972 Donald Bacon estimated that collection costs for a *relatively simple* VAT integrated with the existing income tax system would not be much more than $70 to $150 million.[21] With net revenues from a 3 percent VAT reckoned at $10.5 billion, such collection costs would be only 0.67 to 1.43 percent of collections.

---

[18] National Economic Development Office, *Value Added Tax* (London: Her Majesty's Stationery Office, 1971), p. 41.

[19] John Due, *State Sales Tax Administration* (Chicago: Public Administration Service, 1963), p. 226; quoted in Douglas H. Eldridge, "Equity, Administration and Compliance and Intergovernmental Fiscal Aspects," *The Role of the Direct and Indirect Taxes in the Federal Revenue System* (Princeton: Princeton University Press, 1964), p. 162.

[20] Eldridge, "Equity, Administration and Compliance," p. 161. In 1972 the cost of collecting federal income taxes was 0.51 percent of collections. See Donald W. Bacon, "Administrative and Compliance Procedures Under a Value Added Tax" (Paper delivered to the Tax Institute of American Symposium, November 16, 1972), p. 2.

[21] Bacon, "Administrative and Compliance Procedures," p. 5.

In summary, enactment of a VAT in the United States would necessitate additional governmental administrative costs. The level of these costs might be in the range of 0.67 to 3 percent of collections, compared to the cost of collecting present federal taxes of 0.47 percent of collections.

Impact of a VAT on business compliance costs.   A VAT would increase the cost of tax compliance for all businesses because it would require a new tax form and new accounting entries for collections and credits. At the retail level the compliance costs would be particularly significant because of the diversity of goods (some of which might be taxed at different rates) and the large number of transactions. However, businessmen in Europe have not found compliance with the VAT unduly burdensome once the transition period is over. As with the government, business would find compliance with the tax vastly simplified if there were a single rate and a minimum of exemptions.[22]

Summary of the economic impact of a VAT in the United States

No tax in itself is positively desirable, except perhaps those designed for regulatory rather than revenue purposes. The question addressed in this chapter is not whether the adoption of a VAT is desirable in and of itself. Rather, the question is whether, if more revenue is needed, it would be better to (1) adopt a VAT, (2) increase other taxes, or (3) resort to deficit financing. If the assumption is made that additional revenues are necessary and that deficit financing is not desirable, then the task is to select the tax alternative that would do the least damage to the economy.

Exhibit 4–4 summarizes and, of necessity, simplifies the economic considerations in introducing a VAT versus increasing existing federal taxes in this country. The following summary uses this exhibit as a guide.

1. With its broad tax base, a VAT would have the capacity to raise substantial revenues at a low tax rate. To match the approximate $10.5 billion yield from a 3 percent VAT (minus revenues lost through adjustments in the individual income tax), any of the existing taxes below would have to be increased roughly as follows:

a)   Corporate income tax rates — from 48 percent to about 63 percent
b)   Individual income taxes — a surcharge of about 12 percent
c)   The payroll tax rate — an increase of about 27 percent
d)   Property taxes — an increase of about 30 percent

2. A VAT of the consumption type would not be a factor in investment decisions. Unless the corporate income tax is fully shifted, an increase in that tax would reduce the availability of funds and the incentive to invest. Even if shifted, a high rate on this tax distorts business investment decisions. Higher payroll taxes might encourage investment in labor-saving equipment. Higher property taxes would discourage investment in real estate.

---

[22] For further discussion of business compliance costs, see Chapter 6.

Because it taxes consumption but not savings, a VAT might, in theory, provide some encouragement to savings. In contrast, the character and incidence of the individual income tax is such that an increase in the tax would have the immediate effect of reducing savings. An increase in payroll taxes or in property taxes would decrease savings, but not so much as higher individual income taxes; for income taxes have a bigger impact on high-income groups, who tend to save a greater percentage of their disposable income.

3. The introduction of a VAT in this country would have two immediate economic effects: (1) a rise in prices as companies passed the tax forward to consumers and (2) a reduction in total unit sales to consumers below the level they would otherwise attain (to the extent that consumers did not use savings to maintain their pre-VAT level of consumption). A VAT would thus cause at least a temporary decline in the growth rate of consumption; but increasing any other tax, particularly increasing taxes paid by individuals, would also affect the growth of consumption.

Although some companies would experience a dip in their growth rates after the implementation of a VAT, others would benefit from increased government expenditures.

4. There is a clear risk that a VAT would provide a stimulus to cost/push inflation. Some other taxes have a similar potential but in not quite so immediate or direct a manner.

5. Viewed by itself, the VAT may have undesired differential effects on various income groups. Any regressive effects of a VAT can be explicitly compensated for in the design of the VAT itself or in supplementary fiscal measures undertaken at the time of VAT introduction. However, no adjustments can make the VAT as progressive as the individual income tax.

6. From the point of view of business, the VAT is a neutral tax. It minimizes tax factors in business decisions since it falls equally on all businesses regardless of their type of organization, efficiency, capital or labor intensity, and use of equity or debt financing. This is in marked contrast to the corporate income tax, payroll taxes, and business property taxes.

7. Under GATT provisions, indirect taxes such as the VAT may be rebated on exports and equivalent taxes imposed on imports. Rebates of direct taxes (corporate income taxes, payroll taxes, property taxes) are not permitted.

A VAT as a supplementary indirect tax would initially have a neutral impact on the balance of payments, since it would not increase export prices or make domestic goods less competitive with imports. However, to the extent that the VAT reduced consumer demand, it might reduce imports, if the higher government revenues derived from the tax were not spent in such a way as to encourage imports. If the VAT stimulated a cost/push inflation, it might eventually reduce our ability to compete on the international market.

In contrast to the VAT, an increase in a direct business tax, such as the corporate income tax, would clearly hurt the country's balance of payments to the extent that

EXHIBIT 4-4

Impact of a VAT on the United States compared with impact of increases in certain existing taxes

	Value Added Tax	Corporate income tax		Individual income tax	Payroll tax	Property taxes
		Shifted	Not shifted			
Rate required to yield $10.5 billion, equal to yield of 3% VAT minus revenues lost through adjustments in the individual income tax*	3%	63%	63%	12% surcharge	Increase of 27%	Increase of 30%
Government spending	.... Increase in government revenues and expenditures					
Total spending — Investment (consumer savings and business investment)	Some encouragement to savings	Mixed effect on savings and investment	Discourages savings and investment	Discourages savings	Slight discouragement of savings; some encouragement of investment	Discourages investment in real estate
Total spending — Consumption (lower consumption via higher prices or lower disposable income)	Higher prices	Higher prices	Lower disposable income (to shareholders)	Lower disposable income	Lower disposable income and somewhat higher prices	Lower disposable income; higher prices for goods affected by property taxes
Demand/pull inflation	.... When country is at or above full employment rate, increase in taxes with no increase in government expenditures will tend to deflate the economy					

Inflationary effects	Immediate higher prices	Eventual higher prices	No effect	Immediate lower disposable income; probably eventual higher prices	Immediate lower disposable income; eventual higher prices	Immediate lower disposable income; eventual higher prices
Equity	Regressive	Largely regressive	Mostly progressive	Progressive	Mostly regressive	Partly regressive partly proportional
Neutrality to business	Neutral	Affects certain types of companies (and their prices) more than others	Tends to distort normal business decisions	Neutral for corporations; hurts unincorporated businesses	Hurts labor-intensive firms; some effect on normal business decisions	Hurts businesses particularly affected by property taxes
Balance of payments	Neutral initially; may reduce demand for some imports; may increase export prices eventually	Higher export prices eventually; firms less able to compete with imports	Reduces capital flowing into country for investment	May reduce demand for some imports; may eventually increase export prices	Slightly higher export prices; firms less able to compete with imports; may reduce demand for some imports	May reduce demand for some imports; may eventually increase export prices
Federal Administrative costs	Increased administrative costs	....	Very little increase in administrative costs	....		
Business compliance costs	Increased compliance costs	....	Very little increase in compliance costs	....		

* See Exhibit 4-1.

the increase in the tax was shifted forward in the form of higher prices and the higher prices reduced exports and made U.S. companies less able to compete with imports. If it is assumed that the corporate tax is not shifted, higher corporate taxes would still hurt our balance of payments, for it would reduce the corporate rate of return and thus attract less capital from abroad. Higher taxes on individuals, whether income taxes, payroll taxes, or property taxes, would reduce disposable income and thus depress the demand for imports unless the revenues from such taxes were spent in such a way as to encourage imports. Eventually, however, because they stimulate wage demands, even taxes on individuals may push prices up and therefore make U.S. goods less able to compete at home or abroad.

8. Federal administrative costs would be greater for a VAT than for an increase in existing taxes. In the latter case, the administrative load would not change, while a VAT would require a significant number of new personnel. Given the limited data available, it has been estimated that the governmental administrative cost of a low-rate VAT might be in the range of 0.67 to 3 percent of tax collections. This is higher than the cost of collecting existing federal taxes—0.47 percent of collections.

9. Business would face increased compliance costs with the introduction of a VAT as opposed to increases in existing business taxes.

These are the issues to be considered in determining whether a VAT might be the least damaging means of raising additional revenues. The relative weighting of these considerations, however, will depend on the detailed characteristics of the VAT in the United States and the condition of the economy at the time the tax (or an alternative) is introduced.

5

Impact of the Value Added Tax on different types of industries

THE VAT theoretically is neutral toward business. As was indicated in Chapter 4, the VAT is supposed to be a tax on consumption, not business, for it is normally passed forward and finally paid by the consumer. Furthermore, almost all types of businesses share the burden of collecting the tax. Thus the VAT is designed not to distort business decisions as most business taxes do.

The theoretical neutrality of a VAT, however, can be diminished if special provisions are written into the VAT—that is, if any important segments of the economy are exempted from the VAT or if certain goods or services are taxed at some rate other than the standard VAT rate.

Even without such provisions, the VAT may have an uneven impact on business because of the secondary effects of the price increases engendered by a VAT. Businesses generally add the VAT on to their prices and thus pass the tax on to their customers. The increase in prices induced by the VAT may then immediately trigger demands for higher wages. Some industries are likely to be hurt more by a rise in wages than others. Those particularly hard hit by escalating wages may have to increase their prices more than other industries. Thus, while a VAT initially causes more or less even price increases throughout the economy, it may eventually cause some prices to rise faster than others.

Even the more or less uniform price increases initially spawned by a VAT may hurt the sales of some industries more than others. Unless savings are tapped, consumers faced with higher prices will be compelled to reduce their consumption below the level that would have occurred without the VAT; and they are likely to reduce (or not increase) their consumption of some goods and services more than others. The sales of certain industries may be particularly hard hit by consumers' efforts to economize. If the government promptly spends all its VAT revenues, the decline in consumer spending should be matched by a rise in government spending. The government's consumption pattern, however, will most likely differ from that of the private consumer, and this may cause some sales to increase while others decline (or at least grow less rapidly).

Thus, while a single-rate VAT with a minimum of exemptions is initially neutral toward business, the indirect effects of the tax may have a differential impact on different types of industries. The likely primary and secondary effects of a VAT on industries of various characteristics are discussed in the next section and sum-marized in Exhibit 5-1. The succeeding section, along with Exhibits 5-2 through 5-10, compares the impact of a VAT with the impact of certain tax alternatives. The final section shows the reader how he can use these data to estimate the effect of a VAT versus the alternatives on his own industry.

Impact of a VAT on industries with various characteristics[1]

A VAT will affect different industries in different ways. In some instances, the VAT (unlike other taxes) is neutral between industries with opposite character-istics; in other instances, the VAT has more of an adverse effect on industries with one particular characteristic than on those with the contrary characteristic.[2]

Largely incorporated industries. The VAT should not have a differential impact on corporations vis-à-vis incorporated firms.

Industries with a high debt/equity ratio. The VAT is neutral between industries with high and low debt/equity ratios.

Industries with a high return on equity or sales. Since the VAT is not a tax on profits, it is technically neutral between profitable and unprofitable industries. How-ever, industries with comparatively high profits can more easily absorb all or part of the VAT instead of passing it forward, if this is necessary to protect their sales. Such industries also can better afford any increase in their labor costs or other purchases caused indirectly by a VAT. Absorbing the VAT or higher costs would, of course, reduce profits and make the industry less attractive to investment capital. But industries with comparatively high profit margins would be in a better position to respond to any market changes produced directly or indirectly by the VAT.

Capital-intensive industries. The VAT is theoretically neutral between capital-intensive and labor-intensive industries. A consumption type VAT does give com-panies credit for the VAT paid on capital purchases. This is not supposed to give a special advantage to capital-intensive industries; it is designed only to eliminate any tax deterrent to capital investment. It may, however, have the psychological effect of encouraging capital purchases and may make labor-intensive industries feel that they are somehow put at a disadvantage. A more tangible disadvantage to labor-intensive industries occurs if the VAT stimulates demands for wage increases. Any wage increases triggered by a VAT might give capital-intensive industries a dual advantage; not only might wage increases (at least in some cases) have less impact on them than on labor-intensive industries, but the cost of their capital purchases might not rise as rapidly as other costs since capital goods are generally not produced in labor-intensive industries. A VAT thus may indirectly encourage higher capital intensiveness.

---

[1] So far as is known, no studies have been done in Europe of the impact of the VAT on various industries. Therefore, any estimate of the impact of a VAT on a given industry must be based on economic theory rather than on existing data. The analysis here is a very general, simplified one.

[2] These characteristics were chosen for analysis because they affect the impact either of a VAT or of an al-ternative tax.

Industries with sizeable assets in land. A VAT theoretically favors landowners since the sale and leasing of land is normally not subject to the VAT. However, it should be remembered that work done on the land is traditionally subject to the VAT whether it be forestry, farming, or construction work. Large landowners have an asset not subject to the VAT, but industries with considerable assets in capital goods also have assets not subject to the VAT, as the VAT paid on capital purchases is, in effect, refunded (with a consumption type VAT). Thus, large landowners, who are not heavy users of labor, would be like other capital-intensive industries and would probably be affected less by the VAT than labor-intensive enterprises.

Industries with sizeable assets in buildings. If the VAT is imposed on construction work, then the building industry would receive the same tax treatment as any other industry. However, the building industry, being labor-intensive, would be particularly hard hit by any wage increases triggered by the VAT, and building costs might rise more rapidly than costs in some other sectors of the economy. This would tend to raise the value of existing buildings.

If the VAT is imposed on the sale of newly constructed buildings but not on the sale of older buildings, pre-VAT buildings would enjoy a price advantage over new ones.[3] This could have a depressing effect on the housing industry until market forces push up prices of pre-VAT houses to a level comparable with those of post-VAT houses (and in the process gave a windfall to owners of pre-VAT buildings).

If the VAT is not imposed on housing rentals, investment in new apartment buildings would be temporarily discouraged: The owner could not recoup any VAT paid on construction of the building by collecting a VAT on his rents, and the owner of a post-VAT building would either have to charge higher rents or accept lower profits than the owner of a pre-VAT building. In time, of course, the value of pre-VAT apartment buildings would rise to a level where they would no longer enjoy a price advantage over new buildings, and there would no longer be any discouragement of investment in new apartments.

If the rental of business property (unlike housing) should be subject to the VAT, the new tax should not affect builders and owners of such property. By charging a VAT on the rental of business property, the owners of such property could recoup any VAT paid on purchases made to construct the building. The owner of a pre-VAT building would have a bigger VAT bill, since he would have no VAT credits for his purchases; but this should impose no tax burden on the owner of commercial property (whether pre- or post-VAT), since normally the VAT would be added onto the rent and therefore paid not by the owner, but by the business using the property. A nonexempt business using the property should not be unduly burdened, since any VAT paid on the rental of a building could be used as a credit against the VAT due on the sales of business.

If, on the other hand, the rental of business property should *not* be subject to the

---

[3] Concern over the alleged price advantage afforded pre-VAT buildings by the introduction of the tax caused the British to zero-rate building construction in their forthcoming VAT and caused the Swedes to reduce the VAT base to 60 percent of the actual cost of new buildings. (See Chapter 1, p. 9 and Chapter 2, p. 18.)

VAT, any VAT levied on the construction of such buildings would be passed on through higher rents; but the tenants would receive no credit on their tax bill for the VAT cost hidden in the rent. Exempting the rental of business property from the VAT would give an advantage to owners of older buildings with no VAT costs to cover and would give them a windfall as market forces pushed up the value of their buildings to eliminate the price differential between pre- and post-VAT buildings.

It would be a matter of indifference whether a VAT were imposed on the sale of an older building by one nonexempt company to another. Any VAT paid by the buyer could be credited against the VAT due on the buyer's sales.

Industries with industry-wide collective bargaining or strong labor unions. If the VAT were included in the cost-of-living index, introduction of a VAT and the resultant price increases would immediately cause wages to go up in industries with wage contracts tied to the cost of living. Even industries without such clauses in their wage contracts would find it difficult to resist demands for higher wages if their workers were organized in strong labor unions. For this reason, some capital-intensive industries might be hurt as much by VAT-triggered wage increases as labor-intensive industries, which tend to be composed of small firms where union strength is comparatively weaker. In short, the impact of a VAT on an industry's wage bill would depend both on the size of its labor force and on the muscle of its unions. The upward pressure a VAT is likely to exert on wages would be reduced, but by no means eliminated, if the VAT were *not* included in the cost-of-living index.

Industries making purchases from diversified sources. If a VAT should trigger a cost/push inflation, companies making purchases from a variety of industries may be able to make substitute purchases if the costs of some items rise faster than others. An industry's costs, of course, will be affected by whether its own purchases are primarily from industries hurt in some way by the VAT.

Industries with a high import cost component. Since the VAT is levied equally on domestic and imported goods, the tax would give no advantage to industries purchasing imports versus those purchasing domestic goods. However, if the VAT triggers a cost/push inflation, imports might, in time, become comparatively cheaper than domestic goods.

Importers complain that they are out-of-pocket for the VAT paid on their purchases for a longer time than companies which purchase domestically.[4] This occurs because importers must pay the VAT on imports when the goods cross the border, while other types of companies, who buy on credit, do not pay the VAT on their purchases until some time after the purchase is actually made. Denmark, for a time, compensated for this by imposing a slightly lower VAT on goods when they came into the country, while imposing the normal VAT on subsequent sales of the imported goods, so that the net effect of the tax remained the same. However, in 1970 Denmark abolished the reduced rate for imports.[5] Another possible way of

---

[4] Alan Tait, *Value Added Tax* (London: McGraw-Hill, 1972) p. 142.
[5] International Bureau of Fiscal Documentation, *Value Added Taxation in Europe* (Amsterdam, 1972), "Denmark," p. 10.

relieving the cash flow problem the VAT creates for importers might be to give importers a longer period to pay their VAT bills, as is done sometimes in Sweden.

Industries with high elasticity of demand. Industries with high elasticity in the demand for their product would be able to sell less if the VAT were added on to their prices, for in such industries price increases depress sales. Of course, initially the VAT would cause more or less uniform price increases throughout the economy, so no industry would be put at a comparative disadvantage. But consumers, finding that their wages would buy fewer goods than before the VAT, would be likely to reduce their consumption of certain goods and services more than others. Of course, when the government spends its VAT revenues, the sales of some industries might rise above their pre-VAT level. The impact of a VAT on an industry's sales thus depends both on the elasticity of demand for the industry's products and on the way the government spends its revenues. The VAT's effect on sales would also be colored by the condition of the economy at the time the VAT is introduced. In an expanding economy, certain industries might experience a reduced rate of growth because of the VAT, but few are likely to suffer any actual reduction in sales.

Industries with high product substitutability (high cross-elasticity). Since initially a VAT causes more or less uniform price increases through the economy, generally it should not affect the competitiveness of one product vis-à-vis a substitute product. In the long run, however, a VAT could cause some product switching for two reasons: (1) Consumers faced with reduced buying power because of the VAT might try to economize by switching to cheaper products; and (2) if VAT-triggered wage increases lead eventually to differential price increases, some products might become more expensive than competing products.

Industries with intense price competition. Any VAT-induced reduction in consumer demand may particularly affect industries with intense price competition arising from such factors as excess capacity in relation to demand. In such industries, companies might feel they could not pass the VAT forward to their customers as businesses generally do. Thus, the VAT, although designed to be a tax on consumption, might become a business cost in industries with great price competition.

Industries with diversified markets. If the VAT should cause sales of some products to fall, companies with diversified markets might be better able to compensate for any shrinking sales by promoting sales of other products or in other areas which are less affected by the VAT or which are benefiting from higher government expenditures.

Producers of capital goods. If the VAT should trigger demands for wage increases, it may prompt companies to invest in labor-saving equipment and thus promote the sale of capital goods. Furthermore, a consumption type VAT, with its provision for credits for any VAT paid on capital purchases, ensures that there is no tax deterrent to capital investment. But, if a VAT-induced reduction in consumer demand is not fully compensated for by higher government spending, business might become reluctant to expand, and the sale of capital goods would fall.

Industries doing much exporting. The introduction of a VAT has initially no effect on exports since VAT's customarily zero-rate exports (that is, exempt export sales from the tax and refund any VAT paid on purchases to produce the export). Both before and after the tax is introduced, exporters pay no VAT. The price at which exporters sell their goods abroad need not change, and, other things being equal, the demand for exported goods need not change. In this respect, exporters might enjoy an advantage over their competitors selling on the domestic market, for the VAT may dampen some domestic sales.

In the long run, however, a VAT might trigger an inflationary spiral, which could increase the cost of producing export goods, particularly those goods manufactured by labor-intensive companies. If exporting industries raised their prices to compensate for increasing costs, the demand for their goods might fall (unless, of course, the demand for the exports was relatively inelastic).

Even without the possible inflationary impact of the VAT, the tax affects the cash flow of exporters, for such companies must actually pay the VAT on their purchases and then wait for these VAT payments to be refunded. This effect, however, occurs only when the VAT is first instituted. Exporters continue to pay the VAT on their purchases, but, after a time, VAT rebates for past purchases should be received as new purchases are made.

Industries competing with imports. Initially the VAT would not affect the competitive position of domestic products vis-à-vis imports, for both domestic goods and imports would have the same VAT levied on them. If, however, the imposition of a VAT sets off an inflationary spiral, then eventually industries which have to compete with imports would be hurt. Domestic goods would cost more to produce, while imported goods would not rise in price — unless, of course, the countries producing the goods imported into the United States suffered from a similar inflation or unless offsetting changes were made in exchange rates.

VAT versus increases in existing taxes

How would these VAT effects on industries with different characteristics compare with the effects of possible increases in existing taxes? As was indicated in Chapter 3, it seems likely that a U.S. VAT would be levied principally to raise additional revenues. Although some tax changes might be made when the VAT is introduced, a VAT would serve primarily not as a substitute for existing taxes, but as an alternative to increases in those taxes. Some of the possible alternative means of raising additional revenues were listed in Chapter 3, and the revenues likely to be generated by various alternatives and the general impact on the economy of each were outlined in Chapter 4. What would be the differential impact on business of a VAT versus some of these alternatives? Which tax alternative would be preferable from the point of view of various kinds of industries? This discussion will not attempt to analyze the impacts on specific industries; it will simply survey the factors any given industry should consider in determining which of the various tax alternatives would hurt it the least.

The impact of various tax changes on industries with different characteristics is indicated in the ten exhibits on pages 108–37. Exhibit 5–1 summarizes the preceding analysis of the VAT's impact on industries with various characteristics. Successive exhibits outline, in a greatly simplified form, the impacts of alternative revenue sources: Exhibit 5–2, increasing corporate income tax rates; Exhibit 5–3, eliminating the 7 percent investment credit and reducing depreciation allowances on the corporate income tax; Exhibit 5–4, increasing capital gains taxes on individuals; Exhibit 5–5, imposing a surcharge on the individual income tax; Exhibit 5–6, reducing the deductions allowed on the individual income tax; Exhibit 5–7, increasing payroll taxes; Exhibit 5–8, increasing business property taxes; and Exhibit 5–9, increasing residential property taxes. Exhibit 5–10 summarizes the preceding nine exhibits so that the impacts of the alternative taxes on industries with different characteristics can be compared. A more detailed comparison of the differential impact of these nine tax alternatives on industries with a given characteristic is made in Appendix B. In estimating the impacts of these tax alternatives, allowance must be made for the fact that a tax impact can be significantly altered by the way the government spends the revenues derived from the tax, and this factor is, of course, unknown at this time.

In very general terms, industries with each of the following characteristics would be affected most by the tax alternative indicated:

1. *Largely incorporated industries:* Of all the tax alternatives, industries with many corporations would be hit hardest by an increase in the corporate tax, whether the increase took the form of higher rates, elimination of the investment credit, or reduction in depreciation allowances.

2. *Industries with a low debt/equity ratio:* High-equity industries also would be hit hardest by an increase in the corporate income tax, whatever form the increase took.

3. *Industries with a high return on equity or sales:* Profitable incorporated industries also would be hurt most by an increase in the corporate income tax, particularly if the increase took the form of higher rates. Profitable unincorporated industries would be hit most by a surcharge on the individual income tax.

4. *Capital-intensive industries:* Of the various tax alternatives, capital-intensive industries would be hit hardest by an increase in the corporate income tax, particularly if the increase took the form of elimination of the investment credit or a reduction in depreciation allowances.

5 and 6. *Industries with sizeable assets in either land or buildings:* Such industries would be hurt most by an increase in business property taxes. It should be remembered, however, that business property taxes might increase at different rates in different areas and thus affect one company much more than a similar company in another area.

7. *Industries with industry-wide collective bargaining or strong labor unions:* Such industries might be affected more by the VAT than the

other tax alternatives, since the VAT is likely to trigger demands for wage increases by at least the amount of the VAT.

8. *Industries making purchases from diversified sources:* Industries with alternative sources of supply might be better able to take advantage of the differential price increases likely to be caused by higher corporate income taxes, business property taxes, or payroll taxes and, to a lesser extent, by other tax changes.

9. *Industries with a high import cost component:* Any tax change which caused domestic prices to rise faster than import prices would give an advantage to industries purchasing many imported goods. In the short run, higher payroll taxes might cause the biggest price differential between domestic and imported goods, but, in the long run, higher corporate income taxes might cause an even greater price differential because of the steep increase in this tax required to raise sizeable revenues.

10. *Industries with high elasticity of demand:* Industries with high elasticity in the demand for their product would probably have their sales dampened the most by the VAT. A surcharge on the individual income tax or an increase in payroll taxes would also hurt the sales of such industries.

11. *Industries with high product substitutability (high cross-elasticity):* Industries for whose products substitutes are readily available may lose customers if a tax change causes their prices to rise faster than the prices of the alternative products. The taxes most likely to cause differential price increases are the corporate income tax, and, to a lesser extent, payroll taxes and business property taxes.

12. *Industries with intense price competition:* Industries with intense price competition because of such factors as excess capacity in relation to demand would be hit hardest by the VAT since, unlike most industries, they might be unable to shift the tax forward and might, therefore, end up with a tax cost not borne generally by business.

13. *Industries with diversified markets:* Possession of diversified markets is an advantage to a company no matter what change is made in the U.S. tax structure.

14. *Producers of capital goods:* Producers of capital goods would be most likely to suffer a drop in sales if the corporate income tax were increased, particularly if the increase took the form of an elimination of the investment credit or a reduction in depreciation allowances.

15. *Industries with large exports:* Big exporters would be hurt most by an increase in the corporate income and payroll taxes, for these are the tax alternatives most likely to make them less competitive on the international market.

16. *Industries competing with imports:* Industries suffering from import competition would be hurt most by a rise in either corporate income taxes or payroll taxes.

General impact of the alternative tax changes on various industries

What does all this mean for a particular industry or company? In addition to its initial impact, any tax change has subtle, complex, and interacting secondary and tertiary effects. These effects depend, in part, on the rate of the tax. To raise revenues equal to those the government might net from a 3 percent VAT, corporate income taxes would have to be increased more than 30 percent. (See Chapter 4.) The impact of the VAT at such a low rate would touch many more companies but would in general affect any one company and any one industry less than such a steep increase in the corporate income tax. The effect of an increase in payroll taxes is diffused because half of the tax is nominally paid by employers and half nominally by employees. The effects of increasing property taxes are difficult to analyze since the rates, assessments, and determination of what is taxable vary so much from district to district. Elimination of the deductions for property taxes and mortgage interest on the individual income tax would have the most immediate impact on the housing industry, while increases in the rates on the individual income tax would have a more generalized effect on the economy. The effect of any tax change would be very much influenced by what the government did with the revenues generated by the new tax and by the state of the economy at the time of the tax change.

Because gauging the impact of any tax is so complex, it is impossible to say categorically that any particular tax change would be especially harmful to any particular industry. In general, however, it can be said that an increase in the corporate income tax would impose an especially heavy burden on industries that are highly incorporated, profitable, and capital-intensive, such as communications, chemicals, utilities, and tobacco processing. The finance and insurance industries also would be hard hit by higher corporate income taxes. An industry that was largely unincorporated, had low profits, was labor-intensive, or had a high debt/equity ratio, would be much less affected by even a steep increase in the corporate income tax. Some industries hit relatively lightly by this tax are the service industries, real estate, agriculture, medical and educational services, and amusements.

Labor-intensive industries of all types would be hit most heavily by an increase in payroll taxes. The service industries, metal mining, ordnance, textiles, apparel, footwear, leather and rubber, furniture, and finance and insurance would particularly feel the impact of such a tax increase. Companies with sizeable real estate holdings would be affected most by a rise in business property taxes. Higher residential property taxes would have their most immediate impact on the housing and related industries as would elimination of the deduction for property taxes and mortgage interest on the individual income tax. Increasing capital gains taxes would reduce the private funds available for investment in high equity companies.

A surcharge on the individual income tax would put unincorporated firms at a disadvantage unless an equivalent surcharge were also imposed on the corporate income tax.

Of all these taxes, the VAT is the one most neutral toward businesses of all types. The differential impact of the VAT arises largely because of the price increases induced by a VAT. Any tax tends directly or indirectly to push up wages and prices, and this not only increases an industry's labor bill but also the cost of its purchases. An industry should, therefore, be concerned not only with the immediate impact of a tax change on its after-tax profits but also with the eventual influence of the change on wages and prices paid by the industry. These effects should be of particular concern to an industry seeking to analyze the potential impact of a VAT, for a VAT probably generates the greatest immediate inflationary pressure of any tax. If a 3 percent VAT pushes prices up approximately 3 percent, will wages go up 3 percent or more? How will this affect the particular industry and its relative competitive position? Does the industry make many purchases from suppliers that would be hard hit by rising wages either because they are labor-intensive or because they have strong labor unions?

If an industry increases its prices, first to shift the VAT forward and then to reflect higher wage and purchasing costs, what effect will this have on sales? Will the industry be compelled to absorb some of these higher costs in order to protect its sales? Are profit margins in the industry such that it could afford to absorb some of these higher costs? Could the industry compensate for these higher costs by changing its production processes, becoming more capital-intensive, shortening its distribution lines or increasing its vertical integration?

As the VAT shifts spending from the private to the public sector, how will this affect an industry's sales? How would a particular industry be affected by any exemptions granted in a VAT? Would a multiple VAT rate be particularly burdensome to an industry?

Determination of the impact of the various tax alternatives on a particular industry

Evaluation of the effect of a VAT on a particular industry requires six steps:

1. *Analysis of the industry's characteristics* (or those of a majority of companies in the industry).
2. *Comparison of the differential impact of a VAT versus the various tax alternatives on an industry with such characteristics.* For this comparison, the industry characteristics determined in step 1 can be matched with the data in Exhibits 5–1 through 5–10. At this point, the analysis may present contradictory evidence. An industry may find that one of its characteristics makes it particularly vulnerable, say, to an increase in the corporate income tax, while another characteristic makes it dubious about the VAT. An attempt must then be made to weight the various factors.
3. *Analysis of the industry's particular combination of characteristics in order to weigh the importance of the various tax impacts.* For example, increasing the corporate income tax hits only profitable corporations. Such an increase would not have a direct impact on a company which was incorporated but not profitable or a company which was profitable but not incorporated — no matter what other

characteristics the company might have. Or again, although an increase in the corporate income tax generally would make U.S. industry less able to compete on the international market, some industries may produce goods for which the demand abroad is inelastic, that is, goods whose sales abroad are not likely to fall because of a tax-induced price increase. In short, one industry characteristic may make another industry characteristic irrelevant in terms of the impact of a given tax alternative.

4. *Determination of which characteristics are of major importance to the industry.* For example, an industry may make sizeable sales abroad, but, if exports constitute only a small fraction of its total sales, the industry should not weigh too heavily the impact of the various tax alternatives on big exporters.

5. *Quantification* (as much as possible) *of the impact of the various tax alternatives.* Consideration must be given both to the likely tax rates and the size of the industry's profits, wage bills, and so forth. For example, equal revenues could be raised by a 3 percent VAT or by an increase in corporate income taxes of over 30 percent. Would an industry be hurt more by a VAT-induced 3 percent rise in its wage bill or by a 30 percent plus increase in the tax on its profits?

6. *Some estimation of the way the revenues generated by the various tax changes are likely to be spent and the likely impact on the particular industry of this higher government spending.*

Determination of the impact of the various tax alternatives on a particular company

The impact of a VAT or any tax change on a particular company is, of course, influenced by the general impact of the tax on the company's industry. However, if a company had characteristics untypical of its industry, it might be affected quite differently from its competitors. For example, a steep increase in the corporate income tax might have relatively little impact on the construction industry, which is largely unincorporated, but it would certainly hurt a corporation in the industry; and the effect would be compounded by the fact that many of the corporation's competitors would be touched relatively little by the tax increase. In sum, a tax change which had an adverse effect on one segment of an industry might give a competitive advantage to another.

To determine the impact of the various tax alternatives on a given company, an analysis must first be made of the company's characteristics. A determination must then be made as to how the company differs from the majority of companies in its industry. With this information and the data in Exhibits 5–1 through 5–10, an analysis can be made of the differential impact of the various tax alternatives on the given company versus its competitors.

A company will also be affected by the impact of the various tax alternatives on its cash flow, its working capital, its interest costs, its compliance costs, and its operating profits. The effect of a VAT on such factors is outlined in the next chapter.

EXHIBIT 5–1
Impact of a VAT (selected factors tending to make a VAT affect industries with one characteristic more than industries with the opposite characteristic)

Characteristic of industries	Industries hurt directly by a proportionately higher tax burden or indirectly by a relative decrease in profits, a comparative decrease in sales, or a relatively greater increase in costs (−)	Neutral impact (0)	Industries aided directly by a proportionately lower tax burden or indirectly by a relative increase in profits, a comparatively smaller reduction in sales, or a relatively smaller increase in costs (+)
1. Highly incorporated industries (versus largely unincorporated industries)	N.A.	VAT taxes equally corporations and unincorporated companies.	N.A.
2. High debt/equity ratio	N.A.	VAT taxes equally companies with high and low debt/equity ratio.	N.A.
3. High return on equity (or on sales)	N.A.	A company's VAT bill is little affected by its profitability.	Industries with comparatively high profits can more easily absorb any higher costs or reduced sales caused by the VAT. They can also afford to absorb the VAT if necessary to protect their sales.
4. High capital intensiveness (Labor-intensive industries would be affected in the opposite way.)	N.A.	VAT taxes equally capital-intensive and labor-intensive industries.	Companies receive credit for the VAT paid on capital purchases. This does not benefit labor-intensive companies. If the VAT pushes prices up and this then triggers demands for higher wages in a cost/push inflation, labor-intensive industries would be hurt more by rising wage bills.
5. Sizeable assets in land	N.A.	Work done on the land (construction, forestry, etc.) is subject to the VAT just as is the value added in other types of work.	The sale and leasing of land would probably not be subject to the VAT.
6. Sizeable assets in buildings	If the leasing of commercial and industrial buildings were not subject to the VAT, the owner of a post-VAT building would have paid a VAT when he purchased the building, and the VAT would become a hidden cost in the rents he charged and not a separately listed item which tenant businesses could deduct from their own VAT liability. If the VAT triggers wage increases, this should lead to higher prices charged by the labor-intensive construction industry.	Construction, alteration, repair and maintenance work would probably be subject to the VAT like work done in other segments of the economy. Like the sale of most goods, the sale of newly constructed buildings would probably be subject to the VAT.	Leasing of residential property (other than hotel rooms) would probably not be subject to the VAT. In most cases the sale of older buildings would not be subject to the VAT. The owner of a pre-VAT building could sell or rent the building at a lower price or a higher profit than the owner of a post-VAT building, at least in the short run.

NOTE: N.A. = Not applicable (given column does not apply to an industry with that characteristic).

EXHIBIT 5–1 (*Continued*)

Characteristic of industries	*Industries hurt directly by a proportionately higher tax burden or indirectly by a relative decrease in profits, a comparative decrease in sales, or a relatively greater increase in costs (−)*	*Neutral impact (0)*	*Industries aided directly by a proportionately lower tax burden or indirectly by a relative increase in profits, a comparatively smaller reduction in sales, or a relatively smaller increase in costs (+)*
7. Industry-wide collective bargaining or strong unions	If the VAT triggers demands for higher wages, this would particularly affect industries where there is industry-wide collective bargaining or a strong union.	N.A.	N.A.
8. Diversified sources of purchases	N.A.	N.A.	If VAT triggers a cost/push inflation, companies which make purchases from a variety of industries may be better able to make substitute purchases if the cost of some items rises faster than others. An industry's costs will, of course, be affected by whether its purchases are primarily from companies helped or hurt by the VAT.
9. High import cost component	N.A.	The VAT is levied equally on domestic and imported goods.	Since the VAT is likely to trigger a cost/push inflation, imports might in time become comparatively cheaper to buy than domestic goods.
10. High elasticity in the demand for the industry's product (Industries with low elasticity in the demand for their product will be affected in the opposite way.)	The VAT is normally added on to prices and is ultimately paid by consumers. The VAT thus reduces consumers' spending money in somewhat the same way an increase in individual income taxes would. However, a VAT is likely to depress consumer demand more than an increase in the IIT, for the VAT is a more regressive tax. The VAT is shifted forward more immediately, directly and universally than corporate income taxes or other direct business taxes. The resulting increase in prices may reduce the demand for certain goods and have less effect on the sale of other goods.	N.A.	The way the government spends its VAT revenues might increase the sales of certain goods or stimulate the economy in certain parts of the country.
11. High product substitutability (high cross-elasticity)	Industries for whose products purchasers can readily find cheaper substitutes are more likely to suffer from any VAT-induced reduction in consumer demand. Industries whose products enjoy low cross-elasticity are less likely to be affected.	Since the VAT is largely neutral in its impact on business, in many cases the tax should not affect the competitiveness of one product vis-à-vis a substitute product.	N.A.

5. Impact of the VAT on different types of industries 109

Characteristic of industries	Industries hurt directly by a proportionately higher tax burden or indirectly by a relative decrease in profits, a comparative decrease in sales, or a relatively greater increase in costs (−)	Neutral impact (0)	Industries aided directly by a proportionately lower tax burden or indirectly by a relative increase in profits, a comparatively smaller reduction in sales, or a relatively smaller increase in costs (+)
12. Intense price competition	Companies in industries with intense price competition are more likely to suffer from the VAT-induced reduction in consumer demand than companies in less competitive industries. Companies in industries with intense price competition may not be able to pass forward the VAT to their customers.	Since the VAT is largely neutral in its impact on business, in many cases it should not directly affect the competitiveness of one company versus another in the same industry.	N.A.
13. Diversified markets	N.A.	N.A.	If the VAT cuts the demand for certain products, a company with diversified markets might be able to compensate by increasing its sales in other areas.
14. Producers of capital goods	If the VAT-induced reduction in consumer demand is not fully compensated for by higher government spending, business might become reluctant to expand, and the sale of capital goods would fall.	N.A.	The VAT may stimulate purchases of capital goods for three reasons: (1) Companies receive a rebate of the VAT paid on capital purchases; (2) if the VAT triggers wage increases, companies may invest more in labor-saving equipment; and (3) VAT revenues may be spent in such a way as to stimulate the sale of capital goods.
15. Industries doing much exporting	If the VAT triggers a cost/push inflation, the cost of producing goods for export will rise. Exporters may eventually have to raise their prices, and this may reduce their sales.	Initially the VAT would not affect exports. Before the VAT exporters paid no such tax, and after the VAT exporters are exempt from the tax. Therefore, neither the price nor the sales of exports should be changed by the introduction of the VAT.	While the VAT might reduce consumer demand at home, initially it should not affect export sales.
16. Industries competing with imports	If the VAT triggers a cost/push inflation, the cost of domestic goods may rise faster than the cost of imports. This would hurt the sales of industries competing with imports.	Initially the VAT would not affect the competitive position of domestic producers vis-à-vis imports, for both domestic goods and imports would have the same VAT levied on them.	N.A.

Note: N.A. = Not applicable (given column does not apply to an industry with that characteristic).

EXHIBIT 5–2

Impact of raising corporate income tax (CIT) rates (selected factors tending to make higher CIT rates affect industries with one characteristic more than industries with the opposite characteristic)

Characteristic of industries	Industries hurt directly by a proportionately higher tax burden or indirectly by a relative increase in profits, a comparative decrease in sales or a relatively greater increase in costs (−)	Neutral impact (0)	Industries aided directly by a proportionately lower tax burden or indirectly by a relative increase in profits, a comparatively smaller decrease in sales, or a relatively smaller increase in costs (+)
1. Highly incorporated industries (versus largely unincorporated industries)	Corporations would pay more CIT, but tax burden of unincorporated companies would be unaffected.	N.A.	N.A.
2. High debt/equity ratio (Industries with low debt/equity ratio would be affected in opposite way.)	N.A.	N.A.	Debt financing is encouraged because interest payments on debts are an expense deducted from a company's taxable income, while profits earned by equity capital are subject to the CIT. With high debt/equity ratio, smaller price increases are necessary to maintain net income if CIT is increased. If the CIT is not fully shifted, lower return on equity increases cost of equity financing for established companies and decreases attraction of equity investment in new ventures.
3. High return on equity (or on sales)	Companies with high profits must pay more CIT than low profit companies. If the CIT is shifted, marginal companies enjoy the price umbrella provided by profitable companies, i.e., although paying proportionately less taxes, marginal companies can charge the same prices as profitable companies.	N.A.	If the CIT is not fully shifted, an increase in the CIT may not cost a marginal company many dollars, but even a small increase in its tax bill may hurt the company with low profits more than a large increase would hurt a very profitable company.
4. High capital-intensiveness (Industries with high labor-intensiveness would be affected in the opposite way.)	CIT, although imposed on the profits of any incorporated company, hits capital-intensive companies harder since their profits need to be higher to provide an adequate return on capital investment. If CIT is shifted ultimately to customers, higher CIT rates would increase the prices charged by capital-intensive industries. This would affect particularly the cost of capital goods.	N.A.	N.A.

NOTE: N.A. = Not applicable (given column does not apply to an industry with that characteristic).

EXHIBIT 5-2 (Continued)
Impact of raising corporate income tax (CIT) rates (selected factors tending to make higher CIT rates affect industries with one characteristic more than industries with the opposite characteristic)

Characteristic of industries	Industries hurt directly by a proportionately higher tax burden or indirectly by a relative increase in profits, a comparative decrease in sales or a relatively greater increase in costs (−)	Neutral impact (0)	Industries aided directly by a proportionately lower tax burden or indirectly by a relative increase in profits, a comparatively smaller decrease in sales, or a relatively smaller increase in costs (+)
5. Sizeable assets in land	N.A.	Raising CIT rates would have roughly the same impact on companies with land assets as those with assets in plant and machinery.	N.A.
6. Sizeable assets in buildings	N.A.	Raising CIT rates would have roughly the same impact on companies with assets in buildings as on those with assets in machinery or land.	N.A.
7. Industry-wide collective bargaining or strong unions	N.A.	Since the CIT does not directly affect wages, increasing the CIT should not hurt industries with strong labor unions any more than those with weak unions.	N.A.
8. Diversified sources of purchases	N.A.	If the CIT is not shifted at all, changing the CIT would not change the cost of a company's purchases whether they were bought from many or few sources.	If the CIT is shifted ultimately to customers and thus increases some prices more than others, companies which make purchases from a variety of industries may be better able to make substitute purchases to take advantage of differential price increases. An industry's costs will, of course, be affected by whether its purchases are primarily from companies hurt by higher CIT rates.
9. High import cost component	N.A.	If the CIT is not shifted at all, the comparative prices of imports and domestic goods would not change.	If the CIT is shifted and thus causes a rise in the price of domestic goods, imports would then be comparatively cheaper to buy.
10. High elasticity in the demand for the industry's product (Industries with low elasticity in the demand for their product would be affected in the opposite way.)	If the CIT is shifted ultimately to customers and thus increases prices, it would reduce the demand for certain goods hit by these price increases. The demand for other goods would be less affected by price increases. If CIT is not fully shifted, companies will have fewer retained earnings to invest in capital goods. Demand for such goods will then decline.	Higher CIT rates will not immediately reduce the amount of money in consumers' hands. (Stockholders may receive smaller dividends, but this would not have much impact on consumer demand.) If the CIT is not shifted at all, higher CIT rates would not cause price increases that would dampen sales.	The way the government spends the new revenues might increase the sales of certain goods or stimulate the economy in certain parts of the country.

Note: N.A. = Not applicable (given column does not apply to an industry with that characteristic).

EXHIBIT 5–2 *(Continued)*

Characteristic of industries	Industries hurt directly by a proportionately higher tax burden or indirectly by a relative increase in profits, a comparative decrease in sales or a relatively greater increase in costs (−)	Neutral impact (0)	Industries aided directly by a proportionately lower tax burden or indirectly by a relative increase in profits, a comparatively smaller decrease in sales, or a relatively smaller increase in costs (+)
11. High product substitutability (high cross-elasticity)	If the CIT is shifted ultimately to customers and thus increases prices, customers might switch to substitute products with a smaller price increase. If the CIT is not fully shifted, companies would have less money to invest in improving their products vis-à-vis possible substitute products.	If the CIT is not shifted at all, higher CIT rates would not cause price increases that would encourage switching to other products.	N.A.
12. Intense price competition	Companies in industries with intense price competition would have greater difficulty in shifting the higher CIT to their customers. If the CIT is not fully shifted, companies would have less money to invest in improving their products and thus in improving their ability to compete.	N.A.	If competitiveness is so intense that industry operates at a loss, industry would not be affected by higher CIT.
13. Diversified markets	N.A.	If the CIT is not shifted at all, consumer demand would not generally be reduced by higher CIT rates, and a diversified market would not be of any greater advantage than it is at present. If the CIT is not fully shifted, companies would have fewer retained earnings to invest in capital goods. Producers of capital goods may then have reduced sales even if they have diversified markets.	If the CIT is shifted at all and the resultant increase in prices reduces some sales, a company with diversified markets might be able to compensate by increasing sales in other areas.
14. Producers of capital goods	If the CIT is not fully shifted, companies would have fewer retained earnings to invest in capital goods. If the CIT is not fully shifted, companies would find fewer capital investments profitable. If the CIT is shifted and therefore causes higher prices, this could reduce consumer demand. This, in turn, would discourage businesses from expanding, unless the drop in consumer demand is fully compensated for by higher government spending.	N.A.	The revenues from the higher CIT might be spent in such a way as to stimulate sales of capital goods.

5. Impact of the VAT on different types of industries   113

EXHIBIT 5–2 (Concluded)
Impact of raising corporate income tax (CIT) rates (selected factors tending to make higher CIT rates affect industries with one characteristic more than industries with the opposite characteristic)

Characteristic of industries	Industries hurt directly by a proportionately higher tax burden or indirectly by a relative increase in profits, a comparative decrease in sales or a relatively greater increase in costs (−)	Neutral impact (0)	Industries aided directly by a proportionately lower tax burden or indirectly by a relative increase in profits, a comparatively smaller decrease in sales, or a relatively smaller increase in costs (+)
15. Industries doing much exporting	If the CIT is even partially shifted, the price of goods produced for export will rise and this may reduce sales. If the CIT is not fully shifted, companies would have less money to invest in improving their product, etc. This might eventually hurt companies' ability to sell abroad.	If the CIT is not shifted at all, it will simply reduce the profits of companies hit by higher CIT rates. It would then not discriminate between industries doing much or little exporting.	N.A.
16. Industries competing with imports	If the CIT is shifted at all, the price of domestically produced goods would rise and they might therefore be less able to compete with imports. If the CIT is not fully shifted, companies would have less money to invest in improving their product, etc. This might eventually hurt companies' ability to compete with imports.	If the CIT is not shifted at all, it would simply reduce the profits of all companies hit by higher CIT rates and would not cause a rise in prices that would make domestic goods less competitive with imports.	N.A.

NOTE: N.A. = Not applicable (given column does not apply to an industry with that characteristic).

EXHIBIT 5-3

Impact of eliminating the investment credit and of reducing depreciation allowances on the corporate income tax (selected factors tending to make such changes in the CIT affect industries with one characteristic more than industries with the opposite characteristic)

Characteristic of industries	Industries hurt directly by a proportionately higher tax burden or indirectly by a relative decrease in profits, a comparatively larger reduction in sales, or a relatively larger increase in costs (−)	Neutral impact (0)	Industries aided directly by a proportionately lower tax burden or indirectly by a relative increase in profits, a comparatively smaller reduction in sales, or a relatively smaller increase in costs (+)
1. Highly incorporated industries (versus largely unincorporated industries)	Corporations would pay more CIT, but tax burden of unincorporated companies would be unaffected.	N.A.	N.A.
2. High debt/equity ratio (Industries with low debt/equity ratio would be affected in opposite way.)	N.A.	N.A.	Debt financing is encouraged because interest payments on debts are an expense deducted from a company's taxable income, while profits earned by equity capital are subject to the CIT. With high debt/equity ratio, smaller price increases are necessary to maintain net income if CIT is increased. If the CIT is not fully shifted, lower return on equity increases cost of equity financing for established companies and decreases attraction of equity investment in new ventures.
3. High return on equity (or on sales)	Companies with high profits must pay more CIT than low profit firms. If the CIT is shifted, marginal companies enjoy the "price umbrella" provided by profitable companies, that is, although paying proportionately less taxes, marginal companies can charge the same prices as profitable companies.	N.A.	If the CIT is not fully shifted, an increase in the CIT may not cost a marginal company many dollars, but even a small increase in its tax bill may hurt the company with low profits more than a large increase would hurt a very profitable company.
4. High capital-intensiveness (Labor-intensive industries would be affected in the opposite way.)	Corporations would not be allowed an investment credit or such generous depreciation allowances on their capital equipment. This would hurt capital-intensive industries much more than labor-intensive industries. If the CIT is shifted ultimately to customers, this change in the CIT would increase the prices charged by capital-intensive industries. This would affect particularly the cost of capital goods.	N.A.	N.A.

NOTE: N.A. = Not applicable (given column does not apply to an industry with that characteristic).

5. Impact of the VAT on different types of industries   115

EXHIBIT 5–3 (Continued)
Impact of eliminating the investment credit and of reducing depreciation allowances on the corporate income tax (selected factors tending to make such changes in the CIT affect industries with one characteristic more than industries with the opposite characteristic)

Characteristic of industries	Industries hurt directly by a proportionately higher tax burden or indirectly by a relative decrease in profits, a comparatively larger reduction in sales, or a relatively larger increase in costs (−)	Neutral impact (0)	Industries aided directly by a proportionately lower tax burden or indirectly by a relative increase in profits, a comparatively smaller reduction in sales, or a relatively smaller increase in costs (+)
5. Sizeable assets in land	N.A.	N.A.	Land-owners do not benefit from the investment credit or depreciation allowances. Thus, they would not be hurt by this tax change, while companies whose assets were in plant and machinery would be hurt.
6. Sizeable assets in buildings	Owners of buildings (like owners of machinery) would be hurt by elimination of the investment credity and a reduction in depreciation allowances.	N.A.	N.A.
7. Industry-wide collective bargaining or strong labor unions	N.A.	Since the CIT does not directly affect wages, changing the CIT should not directly affect industries with strong labor unions any more than those with weak unions.	N.A.
8. Diversified sources of purchases	N.A.	If the CIT is not shifted at all, changing the CIT would not change the cost of a company's purchases whether they were bought from many or few sources.	If the CIT is shifted ultimately to customers and thus increases some prices more than others, companies which make purchases from a variety of industries may be better able to make substitute purchases to take advantage of differential price increases. An industry's costs will, of course, be affected by whether its purchases are primarily from companies hurt or helped by the change in depreciation allowances and the elimination of the investment credit.
9. High impost cost component	N.A.	If the CIT is not shifted at all, the comparative prices of imports and domestic goods would not change.	If the CIT is shifted and thus causes an increase in the price of domestic goods, imports would then be comparatively cheap to buy.

NOTE: N.A. = Not applicable (given column does not apply to an industry with that characteristic).

EXHIBIT 5–3 (Continued)

Characteristic of industries	Industries hurt directly by a proportionately higher tax burden or indirectly by a relative decrease in profits, a comparatively larger reduction in sales, or a relatively larger increase in costs (−)	Neutral impact (0)	Industries aided directly by a proportionately lower tax burden or indirectly by a relative increase in profits, a comparatively smaller reduction in sales, or a relatively smaller increase in costs (+)
10. High elasticity in the demand for the industry's product (Industries with low elasticity in the demand for their product would be affected in the opposite way.)	If the CIT is shifted ultimately to customers and thus increases prices, it would reduce the demand for certain goods hit by these price increases and have less effect on the demand for other goods. If the CIT is not fully shifted, companies would have less money to spend on capital goods, and the demand for such goods would fall. This will be accentuated by the fact that capital-intensive companies would be very hard hit by this change in the CIT.	This tax change would not immediately reduce the amount of money in consumers' hands. (Stockholders may receive smaller dividends, but this would not have much impact on consumer demand.)	The way the government spends its new revenues might increase the sales of certain goods or stimulate the economy in certain parts of the country.
11. High product substitutability (high cross-elasticity)	If the CIT is shifted ultimately to customers and thus increases prices, customers might switch to substitute products with smaller price increases. If the CIT is not fully shifted, companies would have less money to invest in improving their products vis-à-vis possible substitute products.	If the CIT is not shifted at all, this tax change should cause no price changes that would encourage switching to other products.	N.A.
12. Intense price competition	Companies in industries with intense price competition would have greater difficulty shifting the higher CIT to their customers. If the CIT is not fully shifted, companies would have less money to invest in improving their products and thus in improving their ability to compete.	N.A.	If competiveness is so intense that industry operates at a loss, industry would not be affected by this change in the CIT.
13. Diversified markets	N.A.	If the CIT is not shifted at all, consumer demand would not generally be affected by this tax change. A diversified market would not be of any greater advantage than it now is. If the CIT is not fully shifted, companies would have less money to spend on capital goods. Producers of capital goods may then have lower sales even if they have diversified markets.	If the CIT is shifted at all and the resultant increase in prices reduces some sales, a company with diversified markets might be able to compensate by increasing sales in other areas.

5. Impact of the VAT on different types of industries   117

EXHIBIT 5-3 (Concluded)

Impact of eliminating the investment credit and of reducing depreciation allowances on the corporate income tax (selected factors tending to make such changes in the CIT affect industries with one characteristic more than industries with the opposite characteristic)

Characteristic of industries	Industries hurt directly by a proportionately higher tax burden or indirectly by a relative decrease in profits, a comparatively larger reduction in sales, or a relatively larger increase in costs (−)	Neutral impact (0)	Industries aided directly by a proportionately lower tax burden or indirectly by a relative increase in profits, a comparatively smaller reduction in sales, or a relatively smaller increase in costs (+)
14. Producers of capital goods	This change in the CIT would make capital investment much less attractive, and sales of capital goods should fall.	N.A.	The revenues from this change in the CIT might be spent in such a way as to stimulate the purchase of capital goods.
15. Industries doing much exporting	If the CIT is shifted at all, the price of goods produced for export should rise, and this may reduce sales. If the CIT is not fully shifted, companies would have less money to invest in improving their product, etc. This might eventually hurt companies' ability to sell abroad.	If the CIT is not shifted at all, it would simply reduce the profits of all industries hit by this tax change. It would then not discriminate between industries doing much or little exporting.	N.A.
16. Industries competing with imports	If the CIT is shifted at all, the price of domestically produced goods rises, and they may therefore be less able to compete with imports. If the CIT is not fully shifted, companies would have less money to invest in improving their product, etc. This might eventually hurt companies' ability to compete with imports.	If the CIT is not shifted at all, it would simply reduce the profits of all industries hit by this tax change and would not cause a rise in prices that would make domestic goods less competitive with imports.	N.A.

NOTE: N.A. = Not applicable (given column does not apply to an industry with that characteristic).

EXHIBIT 5–4

Impact of increasing taxes on capital gains of individuals (selected factors tending to make an increase in capital gains taxes affect industries with one characteristic more than industries with the opposite characteristic)

Characteristic of industries	Industries hurt directly by a proportionately higher tax burden or indirectly by a relative decrease in profits, a comparatively larger decrease in sales, or a relatively larger increase in costs (−)	Neutral impact (0)	Industries aided directly by a proportionately lower tax burden or indirectly by a relative increase in profits, a comparatively smaller reduction in sales, or a relatively smaller increase in costs (+)
1. Highly incorporated industries (versus largely unincorporated industries)	Corporations would be hurt only indirectly by the reduction in the funds available from outside investors.		If taxes are increased only on the capital gains of individuals, only unincorporated industries would be directly affected.
2. High debt/equity ratio (Industries with low debt/equity ratio would be affected in the opposite way.)	N.A.	N.A.	Stockholders would pay higher taxes on capital gains. They therefore would have fewer funds for reinvestment. It is primarily equity capital which enjoys capital gains, and it is therefore primarily those who invested in stocks rather than bonds who would be hurt by heavier taxation in capital gains. Investment in stocks would become less attractive to potential stockholders.
3. High return on equity (or on sales)	Companies with a high return on equity are likely to become less attractive to investors.	Investment in companies with a high return on *sales* (versus equity) generally would not be affected as much by higher capital gains taxes levied on stockholders.	N.A.
4. High capital-intensiveness (Labor-intensive industries would be affected in the opposite way.)		The effect of higher capital gains taxes on capital-intensive versus labor-intensive industries is hard to gauge.	N.A.
5. Sizeable assets in land	Land is generally more likely to enjoy capital gains than, say, machinery. Owners of land would therefore be hurt by heavier taxation of capital gains, and investment in land would become less attractive.	N.A.	N.A.
6. Sizeable assets in buildings	Commercial and residential buildings are generally more likely to enjoy capital gains than, say, machinery. Owners of buildings would therefore be hurt by heavier taxation of capital gains, and investment in buildings would become less attractive.	N.A.	N.A.

NOTE: N.A. = Not applicable (given column does not apply to an industry with that characteristic).

5. Impact of the VAT on different types of industries   119

EXHIBIT 5–4 *(Continued)*

Impact of increasing taxes on capital gains of individuals (selected factors tending to make an increase in capital gains taxes affect industries with one characteristic more than industries with the opposite characteristic)

Characteristic of industries	*Industries hurt directly by a proportionately higher tax burden or indirectly by a relative decrease in profits, a comparatively larger decrease in sales, or a relatively larger increase in costs* (−)	*Neutral impact* (0)	*Industries aided directly by a proportionately lower tax burden or indirectly by a relative increase in profits, a comparatively smaller reduction in sales, or a relatively smaller increase in costs* (+)
7. Industry-wide collective bargaining or strong labor unions	N.A.	Since this tax change should not directly affect wages, there should be no difference in the impact on industries with strong and weak labor unions.	N.A.
8. Diversified sources of purchases	N.A.	Since this change in the tax structure should not lead directly to higher prices, it should not change the cost of a company's purchases whether made from few or many sources.	N.A.
9. High import cost component	N.A.	Since this change in the tax structure should not lead directly to higher prices, the comparative costs of imports and domestic goods should not change.	N.A.
10. High elasticity in the demand for the industry's product (Industries with low elasticity in the demand for their product would be affected in the opposite way.)	If this tax change reduces the availability of equity capital, it should reduce the demand for capital goods.	This tax change is not likely to seriously reduce consumer spending as other changes in the personal income tax would, for heavier taxation of capital gains would hurt principally those with high incomes and a high propensity to save.	The way the government spends its new revenues might increase the sales of certain goods or stimulate the economy in certain parts of the country.
11. High product substitutability (high cross-elasticity)	By reducing the availability of equity capital, this tax change might make it more difficult for a company to improve its product vis-à-vis substitute products.	Since this tax change should not in the short term lead to higher prices, it should not directly cause customers to switch from one product to another.	N.A.
12. Intense price competition	By reducing the availability of equity capital, this might make it more difficult for companies to invest in cost-cutting equipment or to develop improved products.	Since this tax change would not affect the tax burden of business, it should not directly affect price competition in an industry.	N.A.
13. Diversified markets	N.A.	Since this tax change should not seriously reduce consumer spending, diversified markets would be less of an advantage than with other tax changes. Since this tax change is likely to reduce the demand for capital goods of all kinds, producers of capital goods may have lower sales even if they have diversified markets.	N.A.

NOTE: N.A. = Not applicable (given column does not apply to an industry with that characteristic).

EXHIBIT 5–4 *(Concluded)*

Characteristic of industries	*Industries hurt directly by a proportionately higher tax burden or indirectly by a relative decrease in profits, a comparatively larger decrease in sales, or a relatively larger increase in costs (−)*	*Neutral impact (0)*	*Industries aided directly by a proportionately lower tax burden or indirectly by a relative increase in profits, a comparatively smaller reduction in sales, or a relatively smaller increase in costs (+)*
14. Producers of capital goods	Since this tax change would reduce the availability of equity capital, it should reduce the demand for capital goods.	N.A.	The revenues from higher capital gains taxes might be spent in such a way as to stimulate sales of capital goods.
15. Industries doing much exporting	This tax change might make companies less able to invest in the development of new or improved products. Eventually this might reduce export sales.	This tax change would probably not cause immediate price increases that would hurt the sales of exports.	N.A.
16. Industries competing with imports	This tax change might make companies less able to invest in the development of new or improved products. Eventually this might make domestic goods less able to compete with imports.	This tax change would probably not cause immediate price increases that would make domestic goods less able to compete with imports.	N.A.

NOTE: N.A. = Not applicable (given column does not apply to an industry with that characteristic).

5. Impact of the VAT on different types of industries   121

EXHIBIT 5–5
Impact of imposing a surcharge on individual income taxes (IIT) (selected factors tending to make a general increase in individual income taxes affect industries with one characteristic more than industries with the opposite characteristic)

Characteristic of industries	Industries hurt directly by a proportionately higher tax burden or indirectly by a relative decrease in profits, a comparative decrease in sales, or a relatively greater rise in costs (−)	Neutral impact (0)	Industries aided directly by a proportionately lower tax burden or indirectly by a relative increase in profits, a comparative increase in sales, or a relatively smaller increase in costs (+)
1. Highly incorporated industries (versus largely unincorporated industries)	N.A.	N.A.	An increase in IIT rates would not affect corporations but would increase taxes on unincorporated companies.
2. High debt/equity ratio (Industries with low debt/equity ratio would be affected in the opposite way.)	N.A.	Individual income taxes are not imposed on corporations.	For *unincorporated* companies, interest payments on debts are an expense deducted from company's profits and therefore reduce a company's IIT.
3. High return on equity (or on sales)	Profitable *unincorporated* companies would pay proportionately more taxes because of the IIT surcharge than less-profitable unincorporated companies.	Corporations, whether profitable or not, would not be directly affected by this tax change.	Profitable companies could more easily absorb any reduction in sales caused by the surcharge on the IIT.
4. High capital-intensiveness (Labor-intensive industries would be affected in the opposite way.)	For *unincorporated* companies, profits subject to IIT have to be higher for capital-intensive companies to provide an adequate return on capital investment. Thus, a surcharge on the IIT would impose a greater tax burden on capital-intensive companies (if unincorporated).	Individual income taxes are not imposed on corporations, whether capital- or labor-intensive.	Increasing the IIT may trigger demands for higher wages, and this would hurt labor-intensive industries more than capital-intensive ones. However, a IIT surtax should cause less upward pressure on wages than a VAT since a VAT (unlike the IIT) would presumably be included in the cost-of-living index to which many wages are tied.
5. Sizeable assets in land	N.A.	Individual income taxes are not imposed on corporations. For unincorporated companies, a surcharge on IIT would have roughly the same impact on companies with land assets as on those with assets in plant and machinery.	N.A.
6. Sizeable assets in buildings	If the IIT surcharge leads ultimately to higher wages, this should lead to higher prices charged by the labor-intensive construction industry.	Individual income taxes are not imposed on corporations. For unincorporated companies, a surcharge on IIT would have roughly the same impact on companies with assets in buildings, machinery, or land.	N.A.
7. Industry-wide collective bargaining or strong labor unions	If the IIT surcharge triggers demands for higher wages, this would particularly affect industries with industry-wide labor bargaining.	N.A.	N.A.

NOTE: N.A. = Not applicable (given column does not apply to an industry with that characteristic).

EXHIBIT 5–5 (Continued)

Characteristic of industries	Industries hurt directly by a proportionately higher tax burden or indirectly by a relative decrease in profits, a comparative decrease in sales, or a relatively greater rise in costs (−)	Neutral impact (0)	Industries aided directly by a proportionately lower tax burden or indirectly by a relative increase in profits, a comparative increase in sales, or a relatively smaller increase in costs (+)
8. Diversified sources of purchases	N.A.	Companies making purchases primarily from corporations would not in the short run be affected by this tax change.	Companies making purchases from a variety of sources might be better able to make substitute purchases to take advantage of any differential price increases. If the IIT surcharge is shifted ultimately to customers, the prices of unincorporated firms will rise. If the IIT surcharge leads ultimately to higher wages, this in turn may lead to higher prices even for corporations.
9. High import cost component	N.A.	Increasing the IIT would not in the short term increase the price of goods produced by domestic corporations. Thus, there will be no change in the comparative cost of imports vis-à-vis most domestic goods.	If the IIT surcharge is shifted, this would increase the costs of goods produced by domestic unincorporated companies vis-à-vis imports. However, unincorporated companies generally do not compete with imports. If the IIT surcharge leads ultimately to higher wages and if this in turn leads to higher prices, then imports would become comparatively cheaper than domestic goods.
10. High elasticity in the demand for the industry's product (Industries with low elasticity in the demand for their product would be affected in the opposite way.)	A surcharge on the IIT would leave consumers with less money to spend and should therefore reduce the consumer demand for certain goods. A surcharge on the IIT is likely to depress consumer demand more than reducing deductions, for the surcharge would hit people at all income levels. It would not, however, depress consumer demand quite as much as a VAT since the IIT is a more progressive tax.	N.A.	The way the government spends its new revenues might increase the sales of certain goods or stimulate the economy in certain parts of the country.
11. High product substitutability (high cross-elasticity)	Since consumers would have less money to spend, they might switch to less expensive substitute products. If unincorporated firms shifted their higher IIT to customers, customers might switch to products not affected by this tax change.	Since increasing IIT would not in the short term affect the price of goods provided by corporations, there would be no differential price changes to cause customers to switch from the product of one corporation to another.	N.A.

5. Impact of the VAT on different types of industries   123

EXHIBIT 5-5 (Concluded)
Impact of imposing a surcharge on individual income taxes (IIT) (selected factors tending to make a general increase in individual income taxes affect industries with one characteristic more than industries with the opposite characteristic)

Characteristic of industries	Industries hurt directly by a proportionately higher tax burden or indirectly by a relative decrease in profits, a comparative decrease in sales, or a relatively greater rise in costs (−)	Neutral impact (0)	Industries aided directly by a proportionately lower tax burden or indirectly by a relative increase in profits, a comparative increase in sales, or a relatively smaller increase in costs (+)
12. Intense price competition	Companies in industries with intense price competition are more likely to suffer from any reduction in consumer demand caused by the IIT surcharge.	Since the IIT does not impose a tax burden on corporations, it should not directly affect price competition between corporations in the same industry.	N.A.
13. Diversified markets	N.A.	N.A.	Companies with diversified markets are more likely to be able to compensate for decreases in some sales by increasing other sales.
14. Producers of capital goods	If the IIT-induced reduction in consumer demand is not fully compensated by higher government spending, businesses might be reluctant to invest in capital goods.	The IIT surcharge would not directly affect the retained earnings corporations had available for capital investment.	The revenues from the IIT surcharge might be spent in such a way as to stimulate sales of capital goods.
15. Industries doing much exporting	If the IIT is shifted, the surcharge would increase the price of goods produced by unincorporated companies and perhaps reduce the sale of such goods abroad. However, unincorporated firms generally do not export much. If the IIT leads ultimately to higher wages and therefore higher prices, companies might have greater difficulty in selling goods abroad.	A surcharge on the IIT should not in the short term affect the price of goods produced either for export or for the domestic market by corporations.	While demand on the domestic market might fall, sales of export goods should not be immediately be affected by a surcharge on the IIT.
16. Industries competing with imports	If the IIT is shifted, the surcharge would increase the price of goods produced by unincorporated companies and make them less able to compete with imports. However, unincorporated companies generally do not compete with imports. If the IIT leads ultimately to higher wages, companies could not compete as well with imports.	A surcharge on the IIT should not in the short term affect the price of domestic goods produced by corporations and therefore should not make them less competitive with imports.	N.A.

NOTE: N.A. = Not applicable (given column does not apply to an industry with that characteristic).

EXHIBIT 5-6

Impact of reducing deductions permitted on individual income taxes (IIT): Not allowing deductions for mortgage interest payments or residential property taxes, reducing allowable deductions for medical expenses, charitable contributions, etc. (selected factors tending to make such changes in the individual income tax affect industries with one characteristic more than industries with the opposite characteristic)

Characteristic of industries	Industries hurt directly by a proportionately higher tax burden or indirectly by a relative decrease in profits, a comparative decrease in sales or a relatively greater increase in costs (−)	Neutral impact (0)	Industries aided directly by a proportionately lower tax burden or indirectly by a relative increase in profits, a comparatively smaller reduction in sales, or a relatively smaller increase in costs (+)
1. Largely incorporated industries (versus largely unincorporated industries)	N.A.	Individual income taxes are not imposed on corporations. IIT burdens on unincorporated businesses would probably not be directly affected by such changes.	N.A.
2. High debt/equity ratio	N.A.	Individual income taxes are not imposed on corporations. IIT burden on unincorporated businesses would probably not be directly affected by such changes.	N.A.
3. High return on equity (or on sales)	N.A.	Unincorporated firms—whether profitable or not—would probably not find their tax bill affected by such changes in the IIT. Corporations also would not be affected.	Profitable industries can more easily absorb any reduction in sales caused by these changes in the IIT.
4. High capital-intensiveness	N.A.	Individual income taxes are not imposed on corporations. IIT burden on unincorporated businesses would probably not be directly affected by such changes.	Increasing the IIT may trigger demands for higher wages and this would hurt labor-intensive industries. However, reducing deductions on the IIT is much less likely to trigger wage demands than imposing a surcharge on the IIT.
5. Sizeable assets in land	If the deduction for property taxes were no longer allowed, consumers would be less interested in buying land.	Individual income taxes are not imposed on corporations. IIT burden on unincorporated businesses would probably not be directly affected by such changes.	N.A.
6. Sizeable assets in buildings	The housing industry might suffer a sales slump if consumers could no longer deduct mortgage interest payments or property taxes on their IIT.	Individual income taxes are not imposed on corporations. IIT burden on unincorporated business would probably not be directly affected by such changes.	N.A.
7. Industry-wide collective bargaining or strong labor unions	If this change in the IIT triggers demands for higher wages, this would particularly affect industries with industry-wide labor bargaining.	N.A.	N.A.

NOTE: N.A. = Not applicable (given column does not apply to an industry with that characteristic).

5. Impact of the VAT on different types of industries   125

EXHIBIT 5–6 (Continued)
Impact of reducing deductions permitted on individual income taxes (IIT): Not allowing deductions for mortgage interest payments or residential property taxes, reducing allowable deductions for medical expenses, charitable contributions, etc. (selected factors tending to make such changes in the individual income tax affect industries with one characteristic more than industries with the opposite characteristic)

Characteristic of industries	Industries hurt directly by a proportionately higher tax burden or indirectly by a relative decrease in profits, a comparative decrease in sales or a relatively greater increase in costs (−)	Neutral impact (0)	Industries aided directly by a proportionately lower tax burden or indirectly by a relative increase in profits, a comparatively smaller reduction in sales, or a relatively smaller increase in costs (+)
8. Diversified sources of purchases	N.A.	Since this tax change will not directly affect most businesses, it generally should not have a differential impact on prices charged by various types of businesses.	N.A.
9. High import cost component	N.A.	Since this tax change will not directly affect most businesses, it should not cause a differential in the cost of domestic goods versus imports.	N.A.
10. High elasticity in the demand for the industry's product (Industries with low elasticity in the demand for their product would be affected in the opposite way).	This tax change will leave consumers with less money to spend and will therefore reduce the demand for certain goods. However, this tax change is likely to depress consumer demand less than imposing a surcharge on the IIT, for reducing deductions would have its greatest impact on high income people, who generally spend a lower proportion of their income. Elimination of the deductions for property taxes and mortgage interest would hurt housing sales.	N.A.	The way the government spends its new revenues might increase the sales of certain goods or stimulate the economy in certain parts of the country.
11. High product substitutability (high cross-elasticity)	Since this tax change would reduce disposable income, it might cause consumers to switch to less-expensive products.	Since this tax change would not directly affect prices, there should be no differential price increases to cause customers to switch from one product to another.	N.A.
12. Intense price competition	Companies in industries with intense price competition are more likely to suffer from any reduction in consumer demand caused by this tax change.	Since this tax change would not increase a business's tax burden, it should not directly affect price competition between companies in the same industry.	N.A.

NOTE: N.A. = Not applicable (given column does not apply to an industry with that characteristic).

EXHIBIT 5–6 *(Concluded)*

Characteristic of industries	*Industries hurt directly by a proportionately higher tax burden or indirectly by a relative decrease in profits, a comparative decrease in sales or a relatively greater increase in costs (−)*	*Neutral impact (0)*	*Industries aided directly by a proportionately lower tax burden or indirectly by a relative increase in profits, a comparatively smaller reduction in sales, or a relatively smaller increase in costs (+)*
13. Diversified markets	N.A.	N.A.	Companies with diversified markets are more likely to be able to compensate for a decrease in some sales by increasing other sales.
14. Producers of capital goods	If the tax-induced reduction in consumer demand is not fully compensated for by higher government spending, the demand for capital good might fall.	This tax change would not directly affect the retained earnings businesses have available for capital investment.	The revenues from this change in the IIT might be spent in such a way as to stimulate sales of capital goods.
15. Industries doing much exporting	If these changes in the IIT lead ultimately to higher wages, and then higher prices, sales of some exports might fall.	Such changes in the IIT should not in the short term affect the price of goods produced either for export or for the domestic market.	The reduction in consumer demand caused by this tax change should not affect exporters, but would hurt some domestic sales.
16. Industries competing with imports	If these changes in the IIT lead ultimately to higher wages, companies may be less able to compete with imports.	In the short term such changes in the IIT should not affect the price of domestic goods and therefore would not affect their ability to compete with imports.	N.A.

5. Impact of the VAT on different types of industries   127

EXHIBIT 5–7

Impact of increasing payroll taxes (selected factors tending to make higher payroll taxes affect industries with one characteristic more than industries with the opposite characteristic)

Characteristic of industries	Industries hurt directly by a proportionately higher tax burden or indirectly by a relative decrease in profits, a comparative decrease in sales, or a relatively greater rise in costs (−)	Neutral impact (0)	Industries aided directly by a proportionately lower tax burden or indirectly by a comparative increase in profits, a relative increase in sales or a relatively smaller increase in costs (+)
1. Highly incorporated industries (versus largely unincorporated industries)	N.A.	Payroll taxes are not affected by whether or not a company is incorporated.	N.A.
2. High debt/equity ratio	N.A.	Payroll taxes are not affected by a company's debt/equity ratio.	N.A.
3. High return on equity (or sales)	N.A.	The size of a company's payroll taxes is not a function of its profits.	Profitable companies could better absorb the rise in payroll taxes and any resultant increase in wages.
4. High capital-intensiveness (Labor-intensive industries would be affected in the opposite way.)	N.A.	N.A.	Payroll taxes fall more heavily on labor-intensive industries. An increase in the payroll taxes paid by employees may trigger demands for higher wages even though payroll taxes are not included in the cost-of-living index. Labor-intensive industries would be hurt more by rising wages.
5. Sizeable assets in land	N.A.	Payroll taxes are neutral toward companies with different kinds of assets.	N.A.
6. Sizeable assets in buildings	Since the construction industry is labor-intensive, the cost of constructing, altering or repairing buildings would probably rise.	Payroll taxes are not affected by the nature of a company's assets.	N.A.
7. Industry-wide collective bargaining or strong unions	The increased payroll taxes paid by employees may trigger demands for higher wages, and these demands would be harder to resist in industries with strong labor unions.	N.A.	N.A.
8. Diversified sources of purchases	N.A.	N.A.	If higher payroll taxes increase the prices of some companies more than others, businesses which make purchases from a variety of industries may be better able to purchase substitute goods less affected by price increases. An industry's costs will, of course, be affected by whether its purchases are primarily from companies hurt by higher payroll taxes.

NOTE: N.A. = Not applicable (given column does not apply to an industry with that characteristic).

EXHIBIT 5–7 (*Continued*)

Characteristic of industries	Industries hurt directly by a proportionately higher tax burden or indirectly by a relative decrease in profits, a comparative decrease in sales, or a relatively greater rise in costs (−)	Neutral impact (0)	Industries aided directly by a proportionately lower tax burden or indirectly by a comparative increase in profits, a relative increase in sales or a relatively smaller increase in costs (+)
9. High import cost component	N.A.	N.A.	If payroll taxes increase prices, particularly for goods produced by labor-intensive companies, imports would then become comparatively cheaper to buy.
10. High elasticity in the demand for an industry's product (Industries with low elasticity in the demand for their product would be affected in the opposite way.)	Higher payroll taxes paid by employees reduce take-home pay and therefore diminish consumer demand generally. This would hurt the sale of some goods more than others. If higher payroll taxes lead to higher prices, there would be differential price increases because of the uneven impact of the higher taxes. Sales may drop for goods hard hit by price increases.	If the government promptly spends the revenues from the higher payroll taxes on higher social security benefits, then the sales of most products should not fall.	If the government promptly spends the revenues from the higher payroll taxes on something beside higher social security benefits, this might increase the sale of certain goods or stimulate the economy in certain parts of the country.
11. High product substitutability (high cross-elasticity)	If higher payroll taxes cause differential price increases, consumers may switch to cheaper products when a substitute is readily available. The reduction in disposable income resulting from higher payroll taxes may cause consumers to switch to cheaper products, even where there are no differential price increases.	N.A.	N.A.
12. Intense price competition	Companies in industries with intense price competition would be particularly hard hit by both the higher labor costs and any reduction in consumer demand caused by higher payroll taxes.	N.A.	N.A.
13. Diversified markets	N.A.	N.A.	If higher payroll taxes cut the demand for certain products, companies with diversified markets might be able to compensate by increasing sales in other areas.
14. Producers of capital goods	If higher payroll taxes reduce consumer demand, this may ultimately discourage businesses from expanding, unless the drop in consumer demand is fully compensated for by higher government spending.	N.A.	Higher payroll taxes may stimulate companies to invest in labor-saving equipment.

5. Impact of the VAT on different types of industries   129

EXHIBIT 5-7 (Concluded)
Impact of increasing payroll taxes (selected factors tending to make higher payroll taxes affect industries with one characteristic more than industries with the opposite characteristic)

Characteristic of industries	Industries hurt directly by a proportionately higher tax burden or indirectly by a relative decrease in profits, a comparative decrease in sales, or a relatively greater rise in costs (−)	Neutral impact (0)	Industries aided directly by a proportionately lower tax burden or indirectly by a comparative increase in profits, a relative increase in sales or a relatively smaller increase in costs (+)
15. Industries doing much exporting	If payroll taxes are shifted at all, the price of exports should rise. The sales of some exports then might fall. However, exports produced by capital-intensive industries would be affected less by higher payroll taxes than by higher corporate income taxes.		N.A.
	If higher payroll taxes cause wages to increase, then export prices would rise even if the taxes themselves are not shifted.		
16. Industries competing with imports	Industries would have greater difficulty competing with imports both because of the higher payroll taxes and because of the possible rise in wages. Labor-intensive industries would be particularly hard hit. However, the ability of capital-intensive industries to compete with imports would be affected less by higher payroll taxes than higher corporate income taxes.		N.A.

NOTE: N.A. = Not applicable (given column does not apply to an industry with that characteristic).

EXHIBIT 5–8

Impact of increasing business property taxes (selected factors tending to make an increase in business property taxes affect industries with one characteristic more than industries with the opposite characteristic)

Characteristic of industries	Industries hurt directly by a proportionately higher tax burden or indirectly by a relative decrease in profits, a comparatively larger reduction in sales, or a relatively larger increase in costs (−)	Neutral impact (0)	Industries aided directly by a proportionately lower tax burden or indirectly by a relative increase in profits, a comparatively smaller reduction in sales, or a relatively smaller increase in costs (+)
1. Highly incorporated industries (versus largely unincorporated industries)	N.A.	Property taxes are not normally affected by whether or not a company is incorporated.	N.A.
2. High debt/equity ratio	N.A.	Property taxes are not affected by company's debt/equity ratio.	N.A.
3. High return on equity (or on sales)	N.A.	The size of a company's property taxes is determined by the size of its fixed assets, not directly by its profits.	Profitable companies could more easily absorb an increase in their property taxes.
4. High capital-intensiveness (Labor-intensive industries would be affected in the opposite way.)	Certain of a company's capital investments are subject to property taxes.	N.A.	N.A.
5. Sizeable assets in land	Property taxes are universally imposed on land (and buildings) but not always on all other types of assets. However, at present the size of a company's property tax bill may depend as much on its location as on its holdings.	N.A.	N.A.
6. Sizeable assets in buildings	Property taxes are almost universally imposed on buildings (and land) but not always on other types of assets. However, at present the size of a company's property tax bill may depend as much on its location as on the buildings it owns.	N.A.	N.A.
7. Industry-wide collective bargaining or strong labor unions	N.A.	Since business property taxes do not directly affect wages, increasing such taxes should not affect industries with strong labor unions more than those with weak unions.	N.A.
8. Diversified sources of purchases	N.A.	If property taxes are not shifted to customers at all, higher property taxes would not change the cost of a company's purchases whether they were made from many or few sources.	If property taxes are shifted ultimately to customers and therefore raise the prices of companies hard hit by a rise in these taxes, this will increase the costs of companies making substantial purchases from such firms. Companies which make purchases from a variety of sources might be better able to make substitute purchases to take advantage of differential price increases.

NOTE: N.A. = Not applicable (given column does not apply to an industry with that characteristic).

5. Impact of the VAT on different types of industries   131

EXHIBIT 5–8 (*Continued*)
Impact of increasing business property taxes (selected factors tending to make an increase in business property taxes affect industries with one characteristic more than industries with the opposite characteristic)

Characteristic of industries	Industries hurt directly by a proportionately higher tax burden or indirectly by a relative decrease in profits, a comparatively larger reduction in sales, or a relatively larger increase in costs (−)	Neutral impact (0)	Industries aided directly by a proportionately lower tax burden or indirectly by a relative increase in profits, a comparatively smaller reduction in sales, or a relatively smaller increase in costs (+)
9. High import cost component	N.A.	In general, property taxes do not have a great effect on import-competitive goods. Thus, in most cases, companies could not buy imports for less than domestic goods.	If property taxes increase the price of certain domestic goods, imports would be relatively cheaper to buy than such goods.
10. High elasticity in the demand for the industry's product (Industries with low elasticity in the demand for their product would be affected in the opposite way.)	If property taxes are shifted ultimately to customers and therefore raise prices, the demand for certain goods produced by companies hard hit by these taxes would be reduced. If retail businesses are hard hit by a rise in property taxes and if retailers then raise their prices, this would reduce the demand for certain retail goods. This could affect manufacturers who themselves are not seriously affected by property taxes. Higher property taxes would reduce the attractiveness of investments in land and buildings. This would reduce the sales of companies dealing in these commodities.	For many businesses property taxes are not a significant element in their costs. Thus, a rise in property taxes is not likely to cause much of an increase in prices and may not seriously affect sales of many businesses.	The way new revenues are spent might increase the sales of certain goods.
11. High product substitutability (high cross-elasticity)	If property taxes are shifted ultimately to customers and therefore raise prices, customers may switch to products less affected by property taxes.	For many businesses, property taxes are not a significant element in their costs; thus a rise in property taxes might not cause much of an increase prices or significant switches in products purchased.	N.A.
12. Intense price competition	When property taxes are higher in one area than in another, more highly taxed companies are put at a competitive disadvantage.	For many businesses, property taxes are not a significant element in their costs and therefore do not affect their competitiveness.	N.A.
13. Diversified markets	N.A.	Since business property taxes may not have a significant impact on the sales of many businesses, a diversified market would be of no greater advantage to such businesses than it now is.	Companies dealing primarily in real estate or real estate related industries will suffer reduced sales with higher property taxes. If such companies were diversified, they could compensate by increasing other sales.

NOTE: N.A. = Not applicable (given column does not apply to an industry with that characteristic).

EXHIBIT 5–8 *(Concluded)*

Characteristic of industries	*Industries hurt directly by a proportionately higher tax burden or indirectly by a relative decrease in profits, a comparatively larger reduction in sales, or a relatively larger increase in costs (−)*	*Neutral impact (0)*	*Industries aided directly by a proportionately lower tax burden or indirectly by a relative increase in profits, a comparatively smaller reduction in sales, or a relatively smaller increase in costs (+)*
14. Producers of capital goods	Higher property taxes might in some cases discourage capital investment.	In some cases higher property taxes would probably not affect capital investment, depending on the provisions of the local tax.	N.A.
15. Industries doing much exporting	N.A.	Property taxes generally do not greatly affect the cost of producing export goods. Therefore, higher property taxes are not likely to increase the prices or reduce the sales of U.S. exports.	N.A.
16. Industries competing with imports	N.A.	For many businesses competing with imports, property taxes do not greatly affect their costs. Therefore, higher property taxes generally should not reduce their ability to compete with imports.	N.A.

EXHIBIT 5-9
Impact of increasing residential property taxes (selected factors tending to make higher residential property taxes affect industries with one characteristic more than industries with the opposite characteristic)

Characteristic of industries	Industries hurt directly by a proportionately higher tax burden or indirectly by a relative decrease in profits, a comparative decrease in sales, or a relatively greater rise in costs (−)	Neutral impact (0)	Industries aided directly by a proportionately lower tax burden or indirectly by a relative increase in profits, a comparative increase in sales, or a relatively smaller increase in costs (+)
1. Highly incorporated industries (versus largely unincorporated industries)	N.A.	Residential property taxes are not imposed on companies (unless they own apartment buildings).	N.A.
2. High debt/equity ratio	N.A.	Residential property taxes are not imposed on companies (unless they own apartment buildings).	N.A.
3. High return on equity (or sales)	N.A.	Since higher residential property taxes would not directly affect many businesses, this tax change would initially be neutral toward most businesses whether profitable or unprofitable.	If higher residential property taxes, by reducing disposable income, lead to reduced consumer demand and then eventually higher wages, profitable companies could cope better with a decline in sales and a rise in costs.
4. High capital-intensiveness (Labor-intensive industries would be affected in the opposite way.)	N.A.	Residential property taxes are not imposed on companies (unless they own apartment buildings).	Since property taxes are included in the cost-of-living index, increasing these taxes would presumably lead to demands for higher wages. This would hurt labor-intensive companies more than capital-intensive companies. Any differences in the rate at which property taxes increase in various districts may drive the labor force from one area to another. This would particularly affect labor-intensive companies.
5. Sizeable assets in land	Higher property taxes should make consumers less eager to buy land on which to build a house and should depress land values.	Residential property taxes are not imposed on companies (unless they own apartment buildings).	Higher *local* property taxes may drive homeowners farther and farther away from the city. Land values in rural areas might therefore rise. If there is increasing emphasis on state rather than local property taxes and if this leads to smaller differences in tax rates between various districts, this might increase land values in areas now subject to inordinately high property taxes (while depressing land values in other areas).

NOTE: N.A. = Not applicable (given column does not apply to an industry with that characteristic).

EXHIBIT 5–9 *(Continued)*

Characteristic of industries	Industries hurt directly by a proportionately higher tax burden or indirectly by a relative decrease in profits, a comparative decrease in sales, or a relatively greater rise in costs (−)	Neutral impact (0)	Industries aided directly by a proportionately lower tax burden or indirectly by a relative increase in profits, a comparative increase in sales, or a relatively smaller increase in costs (+)
6. Sizeable assets in buildings	Since higher property taxes are likely to trigger demands for wage increases, this should lead the labor-intensive construction industry to charge more for constructing, repairing or altering buildings. Any differences in the rate at which property taxes increase in various districts may foster differences in the growth rate of various communities. This, in turn, would affect building values in the different communities.	Residential property taxes are not imposed on companies (unless they own apartment buildings).	N.A.
7. Industry-wide collective bargaining or strong unions	The wage demands stimulated by higher property taxes would particularly affect industries with strong labor unions.	N.A.	N.A.
8. Diversified sources of purchases	N.A.	Residential property taxes do not directly affect most prices (other than housing). Therefore, increasing these taxes should not in the short run change the cost of a company's purchases whether made from few or many sources.	If higher property taxes lead to higher wages, and if this leads ultimately to price increases of varying magnitude, companies making purchases from a variety of sources might be able to take advantage of price differentials.
9. High import cost component	N.A.	Since higher residential property taxes would not directly affect most prices, the comparative costs of imports and domestic goods should not change in the short term.	If higher property taxes lead to higher wages and ultimately to higher prices, imports may become comparatively cheaper to buy than domestic goods.
10. High elasticity in the demand for the industry's product (Industries with low elasticity in the demand for their product would be affected in the opposite way.)	Since higher residential property taxes reduce disposable income, consumer demand should be reduced. Sales of some goods will fall more than others. Housing sales would suffer particularly if residential property taxes were increased. If higher residential property taxes lead ultimately to higher wages and then to higher prices, this would hurt the sale of some goods more than others.	N.A.	The way the revenues from the higher taxes are spent might increase the sales of certain goods.

5. Impact of the VAT on different types of industries   135

EXHIBIT 5–9 (Concluded)
Impact of increasing residential property taxes (selected factors tending to make higher residential property taxes affect industries with one characteristic more than industries with the opposite characteristic)

Characteristic of industries	Industries hurt directly by a proportionately higher tax burden or indirectly by a relative decrease in profits, a comparative decrease in sales, or a relatively greater rise in costs (−)	Neutral impact (0)	Industries aided directly by a proportionately lower tax burden or indirectly by a relative increase in profits, a comparative increase in sales, or a relatively smaller increase in costs (+)
11. High product substitutability (high cross-elasticity)	Since higher residential property taxes reduce disposable income, consumers might switch to cheaper substitute products. If residential property taxes increase at different rates in different areas, wages may increase at different rates. In some cases, this may eventually lead to differential price increases in competing products.	Since higher residential property taxes would not directly affect most prices, the comparative cost of competing products generally would not change in the short term.	N.A.
12. Intense price competition	Higher residential property taxes reduce disposable income and thus diminish consumer demand. This could particularly hurt the sales of companies in industries with intense price competition. If residential property taxes increase at different rates in different areas, wages may increase at different rates. This may make it more difficult for a company to compete with others in other areas.	Since higher residential property taxes would not directly affect many businesses, they should often not immediately affect the competitiveness of one company versus another in the same industry.	N.A.
13. Diversified markets	N.A.	N.A.	If higher residential property taxes cut the demand for certain products or reduced sales in areas hard hit by the higher taxes, a company with diversified markets might be able to compensate by increasing its sales in other areas.
14. Producers of capital goods	If the reduction in consumer demand caused by these tax increases is not fully compensated by higher government spending, companies might ultimately be discouraged from investing in capital goods.	Since higher residential property taxes would not directly affect many businesses, they would have no immediate effect on capital investment.	If higher residential property taxes lead ultimately to higher wages, companies may be stimulated to buy labor-saving equipment.
15. Industries doing much exporting	If higher residential property taxes lead ultimately to higher wages, export prices may eventually rise and sales might fall.	Since higher residential property taxes would not directly affect most exporters, export prices should not change in the short term.	N.A.
16. Industries competing with imports	If higher residential property taxes lead ultimately to higher wages, the price of domestic goods may rise faster than the cost of imports.	Since higher residential property taxes would not directly affect many businesses, the competitive position of domestic goods versus imports should not change in the short run.	N.A.

EXHIBIT 5–10

Differential impact of various possible changes in the U.S. tax structure (summary of exhibits 5–1 through 5–9)

Characteristic of industries	VAT	Higher corporate income tax rates	Elimination of investment credit and reduction in depreciation allowances	Increased taxes on capital gains of individuals	Surtax on individual income taxes	Reduction in deductions allowed on individual income taxes	Increased payroll taxes	Increase in business property taxes	Increase in residential property taxes
1. Largely incorporated	0	−	−	−/+	+	0	0	0	0
1a. Largely unincorporated	0	+	+	−	−	0	0	0	0
2. High debt/equity ratio	0	+	+	+	0(+)*	0	0	0	0
2a. Low debt/equity ratio	0	−	−	−	0(−)*	0	0	0	0
3. High return on equity (or on sales)	0/+	−	−	−(equity) 0 (sales)	0/+(−)*	0/+(0)*	0/+	0/+	0/+
4. High capital-intensiveness	0/+	−	−	0	0/+(−)*	0/+	+	−	0/+
4a. High labor-intensiveness	0/−	+	+	0	0/−(+)*	0/−	−	+	0/−
5. Sizeable assets in land	0/+	0	+	−	0	0/−	0	−	−/0/+
6. Sizeable assets in buildings	−/0/+	0	−	−	0/−	0/−	0/−	−	−/0
7. Industry-wide collective bargaining or strong labor unions	−	0	0	0	−	−	−	0	−
8. Diversified sources of purchases	+	+/0†	+/0†	0	0/+	0	+	+/0†	0/+
9. High import cost component	0/+	+/0†	+/0†	0	0/+	0	+	0/+	0/+
10. High elasticity in demand for industry's product	−	0/−	0/−	0/−	−	−	−	0/−	−
10a. Low elasticity in demand for industry's products	+	0/+	0/+	0/+	+	+	+	0/+	+
11. High product substitutability (high cross-elasticity)	−/0	−/0†	−/0†	0/−	0/−	0/−	−	0/−	−/0
12. Intense price competition	−/0	−/+	−/+	0/−	0/−	0/−	−	−/0	−/0
13. Diversified markets	+	0/+	0/+	0	+	+	+	0/+	+
14. Producers of capital goods	+/−	−	−	−	0/−	0/−	+/−	−/0	−/0/+
15. Industries doing much exporting	0/−/+	−/0†	−/0†	0/−	+/0/−	0/+/−	−	0	0/−
16. Industries competing with imports	0/−	−/0†	−/0†	0/−	0/−	0/−	−	0	0/−

+ = Industries aided directly by a proportionately lower tax burden or indirectly by a relative increase in profits. a comparatively smaller reduction in sales. or a relatively smaller increase in costs vis-à-vis industries with the opposite characteristic.

0 = Impact would be neutral between industries with opposite characteristics.

− = Industries hurt directly by a proportionately higher tax burden or indirectly by a relative decrease in profits. a comparatively larger reduction in sales. or a relatively larger increase in costs vis-à-vis industries with the opposite characteristic.

Where there are two or more signs in a box. see previous exhibits for an explanation.

* Sign in parenthesis indicates impact on unincorporated firms with the indicated characteristic.

† The effect of the tax change would be neutral only if the tax were not shifted at all to customers.

NOTE: To produce equal revenues only a low rate VAT would have to be imposed, while substantial increases in the rates of either the corporate income tax (CIT) or the individual income tax (IIT) would be required. For example. the CIT would have to be raised from 48 percent to roughly 63 percent to generate the additional revenues produced by a 3 percent VAT (minus revenues lost by compensating changes in the IIT). The higher rates would mean that the impact of the CIT might in many cases be greater than the impact of the VAT. Although a 12 percent surcharge on the individual income tax would be needed to raise the additional revenues produced by a 3 percent VAT, the higher IIT rate might not have quite the dampening effect on consumer demand as the low VAT because the IIT is a more progressive tax.

5. Impact of the VAT on different types of industries   137

6

Impact of a Value Added Tax on a company's cash flow, working capital, and operating profit

A COMPANY'S SALES and profits will be affected primarily by the general impact of a Value Added Tax on the economy and by the specific impact on its own industry. The company must also consider whether the effect of the tax on other firms in its industry is likely to be the same as the effect on the company itself. Once the larger impact of the tax is analyzed, a company must study the details of the VAT regulations to determine the effect of the tax on the company's actual operations, particularly on its cash flow and operating profit.

IMPACT OF A VAT ON CASH FLOW

The effect of a VAT on cash flow—that is, the inflow or outflow of cash resulting from a VAT—can vary considerably depending on both the detailed provisions of the VAT law and the characteristics of a particular company. Cash flow will also be affected by the VAT rate, but, to eliminate this variable, this chapter expresses cash flow as a fraction of one month's VAT collections on a company's sales. The impact of the VAT on the economy, on the industry, and on the company's sales would also affect cash flow, but, to simplify this analysis, we have assumed that a VAT has no effect on a company's overall sales characteristics, including the number of transactions, the price of goods without tax, and the mix of goods sold. This is, of course, an unrealistic assumption, but it will enable the reader to understand the general direction of the VAT's impact on cash flow and to see the effect on cash flow of variations in either the VAT regulations or in company characteristics.

The terms "VAT cash flow" and "effect of VAT on cash flow" are used interchangeably throughout the chapter. Strictly speaking, "VAT cash flow" should only be used if there is a full shifting of the tax. If this is not the case, the correct terminology would be "effect of VAT on cash flow."

Benchmark examples

To illustrate the impact of a VAT on cash flow two examples have been chosen: a food store with all-cash sales and a 20 percent gross margin; and a department store with 50 percent credit sales, four months' accounts receivable terms, and a 40 percent gross margin.[1] For both of these examples, the company is assumed to have level sales and suppliers' terms of one month. The VAT is assessed on both sales

EXHIBIT 6–1
VAT cash flow for food store with a 5 percent VAT

	Month					
	1	*2*	*3*	*4*	*5*	*6*
1. Sales (VAT excluded) $100.00	$100.00	$100.00	$100.00	$100.00	$100.00
2. Less purchases (VAT excluded)......... 80.00	80.00	80.00	80.00	80.00	80.00
3. Gross margin.................................$ 20.00	$ 20.00	$ 20.00	$ 20.00	$ 20.00	$ 20.00
Cash receipts						
4. Cash sales (VAT included)................ 105.00	105.00	105.00	105.00	105.00	105.00
5. Credit sales (VAT included).............. 0	0	0	0	0	0
6. Total cash receipts (VAT included)......$105.00	$105.00	$105.00	$105.00	$105.00	$105.00
Cash disbursements						
7. Purchases (VAT included) 80.00*	84.00	84.00	84.00	84.00	84.00
8. Net VAT payment to government (line 20)...................................... 0	1.00	1.00	1.00	1.00	1.00
9. Total cash disbursements (VAT included)....................................$ 80.00	85.00	85.00	85.00	85.00	85.00
Cash inflow or outflow						
10. Total cash flow (line 6 − line 9)......... 25.00	20.00	20.00	20.00	20.00	20.00
11. Less pre-VAT gross margin (line 3)...... 20.00	20.00	20.00	20.00	20.00	20.00
12. Cash flow due to VAT ....$ 5.00	0	0	0	0	0
13. Cumulative cash flow due to VAT......$ 5.00	5.00	5.00	5.00	5.00	5.00
14. Cumulative cash flow expressed in months of VAT collections on sales (line 13 ÷ line 15)........................... 1.0	1.0	1.0	1.0	1.0	1.0
VAT remittance						
Balance sheet for accounting period						
15. Liability: VAT assessed on sales........ 5.00	5.00	5.00	5.00	5.00	5.00
16. Asset: VAT credit on purchases .... 4.00†	4.00	4.00	4.00	4.00	4.00
17. Asset: VAT payment due later to government 1.00	1.00	1.00	1.00	1.00	1.00
Calculation of VAT payments‡						
18. VAT payable on sales...................... 0	5.00	5.00	5.00	5.00	5.00
19. Less VAT credit on purchases........... 0	4.00	4.00	4.00	4.00	4.00
20. Net VAT payment to government ......$ 0	1.00	1.00	1.00	1.00	1.00

NOTES: All-cash retailer with 20% gross margin, one-month supplier's terms; one-month accounting period, one-month payment period, invoice collection method.
( ) indicates cash outflow.
* No VAT is levied on these purchases since the $80 represents payment for purchases made the preceding month before the VAT was introduced.
† The store earns a credit for the VAT paid on purchases made in month 1 even though the purchases are not paid for until month 2.
‡ VAT payments are based on VAT credits and liabilities acquired in the preceding month.

---

[1] The retailing industry was selected for our examples because it has a broad range of cash versus credit policies and a variety of gross margin structures. Also compliance costs are likely to be particularly significant for retailers.

and purchases at the time of invoicing (rather than at the time of cash payment); there is a one-month VAT accounting period (the segment of time for which VAT liabilities and credits are calculated); and there is also a one-month tax payment period (the time span between the end of the accounting period and the date the VAT payment to the government is due).

Exhibit 6–1 illustrates the VAT cash flow for our hypothetical food store under a 5 percent VAT; and Exhibit 6–2 does the same for the hypothetical department

EXHIBIT 6–2

VAT cash flow for department store with 5 percent VAT

	Month					
	1	*2*	*3*	*4*	*5*	*6*
1. Sales (VAT excluded)................$100.00	$100.00	$100.00	$100.00	$100.00	$100.00
2. Less purchases (VAT excluded).... 60.00	60.00	60.00	60.00	60.00	60.00
3. Gross margin...........................$ 40.00	40.00	40.00	40.00	40.00	40.00
Cash receipts						
4. Cash sales (VAT included)........... 52.50	52.50	52.50	52.50	52.50	52.50
5. Credit sales (VAT included)......... 50.00*	50.00*	50.00*	50.00*	52.50	52.50
6. Total cash receipts (VAT included)................$102.50	102.50	102.50	102.50	105.00	105.00
Cash disbursements						
7. Purchases (VAT included) .... 60.00†	63.00	63.00	63.00	63.00	63.00
8. Net VAT payment to government (line 20)............ 0	2.00	2.00	2.00	2.00	2.00
9. Total cash disbursements (VAT included)................$ 60.00	65.00	65.00	65.00	65.00	65.00
Cash inflow or outflow						
10. Total monthly cash flow (line 6 − line 9)................ 42.50	37.50	37.50	37.50	40.00	40.00
11. Less pre-VAT gross margin (line 3)..................... 40.00	40.00	40.00	40.00	40.00	40.00
12. Monthly cash flow due to VAT.....$ 2.50	(2.50)	(2.50)	(2.50)	0	0
13. Cumulative cash flow due to VAT ....$ 2.50	0	(2.50)	(5.00)	(5.00)	(5.00)
14. Cumulative cash flow expressed in months of VAT collections on sales (line 13 ÷ line 15)............... 0.5	0	(0.5)	(1.0)	(1.0)	(1.0)
VAT remittance						
Balance sheet for accounting period						
15. Liability: VAT assessed on sales... 5.00‡	5.00	5.00	5.00	5.00	5.00
16. Asset: VAT credit on purchases ... 3.00‡	3.00	3.00	3.00	3.00	3.00
17. Asset: VAT payment due later to government 2.00	2.00	2.00	2.00	2.00	2.00
Calculation of VAT payments						
18. VAT payable on sales................. 0	5.00	5.00	5.00	5.00	5.00
19. Less VAT credit on purchases...... 0	3.00	3.00	3.00	3.00	3.00
20. Net VAT payment to government ....$ 0	2.00	2.00	2.00	2.00	2.00

NOTES: Credit retailer with 40 percent gross margin, 50 percent credit sales, four months' accounts-receivable terms, one-month suppliers' terms; one-month VAT accounting period, one-month payment period, invoice collection method.

( ) indicates cash outflow.

* No VAT is collected on this $50 as it represents payment for sales made before the VAT was introduced.

† No VAT is levied on these purchases since $60 represents payment for purchases made the preceding month before the VAT was introduced.

‡ The store earns a credit for the VAT paid on purchases made in month 1 even though these purchases are not paid for until month 2. The store earns a liability for all $100 of its sales, even though payment for half of these sales will not occur for months.

 VAT payments are based on the VAT credits and liabilities acquired in the preceding month.

store with 50 percent credit sales. As can be seen in line 14 of each exhibit, the VAT's initial impact on cash flow is an *in*flow of 1.0 months of VAT collections on sales for the food store and an *out*flow of 1.0 months of VAT collections on sales for the department store with 50 percent credit sales. The impact is completed in month 1 for the food store but not until month 4 for the department store. Once the initial impact has been achieved, the VAT ceases to change the company's cash flow position, but the VAT's earlier effect on cash flow is never undone.

The food store enjoys a cash inflow due to the VAT because the store receives $5.00 in VAT from its customers in month 1 but does not have to pay any VAT until month 2, when the company pays $4.00 in VAT to its suppliers (for purchases made in month 1) and $1.00 in VAT to the government (the balance due on sales made in month 1). The department store, on the other hand, has a cash outflow due to VAT because it has to pay the VAT on its sales before it receives payment from half of its customers.

In both examples, purchases do not affect the company's cash flow. With suppliers' terms of one month, the VAT credit is earned one month before the company actually pays the VAT on purchases. However, the credit can not be applied until the next accounting period; thus it is used to offset the VAT liability incurred in the second month. Since the payment to the supplier is also due in the second month, the use of the VAT credit on the purchase and the VAT payment on the purchase occur at the same time. The net effect of the VAT purchase credit on cash flow is zero in these particular examples.

In summary, the VAT effect on cash flow depends on two things: (1) whether a company must pay the VAT due on its sales before or after it receives full payment from its customers; and (2) whether a company uses the VAT credit on its purchases before, after, or at the same time as it pays for these purchases.

Variations in company characteristics which affect cash flow

A company's cash flow will be changed if there are any variations in the company characteristics used in the benchmark examples given above.

1. *The higher the percentage of credit sales a company has, the greater will be its cash outflow due to VAT.* In the case of the department store example cited above, if the percentage of its credit sales were increased from 50 percent to 75 percent of all sales (with four months' terms), the company's cash outflow would increase by 1.0 months of VAT collections. (See Exhibit 6–3.)
2. *The longer the terms of a company's accounts receivable, the greater will be its cash outflow due to VAT.* For the department store with 50 percent credit sales, every two months' increase in accounts receivable terms increases cash outflow by one month's VAT collections on sales—the same effect as increasing the percentage of the company's credit sales from 50 percent to 75 percent. The general effect on cash flow can be seen by calculating the company's average receivables turnover; that is, multiplying the company's accounts receiv-

EXHIBIT 6-3

Effect of percentage of credit sales and accounts receivable terms on VAT cash flow

		VAT cash flow				
		Accounts receivable terms				
Percent of credit sales	Cash	2 months	4 months	6 months	8 months	12 months
None	1.0	N/A	N/A	N/A	N/A	N/A
25	N/A	0.5	0	(0.5)	(1.0)	(2.0)
50	N/A	0	(1.0)	(2.0)	(3.0)	(5.0)
75	N/A	(0.5)	(2.0)	(3.5)	(5.0)	(8.0)
100	N/A	(1.0)	(3.0)	(5.0)	(7.0)	(11.0)

NOTES: VAT cash flow figures are expressed in terms of one month's VAT collections on sales.

Department store with 40 percent gross margin; one-month suppliers' terms; invoice collection method, one-month VAT accounting period, one-month VAT payment period.

N/A = not applicable.

( ) indicates VAT cash outflow.

☐ indicates benchmark example.

able terms by its percentage of credit sales. Increasing either the accounts receivable terms or the percentage of credit sales increases the cash outflow due to VAT, since either factor will increase the company's average receivable turnover. If both the accounts receivable terms and the percentage of credit sales are increased, the effect on the average receivable turnover and therefore on VAT cash outflow is multiplied. For example, increasing the department store's accounts receivable terms from 4 to 6 months *and* increasing the percentage of credit sales from 50 to 75 percent would raise the store's VAT outflow from 1 to 3.5 months VAT collections on sales. On the other hand, reducing both the accounts receivable terms *and* the percentage of credit sales reduces the impact on a company's VAT cash flow of the reduction in either factor alone. For example, if the department store's accounts receivable terms are reduced from 4 to 2 months and if the percentage of credit sales is reduced from 50 to 25 percent, the store's VAT cash flow is changed from an *out*flow of 1.0 months to an *in*flow of 0.5 months of VAT collections on sales. This is illustrated in Exhibit 6-3.

3. *The longer the terms of a company's suppliers, the greater the cash inflow the company will have from the VAT paid on its purchases.* For both the food store and the department store cited above, the lengthening of suppliers' terms by one month provides an increase in the VAT cash flow equal to the VAT on one month's purchases (0.8 for the food store whose purchases equal 80 percent of its sales and 0.6 for the department store whose purchases equal 60 percent of its sales). This is illustrated in Exhibit 6-4.

4. *In some circumstances, VAT cash flow is affected by the company's gross margin (or value added).* For example, if a company's cash flow position is enhanced by the VAT levied on its purchases, as when suppliers' terms are lengthened, the effect will be greater for the company whose purchases are a larger percentage of its sales.

6. Impact of VAT on company's cash flow, working capital, operating profit   143

EXHIBIT 6–4
Effect of companies' terms on VAT cash flow

		VAT cash flow				
		Department store with 50% credit sales				
	Food store	Accounts receivable terms				
Suppliers' terms	Cash	Cash	2 months	4 months	6 months	12 months
Cash	0.2	0.4	(0.6)	(1.6)	(2.6)	(5.6)
1 month	1.0	1.0	0	(1.0)	(2.0)	(5.0)
2 months	1.8	1.6	0.6	(0.4)	(1.4)	(4.4)

NOTES: Cash flow figures are expressed as a fraction of one month's VAT collections on the company's sales.
One-month VAT accounting period; one-month VAT payment period; invoice collection method.
( ) indicates cash outflow.
☐ indicates benchmark examples.

5. *Growing sales affect a company's VAT cash flow.* For a company with cash customers, growing sales mean increased VAT collections each month. Since such a company has the advantage of immediate VAT collections and delayed tax payments, its growing VAT collections increase its cash inflow due to VAT. On the other hand, the company with credit customers must pay its VAT before it collects the tax from its customers. For such a company, growing sales will

EXHIBIT 6–5
VAT cash flow under level versus seasonal sales patterns

	Level sales			Seasonal sales		
Month	Sales (including VAT)	Purchases (including VAT)	Cumulative cash flow due to VAT	Sales (including VAT)	Purchases (including VAT)	Cumulative cash flow due to VAT
July	$ 105.00	$ 63.00	$2.50	$ 105.00	$ 63.00	$2.50
August	105.00	63.00	0	105.00	63.00	0
September	105.00	63.00	(2.50)	105.00	63.00	(2.50)
October	105.00	63.00	(5.00)	105.00	126.00	(5.00)
November	105.00	63.00	(5.00)	105.00	31.50	(6.00)
December	105.00	63.00	(5.00)	210.00	31.50	(2.50)
January	105.00	63.00	(5.00)	52.50	63.00	(8.75)
February	105.00	63.00	(5.00)	52.50	63.00	(8.00)
March	105.00	63.00	(5.00)	105.00	63.00	(6.00)
April	105.00	63.00	(5.00)	105.00	63.00	(2.50)
May	105.00	63.00	(5.00)	105.00	63.00	(3.75)
June	105.00	63.00	(5.00)	105.00	63.00	(5.00)
Total for year	$1,260.00	$756.00	($5.00)	$1,260.00	$756.00	($5.00)
July				$ 105.00	$ 63.00	($5.00)
August				105.00	63.00	(5.00)
September				105.00	63.00	(5.00)
October				105.00	126.00	(5.00)
November				105.00	31.50	(6.00)

NOTES: Cumulative cash flow for level and seasonal sales cannot be calculated from data on sales and purchases presented in this exhibit, due to accruals of VAT credits and liabilities, which are not shown here. These accruals and the resultant cumulative cash flow were calculated by the same method used in Exhibit 6–2.
Both cases are department store retailers with $1,200.00 in annual sales, 50 percent credit sales, 40 percent gross margin; 5 percent VAT rate; one-month suppliers' terms; four months' accounts receivable terms; one-month accounting period; one-month tax payment period; invoice collection method.
( ) indicates outflow.

steadily increase accounts receivable and will thus accentuate the cash outflow due to VAT.

6. *A company with seasonal sales will have the same cumulative VAT cash flow as an equivalent company with level sales. However, with seasonal sales, the movement of the VAT-related cash account varies widely.* This is illustrated in Exhibit 6–5, which presents two examples of department stores, one with level sales and one with seasonal sales. The seasonality pattern is a simplified version of that of a typical department store, but the simplification does not affect the overall cash flow or the general conclusions of this section. The exhibit shows that both the department store with level sales and the one with seasonal sales have a net permanent cash outflow of $5.00 due to the introduction of a VAT of 5 percent. The movement of the VAT-related cash account within the year varies widely for the seasonal case, but this does reach a steady state after one year. Note that in November of the second year the department store with seasonal sales has a $6.00 balance in VAT cash outflow, just as it does in November of the first year. Thus, the flow for the remainder of the second year will be the same as for the first year, assuming the sales and purchase patterns are the same in both years.

Variations in VAT provisions which affect cash flow

A company's cash flow is affected not only by the characteristics of the company but also by the specific provisions of the VAT.

Effect of VAT collection methods on cash flow. There are two standard VAT collection methods: (1) the invoice method, which recognizes both the VAT credit on purchases and the VAT liability on sales at the time of invoicing;[2] and (2) the cash method, which recognizes both taxable events at the time of cash payment. In theory, two other variations are possible: (1) using the invoice method for purchases and the cash method for sales; and (2) the reverse of this, namely using the cash method for purchases and the invoice method for sales. In fact, these mixed methods have never been used in any of the European countries with a VAT, and it is unlikely they would be used in a U.S. VAT. The invoice method (used in our benchmark examples) is the standard one in Europe, but Sweden gives all companies the option of electing the cash method, and a few other countries give certain types of companies this option.

With the cash collection method, a company cannot claim the VAT credit on purchases until the purchase is actually paid for. Since it is normally impossible to utilize the VAT credit on purchases on the same day the VAT is paid on the purchase, purchases hurt any company's VAT cash flow position under the cash collection method. In contrast, under the invoice collection method purchases may have a

---

[2] Generally in Europe the effective date of an invoice is not the date it is written but the date the goods or services are delivered.

neutral impact on, or even enhance, a company's VAT cash flow if the company can use its VAT credit on purchases at the same time as, or even before, paying for the purchases.

The different collection methods, however, do not affect the VAT liability on sales for companies whose customers all pay cash. With such a company, its sales are invoiced at the time they are paid for. Therefore, levying the VAT on sales at the time of invoicing or at the time of payment makes no difference in its cash flow.

In contrast, the cash flow of a company with credit sales is affected by whether sales are recognized at the time of payment. If a company's customers pay their bills more slowly than the company pays its suppliers, the company has a better VAT cash flow position with the cash collection method than with the invoice collection method.

While purchases always hurt a company's VAT cash flow position with the cash collection method, sales under this method always help the company's VAT cash flow position, for the company collects the VAT on its sales before having to pay its VAT bill. Since a company's sales are normally larger than its purchases, the cash collection method produces a VAT cash inflow for most companies. The invoice collection method, on the other hand, generally causes a VAT cash outflow for companies with credit customers.

Exhibit 6–6 illustrates the effect of the various VAT collection methods on the VAT cash flow of the two stores used for our original benchmark examples. In these examples, the food store with all cash sales has a better cash flow position with the invoice method, because then it can use the VAT credit on its purchases during the same month it pays for the purchases rather than a month later. On the other hand, the department store with 50 percent credit sales is better off with the cash method because then its VAT liability on its sales does not occur until it receives payment from its credit customers.

EXHIBIT 6–6
Effect of tax collection methods on VAT cash flow

	VAT cash flow	
Tax collection method	Food store with all-cash sales	Department store with 50% credit sales
Invoice method (invoice method for both purchases and sales)	1.0	(1.0)
Cash method (cash method for both purchases and sales)	0.2	0.4
Cash method for purchases, invoice method for sales	0.2	(1.6)
Invoice method for purchases, cash method for sales	1.0	1.0

NOTES: Cash flow figures are expressed as a fraction of one month's VAT collections on sales.
One-month suppliers' terms for both stores; four month's accounts receivable terms for department store; one-month VAT accounting period; one-month VAT payment period.
( ) indicates cash outflow.
☐ indicates benchmark examples.

It should be noted that with the cash collection method a company's VAT cash flow position is not affected by its suppliers' terms, accounts receivable terms, or its percentage of credit sales. All that affects a company's VAT cash flow is its gross margin (or value added). In Exhibit 6–6 the food store and the department store have different VAT cash flows under the cash collection method only because the food store's gross margin is 20 percent and the department store's gross margin is 40 percent.

Effect of VAT remittance procedures on cash flow. There are two elements in the VAT remittance procedure: (1) the accounting period—that is, the segment of time for which VAT liabilities and credits are calculated; and (2) the tax payment period—that is, the time span between the end of the accounting period and the date the VAT payment to the government is due. In the benchmark examples cited above, it is assumed that both the accounting period and the tax payment period were one month. However, the accounting period might well be two or even three months, and the payment period might conceivably be as much as two months. For most companies, cash inflow increases as the accounting period and the tax payment period, or both, increase. However, exporters and other companies which collect a VAT refund rather than paying a VAT bill would have their cash flow adversely affected by a longer VAT accounting period. In the VAT countries which have an accounting period longer than one month, exporters are given the option of using a one-month accounting period. Exhibit 6–7 illustrates how longer accounting periods and longer tax periods help the cash flow positions of most companies.

The advantage a company derives from longer VAT remittance periods is affected by the company's gross margin or value added. The larger a company's gross margin, the more its VAT cash flow position is helped by longer VAT accounting and payment periods. As can be seen in Exhibit 6–8, a company with a 20 percent gross margin has its cash flow position improved by 0.4 months of VAT collections on sales if the accounting and payment periods are stretched from 1 month/1 month

EXHIBIT 6–7

Effect of VAT remittance procedures on cash flow

	VAT cash flow			
	Food store with all-cash sales and with 20% gross margin		Department store with 50% credit sales and with 40% gross margin	
	Payment period		Payment period	
Accounting period	1 month	2 months	1 month	2 months
1 month	1.0	1.2	(1.0)	(0.6)
3 months	1.2	1.4	(0.6)	(0.2)
6 months	1.5	1.7	0	0.4

NOTES: Cash flow figures are expressed as a fraction of one month's VAT collections on sales; one-month suppliers' terms, four months' accounts receivable terms for department store; invoice collection method.

( ) indicates cash outflow.

☐ indicates benchmark examples.

EXHIBIT 6–8
Effect of gross margin on VAT cash flow

		VAT cash flow			
		20% gross margin		40% gross margin	
Tax collection method	Remittance procedure (accounting and payment periods)	Cash terms	4 months' accounts receivable terms	Cash terms	4 months' accounts receivable terms
Invoice ....1 month/1 month		☐1.0	(1.0)	1.0	☐(1.0)
Invoice ....3 months/2 months		1.4	(0.6)	1.8	(0.2)
Cash..................1 month/1 month		0.2 (mo. 2)	0.2 (mo. 10)	0.4 (mo. 2)	0.4 (mo. 6)
Cash..................3 months/2 months		0.6 (mo. 2)	0.6 (mo. 9)	1.2 (mo. 6)	1.2 (mo. 9)

NOTES: Cash flow figures are expressed as a fraction of one month's VAT collections on sales.
If the initial impact is completed after month 6, it is noted in parentheses. With cash collection method, the month in which initial impact is completed is noted for all cases in order to show the effect on its timing of varying gross margins and terms.
50% credit sales where applicable; one month suppliers' terms.
( ) indicates cash outflow.
☐ indicates benchmark example.

to 3 months/2 months. The company with a 40 percent gross margin has its cash flow position improved by 0.8 months of VAT collections on sales with the longer remittance procedure. This applies with both the cash and the invoice collection methods, and it applies whether or not the company has any credit sales.

Effect of VAT type on cash flow. The consumption type VAT, which allows immediate credit for the VAT on capital expenditures, can enhance a company's cash flow because of the customary elapse of time between the invoicing of the purchase and payment for it. If more than one month elapses between the two, and if the invoice method is used, the company enjoys a VAT cash inflow until the capital purchase is paid for. After that the net cash effect is zero.

On the other hand, the gross product and the income types of VAT would have an adverse effect on a company's cash flow. With the gross product type, which allows no credit for the VAT on capital expenditures, there would be a net outflow of funds equal to the VAT payable on the capital items. With the income type, the cash effect would also be negative because the credit on the VAT paid on the purchase would be amortized according to the depreciation schedule of the capital item.

Credit for excess VAT. Sometimes a company is owed a VAT refund by the government. This occurs primarily with exporters who are entitled to a rebate of any VAT paid on purchases made to produce the export goods. But companies with seasonality in their sales or purchases and companies making sizeable capital purchases may also be entitled to a VAT refund. In Europe, exporters are usually allowed to use a one-month VAT accounting period and to apply for their VAT refund at the end of each month. However, many countries allow nonexporters to apply for a refund at the end of their VAT accounting period only if the VAT credit is sizeable and/or a regularly recurring one. When a VAT refund is not paid by the government, a company must carry the VAT credit on its books until the credit is used up by subsequent VAT liabilities or until the company becomes eligible for a refund check either because its VAT credit has grown to the prescribed size or because the end of the tax year has arrived. This, of course, hurts the company's cash flow position until all the VAT credit can be used. Even when a company may apply for its VAT refund at the end of the VAT accounting period, there may be a lapse of time between the time the VAT was paid on purchases and the time the check for the VAT refund is actually received by the company. Obviously, it is to the advantage of any business likely to be entitled to VAT refunds to have a short VAT accounting period, to have VAT refunds actually paid rather than just credited, and to have the government required to mail VAT refund checks with reasonable promptitude, not just at the end of the quarter or the year.

Summary of the company characteristics which affect VAT cash flow

The company characteristics which affect VAT cash flows are as follows:

1. *Suppliers' terms:* Longer suppliers' terms help and shorter suppliers' terms hurt a company's VAT cash flow under the invoice collection method but have no effect with the cash collection method.
2. *Accounts receivable terms:* Shorter accounts receivable terms help and longer accounts receivable terms hurt a company's VAT cash flow under the invoice collection method but have no effect with the cash collection method.
3. *Percentage of credit sales:* A lower percentage of credit sales helps and a higher percentage hurts a company's VAT cash flow under the invoice collection method but has no effect with the cash collection method.
4. *Growing sales:* Growing sales help the VAT cash flow position of a company with all cash sales under any collection method; growing sales hurt the cash flow position of a company with credit sales under the invoice collection method and help the cash flow position of such a company under the cash collection method.
5. *Seasonality in sales and/or purchases:* Seasonality in sales or purchases causes fluctuations in a company's VAT cash flow position but does not affect its *average,* long-term cash flow position.
6. *Capital expenditures:* With a consumption type VAT with the invoice collection method, capital expenditures help a company's VAT cash flow position temporarily if time elapses between utilization of the VAT credit from the capital purchase and the payment for that purchase. With other types of VAT, capital expenditures always hurt a company's VAT cash flow position.
7. *Gross margin or value added:* If purchases either hurt or help a company's VAT cash flow position, then cash flow will be affected by the company's gross margin or value added (that is, by the difference between its purchases and its sales). Purchases hurt the VAT cash flow position of all companies with the

cash collection method, and the adverse effect is greater for a company with a smaller gross margin (that is, whose purchases constitute a higher percentage of its sales). With the invoice collection method, purchases help a company's VAT cash flow position when suppliers' terms are long enough to enable a company to utilize the credit for the VAT on its purchases before actually paying for these purchases. In this instance, the beneficial effect on a company's VAT cash flow position is greater, the smaller the company's gross margin or value added. A company's gross margin or value added also affects the advantage a company derives from longer VAT accounting and payment periods: The larger a company's gross margin, the more its VAT cash flow position is helped by longer VAT remittance periods.

Summary of the VAT characteristics which affect cash flow

1. *Invoice versus cash collection method:* The cash collection method (with VAT credits and liabilities recognized at the time of cash payment) is advantageous to companies with credit sales (if their accounts receivable terms are longer than their supplier terms). The invoice collection method (with VAT credits and liabilities recognized at the time of invoicing)[3] is advantageous to companies with all-cash customers (and to companies whose suppliers' terms are longer than their accounts receivable terms).
2. *VAT remittance procedure:* A longer VAT accounting and/or payment period would help the cash flow position of any company under any collection method, but the advantage would be greatest for a company with a larger gross margin or value added.
3. *Type of VAT:* It is to the advantage of companies of all varieties to have a VAT of the consumption type, which gives business full and immediate credit for any VAT paid on capital purchases.
4. *Refund of excess VAT credits:* For any company which might be entitled to a VAT rebate, it would be advantageous to have a VAT with provision for prompt payment of excess VAT credits.

Overall impact of a VAT on cash flow

Since so many factors can affect a company's VAT cash flow, it is impossible to provide a precise formula to determine the effect of a VAT on a company's cash flow. Exhibits 6–1 and 6–2 illustrate the method a company can use to calculate its own VAT cash flow. Exhibit 6–9 shows the range of VAT cash flow effects likely for our two benchmark examples, the food store with all-cash sales and a 20 percent gross margin and the department store with some credit sales and a 40 percent gross

---

[3] In Europe the effective date of an invoice is normally not the day the invoice is written but the day the goods or services are delivered.

EXHIBIT 6–9
Summary of VAT cash flow effects

	Source of data (exhibit number)	VAT cash flow (expressed as fraction of 1 month's VAT collections on sales)	
		Food store (with all-cash sales and 20% gross margin)	Department store (with some credit sales and 40% gross margin)
Benchmark examples:	6–1, 2	⌈1.0⌉	⌈(1.0)⌉
Positive cash flow factors:			
Suppliers' terms: 2 months versus 1 month	6–4	+0.8	[+0.6]*
Accounts receivable terms: 2 months versus 4 months⎫	6–3	N/A	[+0.5]*
Percentage of credit sales: 25% versus 50% ⎭			
Collection method: cash versus invoice	6–6	N/A	+1.4*
Remittance procedure: 3 month versus 1 month	6–7	+0.4	+0.8
accounting period; 2-month versus 1 month payment period			
Positive factors subtotal		+1.2	+2.2
Negative cash flow factors:			
Suppliers terms: 0 months versus 1 month	6–4	[–0.8]*	–0.6
Accounts receivable terms: 12 months versus 4 months⎫	6–3	N/A	–10.0
Percentage of credit sales: 100% versus 50% ⎭			
Collection method: cash versus invoice	6–6	–0.8*	N/A
Negative factors subtotal		–0.8	–10.6
Range of effects on VAT cash flow:			
Benchmark plus positive effects		1.0 + 1.2 = 2.2	(1.0) + 2.2 = 1.2
Benchmark plus negative effects		1.0 + (0.8) = 0.2	(1.0) + (10.6) = (11.6)
Range of cash flow effects		0.2 to 2.2	(11.6) to 1.2

NOTES: N/A indicates not applicable; ( ) indicates VAT cash outflow; ☐ indicates benchwork examples.

* With the cash collection method, VAT cash flow is not affected by suppliers' terms, accounts receivable terms, or percentage of credit sales. Therefore, a company's VAT cash flow is affected *either* by the switch from the invoice to the cash collection method *or* by changes in other factors.

margin. In the case of the food store, the VAT could create a cash *in*flow of from 0.2 to 2.2 months of VAT collections on sales. With a 3 percent VAT, such a store would enjoy, because of VAT, a cash inflow of from 0.6 to 6.6 percent of its monthly sales receipts (3 percent times 0.2 to 2.2 months of VAT collections on sales); the cash inflow due to VAT would be 0.05 to 0.55 percent of its annual sales (the monthly figure divided by 12). In the case of the department store, the VAT effect could range from an *in*flow of 1.2 months of VAT collections on sales to an *out*flow of 11.6 months of VAT collections on its sales. With a 3 percent VAT, such a store would have a VAT cash inflow of up to 3.6 percent of its monthly sales or a VAT cash outflow of up to 34.8 percent of its monthly sales. As a percentage of annual sales, the VAT cash flow effect would range from a positive 0.3 percent to a negative 2.9 percent.

It should be remembered that, if sales and purchases remain level, a VAT normally changes a company's cash flow position only during the first months after the tax is introduced. After a period of varying length, depending on the characteristics of both the VAT and the company, the company's VAT cash flow may reach a steady state. The VAT may no longer change the company's cash flow, for VAT receipts and VAT payments eventually become equal if sales and purchases do not change. However, the VAT's initial impact on cash flow is never undone. The company's cash position is permanently enchanced or diminished by the extra dollars it took in or paid out during the first few months after the VAT was introduced.

VAT IMPACT ON WORKING CAPITAL

If the VAT hurts or enhances a company's cash position, then it will diminish or increase the company's working capital. The impact of the VAT on working capital will depend, of course, both on the percentage of annual sales receipts that are affected by the VAT cash flow and on the percentage of sales that working capital constitutes. With the range of VAT cash flow outcomes indicated in the preceding section, a 3 percent VAT would affect working capital as shown in Exhibit 6–10.

This exhibit, of course, does not present all possible variations in company characteristics or working capital, but it does give a general picture of the impact of the VAT on companies' working capital. This exhibit indicates that a VAT might increase a company's working capital by as much as 7 percent or diminish it by as much as 4.2 percent.

VAT IMPACT ON OPERATING PROFIT

The VAT can affect a company's operating profit even if the tax is fully passed forward to the company's customers, as it generally is. A company's operating profit can be affected by three things: interest savings or costs due to VAT cash flow; compliance costs; and the breakage and bad debt policies prescribed by the VAT regulations.

Interest savings or costs due to VAT cash flow

As was demonstrated earlier in this chapter, a VAT creates an inflow or outflow of cash depending on the elements of the tax policy and the characteristics of the company. Any VAT cash inflow enjoyed by a company should earn it interest or save it interest on money it would otherwise borrow. On the other hand, any VAT cash outflow suffered by a company should generally cost it interest. Exhibit 6–11 uses the VAT cash flow data from earlier exhibits and assumes an 8 percent annual interest rate to calculate the VAT-caused interest savings, or costs, for five types of companies. The assumed VAT rate is 3 percent of sales.

The analysis of the first three companies with credit sales assumes that companies which suffer a VAT cash outflow incur an interest cost. This assumption is not valid for the portion of accounts receivable on which interest is charged. Retailers who have deferred payment plans or revolving credit accounts typically charge interest at rates of 12 to 18 percent on the outstanding balance in such accounts. Thus the VAT which credit customers owe such a retailer earns the retailer more interest than it costs him. In such a case, an increase in accounts receivable due to VAT can create both a negative cash flow and a positive contribution to profit.

To demonstrate the effect of interest earned on accounts receivable, Exhibit 6–11 includes the case of a credit retail company (company #4), which has the same overall characteristics as company #3 except that it has a deferred payment plan,

EXHIBIT 6-10
The effect of a VAT on cash flow and working capital with different types of companies

	Company characteristics				VAT cash flow as fraction of monthly VAT collections				VAT cash flow as percentage of annual sales with 3% VAT†				Working capital as % of sales	VAT cash flow as percentage of working capital‡			
	Value added or gross margin	Credit sales	Average accounts receivable terms	Accounts receivable outstanding	Collection method				Collection method					Collection method			
					Invoice	Invoice	Cash	Cash	Invoice	Invoice	Cash	Cash		Invoice	Invoice	Cash	Cash
					Remittance procedure				Remittance procedure					Remittance procedure			
Type of company					1/1	3/2	1/1	3/2	1/1	3/2	1/1	3/2		1/1	3/2	1/1	3/2
	Percent of sales	Percent of sales	Months of sales	Months of sales	Months of VAT collections				Percent of sales				% of sales	Percent of working capital			
Company with all cash sales	20	0	0	0	1.0 / 6-1*	1.4 / 6-7*	0.2 / 6-6*	0.6 / 6-8*	0.25	0.35	0.05	0.15	5.0	5.0	7.0	1.0	3.0
Company #1 with credit customers	40	50	4	2	(1.0) / 6-2*	(0.2) / 6-7*	0.4 / 6-6*	1.2 / 6-8*	(0.25)	(0.05)	0.1	0.3	10.0	(2.5)	(0.5)	1.0	3.0
Company #2 with credit customers	40	50	6	3	(2.0) / 6-3*	(1.2)	0.4	1.2	(0.5)	(0.3)	0.1	0.3	20.0	(2.5)	(1.5)	0.5	1.5
Company #3 with credit customers	40	50	12	6	(5.0) / 6-3*	(4.2)	0.4	1.2	(1.25)	(1.05)	0.1	0.3	30.0	(4.2)	(3.5)	0.3	1.0

NOTES: Remittance procedures: 1/1 indicated one-month accounting period and one-month tax payment period; 3/2 indicates a three-month accounting period and a two-month payment period.

( ) indicates cash outflow or negative effect

In these examples, it is assumed all companies have one-month suppliers' terms.

*Exhibits from which data are taken.

†Multiply cash flow as fraction of monthly VAT collections by 3% to obtain VAT cash flow as percentage of monthly sales. Then divide by 12 to obtain VAT cash flow as percentage of annual sales.

‡Divide cash flow as percentage of annual sales by working capital as percentage of sales to obtain cash flow as percentage of working capital.

with its accounts receivable earning 18 percent interest. With 50 percent credit sales and with a 3 percent VAT, the VAT owed the retailer by his credit customers amounts to 1.5 percent of his sales. Since the credit customers pay the retailer 18 percent interest not only on sales not yet paid for but also on the VAT due on those sales, the interest such a retailer earns on the VAT owed him amounts to 0.27 percent of his sales. This more than compensates for the extra interest this credit retailer has to pay because of his VAT cash outflow. The VAT thus earns such a retailer extra interest rather than costing him extra interest.

EXHIBIT 6–11
Range of interest savings or costs due to VAT cash flow (3% VAT, 8% interest rate)

Type of company	Accounts receivable terms	Cash flow as % of sales (from Exhibit 6–10)				Interest savings or cost ( ) due to VAT cash flow			
		Collection method				Collection method			
		Invoice		Cash		Invoice		Cash	
		Remittance procedure				Remittance procedure			
		1/1	3/2	1/1	3/2	1/1	3/2	1/1	3/2
		.........Percent of sales.........							
Company with all cash sales	Cash sales	0.25	0.35	0.05	0.15	0.02	0.028	0.004	0.012
Company #1 with credit sales	Average 2 months' accounts receivable outstanding	(0.25)	(0.05)	0.1	0.3	(0.02)	(0.004)	0.008	0.024
Company #2 with credit sales	Average 3 months' accounts receivable outstanding	(0.5)	(0.3)	0.1	0.3	(0.04)	(0.024)	0.008	0.024
Company #3 with credit sales	Average 6 months' accounts receivable outstanding	(1.25)	(1.05)	0.1	0.3	(0.10)	(0.084)	0.008	0.024
Company #4 with credit sales (Same as #3 but a retailer with deferred-payment plan)	Average 6 months' accounts receivable outstanding; outstanding receivables earn 18% interest	(1.25)	(1.05)	0.1	0.3	0.17	0.186	0.278	0.294

NOTES: Company with all cash sales has 20 percent gross margin.
Companies with credit sales have 40 percent gross margin, 50 percent credit sales.
All companies have one-month supplier terms.
Remittance procedures: 1/1 = one-month accounting period and one-month tax payment period: 3/2 = three-month accounting period and two-month payment period.
( ) indicates cash outflow or interest costs.

The VAT also always earns extra interest for the company with all-cash sales. And it earns extra interest for any type of company under the cash collection method. But, with the invoice collection method, the VAT is responsible for an extra interest *cost* for companies with credit sales on which they do not earn interest.

Even for companies which earn extra interest because of the VAT, the amount of extra interest would usually not be large enough to compensate for the cost of complying with the VAT, as can be seen in the following sections.

Impact of VAT compliance costs on operating profit

There is universal agreement that the introduction of a new tax system such as the VAT increases a company's cost of tax compliance. With the great diversity that exists among companies, it is at this point impossible to make a precise determination of the level of increased compliance costs. However, some analysis can be made of the variations in company characteristics and in VAT characteristics which can affect compliance costs.

Variables affecting compliance costs. The seven variables which affect compliance costs are: (1) the type of company; (2) its size and sophistication; (3) the VAT rate; (4) the number of VAT rates and exemptions; (5) the type of VAT; (6) VAT remittance procedures; and (7) the regulations about indicating the VAT on invoices.

1. *Type of company.* The first variable affecting compliance costs is the nature of a company and its sales. The greater the variety of goods sold by a company, the greater its VAT compliance costs are likely to be if the VAT has a multiple rate or any significant exemptions. With any VAT, whether a simple one or a complex one, compliance costs are likely to be greater for companies which make many small sales rather than a smaller number of large sales, for a company's bookkeeping costs are affected by the *number* of its transactions, not the *size* of them; and companies which make many different types of transactions may not be able to streamline their compliance procedures so readily as companies making only one type of transaction.

2. *Size and sophistication of company.* The second variable affecting compliance costs is the size and sophistication of the company. In general, compliance costs are likely to be lower for large, sophisticated companies than for smaller ones. More sophisticated enterprises, with greater access to data-processing equipment and advanced accounting techniques, would incur proportionately lower administrative burdens in complying with a VAT than smaller companies which often do not rely on professional accounting services or computerized accounting processes. Larger companies are more likely to have on their staff specialists who can easily handle any problems arising because of the VAT. Larger companies also generate larger VAT collections, and this would reduce their compliance costs as a percent of collections. This was demonstrated in a study of sales tax compliance costs in Ohio. There, retailers (other than department stores) with annual sales of $100,000 to $199,000 had compliance costs of 9.94 percent of their sales tax collections, while the same type of retailers with sales over $400,000 had compliance costs of only 4.64 percent of collections.[3]

3. *VAT rate.* The rate of the VAT also affects compliance costs. A higher tax rate generates larger tax collections but does not increase collection costs; as a re-

---

[3] James C. Yocum, *Retailers' Cost of Sales Tax Collection In Ohio* (Columbus: Ohio State University, 1961), p. 109. Figures given exclude the compliance costs arising from the tax stamps used in Ohio.

sult, compliance costs expressed as a percentage of tax collections are lower. For example, compliance costs of 10 percent of collections with a 1 percent tax are equal to a cost of 5 percent of collections for a 2 percent tax.

4. *Number of VAT rates and exemptions.* The fourth variable affecting compliance costs is the number of VAT rates and the number of VAT exemptions. A multiple-rate VAT is much more costly to administer than a single-rate VAT, particularly for companies selling or buying goods subject to different rates. Exemptions can complicate compliance for companies if some of their sales are exempt and some are not. It has been estimated that multiple VAT rates increase collection costs to the government by 50 to 80 percent, and it is likely that multiple rates would increase the compliance costs of many companies by roughly the same amount.

A system of multiple rates and exemptions increases compliance costs in the following ways. First, it distorts the subtraction/tax credit method of computing the VAT payable. (See Chapter 1.) With this method a company multiplies all sales by the tax rate and subtracts from this amount the tax credits received on purchases. With multiple rates, a company must categorize its sales according to the different rates. If any of its sales are exempt, such sales must be distinguished from taxable sales. And if the sales are exempt but not zero-rated, the company cannot claim credit for the VAT paid on purchases made to produce the exempt goods, and such purchases would have to be distinguished from other purchases.

Multiple rates and exemptions complicate a company's invoicing procedures. The tax must be calculated for each individual item on an invoice rather than on the total sale. With a complex VAT, differences in interpretation of the rate system may have to be settled in court, an expensive and time-consuming process for both the companies involved and the government. Finally, preferential treatment or exemption of entire stages of production distorts the tax structure. For example, if a company collects taxes on its sales at a lower rate than the one it pays on its purchases, it could receive a net tax credit, and, in effect, collect tax refunds from the government. Thus neither party would benefit: The company would still bear the accounting costs associated with the VAT, and the government would lose revenues.

5. *Type of VAT.* If the VAT were not of the consumption type, a company would have to keep separate VAT records on its capital purchases and its other purchases, for the credit given for the VAT paid on the two types of purchases would be different.

6. *VAT remittance procedures.* A VAT with a longer accounting period would require the company to fill out fewer tax forms than would be necessary for a VAT with a shorter accounting period. Compliance costs would be lower if companies were allowed to make only an estimate of the VAT due at the end of each accounting period and a precise calculation were required only at the end of the year.

7. *Indication of VAT on Invoices.* Compliance costs would also be affected by the requirements regarding the indication of the VAT on invoices. Presumably on invoices prepared for business customers a company would be required to indicate the VAT separately; but, if there were a single rate VAT, the invoice could indicate the VAT on the total sale rather than the VAT on each individual item. It is uncertain whether companies selling to consumers would have to indicate the VAT separately on sales slips or whether the VAT would be included in the price of each item (as it generally is in Europe). To include the VAT in the price of every item would increase compliance costs for retailers, particularly if price tags had to indicate not just the VAT-inclusive price but also the price without VAT and the VAT. On the other hand, calculating the VAT at the point of sales would increase the work of sales clerks and might be difficult for them to handle if there were complex provisions about different VAT rates and VAT exemptions. If the VAT is not indicated separately either on the price tag or on the sales slip, retailers would have to prepare special invoices for their business customers who were entitled to a credit for the VAT paid on purchases. This, too, would increase compliance costs. Thus, unless the VAT were very complex, retailers would probably find it easier (and their compliance costs lower) if the VAT were applied at the point of sale (as sales taxes normally are); and retailers with any business customers might find compliance simplified if the VAT were listed separately on all sales slips.

Nature of compliance costs. The direct costs of tax compliance, excluding fixed overhead costs, are of two types: (1) accounting costs, which include maintaining records of purchases and sales and preparing tax returns and reports; and (2) sales costs, which include training sales personnel to handle the new tax, changing cash registers to include the new system, and accounting for the additional time required to calculate the VAT and include it in final sales.

The division of compliance costs between the two types would depend very much on the nature of the company. Sales costs are likely to be much greater for retailers than for other companies. However, if the VAT had to be included in retail price tags, this would reduce sales costs but greatly increase accounting (and pricing) costs.

Range of compliance costs. There is, as yet, no documentation on the compliance costs businesses have experienced with the VAT in Europe. A very rough idea of compliance costs can be gleaned from the data on retail sales tax compliance costs given in Exhibit 6–12. With a 3 percent sales tax, Ohio retailers had compliance costs ranging from 1.23 to 10.77 percent of their tax collections, and the average was 3.93 percent. The Ohio figures include many small retailers, who raise the average considerably. Since American business as a whole probably has a smaller percentage of small companies than the retailing industry, the average cost to a business of complying with a 3 percent VAT might be as low as 2 percent of its tax collections. On the other hand, a VAT requires a company to keep tax records of its purchases as well as its sales, and this factor might bring average business compliance costs up to 4 percent of their VAT collections, the same average experienced by Ohio retailers with a 3 percent sales tax.

If the average cost of complying with a 3 percent VAT were between 2 and 4 percent of the tax collections, compliance costs would be between 0.04 and 0.08 percent of sales.

EXHIBIT 6–12
Direct compliance costs to retailers of state retail
sales taxes

State	Tax rate (percent)	Compliance costs as percentage of tax collections
Ohio retailers* 3		1.23–10.77 (3.93 average)
National department store chain.................2–4		1.1–16

* The cost of tax stamps provisions has been factored out of this data.
SOURCE: James C. Yocum, *Retailers' Costs of Sales Tax Collection in Ohio* (Columbus: Ohio State University, 1961), pp. 85, 87, 90, 93, 95, 98, 100, 102, 105, and Tax Foundation, Inc., *Retail Sales and Individual Income Taxes in State Tax Structures* (New York: Tax Foundation, Inc., 1962), p. 37.

Overall VAT impact on operating profit

To determine the overall VAT impact on operating profit, two factors must be considered: compliance costs, which are estimated to average roughly 0.04 to 0.08 percent of sales; and the interest savings or cost due to VAT. Exhibit 6–13 weighs each of these factors to determine the total VAT impact on operating profit for various types of companies. Obviously the exhibit covers only a very few types of companies; but it does seem to indicate that, although the VAT will make a dent in the operating profits of most companies, the dent generally will be a small one: 0.2 to 3.8 percent of operating profits. And companies whose credit customers pay 18 percent interest on their outstanding bills may find that the VAT increases their operating profits by 1.1 to 3.2 percent.

Other factors affecting operating profit: Breakage and bad debt policy

Two other factors can affect the VAT's impact on a company's operating profit: the VAT provisions about breakage and about bad debts. The impact of these factors, however, can not be quantified, even in a very rough way.

Breakage. Breakage in a tax on sales is the difference between the tax actually collected and the tax due as a statutory percentage of sales. The main reason for this difference arises from the use of bracket schedules to avoid fractional tax collections. For example, all sales between $0.60 and $0.90 may have the same tax levied on them. The difference between tax collected and theoretical tax due arises primarily with companies, such as retailers, that make many small sales.

EXHIBIT 6-13

Calculation of range of VAT impact on profits (3% VAT, 8% interest rate)

Type of company	Assumed operating profit as % of sales	Interest savings or costs as % of sales — Invoice 1/1	3/2	Cash 1/1	3/2	Compliance costs of a VAT as % of sales	Net savings or costs due to VAT as % of sales — Invoice 1/1	3/2	Cash 1/1	3/2	Net savings or costs due to VAT as % operating profit — Invoice 1/1	3/2	Cash 1/1	3/2	Saving or costs as % operating profit (range)
Company with all cash sales	2	.02	.028	.004	.012	(.04)	(.02)	(.012)	(.036)	(.028)	(1.0)	(0.6)	(1.8)	(1.4)	(3.8) to (0.6)
						(.08)	(.06)	(.052)	(.076)	(.068)	(3.0)	(2.6)	(3.8)	(3.4)	
Company #1 with credit sales (2 months' average accounts receivable outstanding)	8	(.02)	(.004)	.008	.024	(.04)	(.06)	(.044)	(.032)	(.016)	(0.75)	(0.55)	(0.4)	(0.2)	(1.25) to (0.2)
						(.08)	(.10)	(.084)	(.072)	(.056)	(1.25)	(1.05)	(0.9)	(0.7)	
Company #2 with credit sales (3 months' average accounts receivable outstanding)	8	(.04)	(.024)	.008	.024	(.04)	(.08)	(.064)	(.032)	(.016)	(1.0)	(0.8)	(0.4)	(0.2)	(1.5) to (0.2)
						(.08)	(.12)	(.104)	(.072)	(.056)	(1.5)	(1.3)	(0.9)	(0.7)	
Company #3 with credit sales (6 months' average accounts receivable outstanding)	8	(.10)	(.084)	.008	.024	(.04)	(.14)	(.124)	(.032)	(.016)	(1.75)	(1.55)	(0.4)	(0.2)	(2.25) to (0.2)
						(.08)	(.18)	(.164)	(.072)	(.056)	(2.25)	(2.05)	(0.9)	(0.7)	
Company #4 with credit sales (same as #3 but with deferred payment plan: outstanding accounts receivable earn 18% annual interest)	8	.17	.186	.278	.294	(.04)	.13	.146	.238	.254	1.625	1.825	2.975	3.175	1.125 to 3.175
						(.08)	.09	.106	.198	.214	1.125	1.325	2.475	2.675	

From Exhibit 6–11 | Assumed values | Interest savings or costs plus compliance costs | Net savings or costs as percent of sales divided by operating profit

NOTES: Remittance procedures: 1/1 = one-month accounting period and one-month payment period; 3/2 = three-month accounting period and two-month payment period. ( ) indicates costs.

The effect on profits of the bracket schedules used with a VAT will be determined by the answers to these questions:

1. Will the VAT paid by a company be a statutory percentage of its sales or will it be the dollar amount actually collected?
2. Will the VAT collected on sales be dictated by a bracket schedule, and, if so, who will benefit from the breakage, if any?
3. How will the bracket schedule be constructed?

These questions can be settled only within the tax structure itself.

Bad debt policy. If the collection method used specifies that the VAT on sales is levied at the time of invoicing rather than at the time of payment, the method of handling bad debts has profit implications for a company. If there is no provision for the deduction of the VAT paid at the time of invoicing on what subsequently turns out to be a bad debt or a cancelled sale, the result is a negative impact on profits. A few European countries recognize this problem and allow a refund of the VAT applicable to bad debts or to sales of goods subsequently returned. If administratively feasible, a VAT in this country should include a similar provision.

SUMMARY

A VAT will affect the cash flow of all companies. With the cash collection method (which recognizes the VAT liability on sales and the VAT credit on purchases at the time of cash payment), the VAT will create a cash *in*flow for all companies except those exempt from the tax. With the invoice collection method (which recognizes VAT liabilities and credits at the time of invoicing), companies with all-cash sales will still enjoy a cash inflow due to the VAT, but companies with credit sales will usually incur a cash *out*flow due to VAT. The invoice method is the one customarily used in Europe.

Although a VAT affects the cash flow position of all companies, it normally does so only during the first months after the tax is introduced. After a period of varying length, depending on the characteristics of both the VAT and the company, VAT receipts and VAT payments should become equal if sales and purchases do not change. However, the VAT's initial impact on cash flow is never undone. The company's cash position is permanently enhanced or diminished by the extra dollars it took in or paid out during the first few months after the VAT was introduced.

The VAT's impact on a company's cash flow position will have two repercussions. First, the VAT will reduce or increase the company's working capital depending on whether the tax causes a cash outflow or inflow. Secondly, if the VAT causes a cash inflow, the company may earn interest on its additional cash. If the VAT causes a cash outflow, it will generally cost the company interest because of the reduction in its working capital. However, companies whose credit customers pay steep interest on their outstanding balances may find that the cash outflow due to VAT earns the company more interest than it costs the company. In such a case, the VAT may have a negative effect on the company's cash flow position and a positive effect on its profits.

The cost of complying with the VAT may consume on the average roughly 0.04 to 0.08 percent of a company's sales. For most companies, compliance costs will be greater than any extra interest earned from their cash inflow due to VAT. However, companies whose credit customers pay steep interest may actually find their operating profits enhanced by the VAT.

7

Determining a company's or an industry's attitude toward a VAT

THE REPRESENTATIVES of an industry and the management of any company will consider many factors in determining their attitudes regarding the possible adoption of a VAT in the United States. As individuals, they will give varying weights to the impact of a VAT on the nation, on their industry, on their company, and on themselves. The foregoing chapters have been designed to provide a background for consideration of a VAT from all of these standpoints.

As one weighs the various relevant considerations regarding a VAT, the dangers of a short-range point of view and narrow perspective must not be ignored. There is always an inclination to appraise proposed action or legislation on the basis of its direct and immediate impact and to determine support or opposition accordingly. Though it is trite to say that a short-range advantage may lead to a long-range disadvantage, the proposition deserves reiteration.

In matters of tax policy, as in other areas, we live in a changing environment. Resistance to change because it is unattractive may lead to alternative changes which will be even more unattractive and adverse. This fact should not be forgotten in the development of a position regarding a VAT.

Determining a thoughtful position on the VAT requires a number of steps, which are outlined in Exhibit 7-1.

Analyzing the impact of tax alternatives on the country

A company or an industry's attitude toward a VAT must be based, first of all, on an analysis of the differential impacts of the various tax alternatives on the on the country as a whole. As was indicated in Chapter 4, no tax is desirable of itself. The question is, rather, which tax alternative is the least bad: Which one will have the fewest adverse effects? When fitted into our existing tax structure,

EXHIBIT 7–1
Determining a position on the VAT

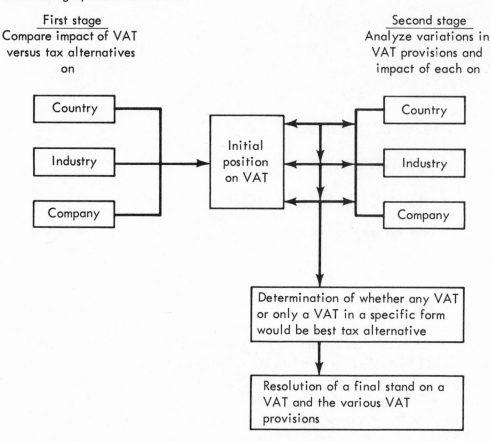

First stage
Compare impact of VAT
versus tax alternatives
on

Country

Industry

Company

Initial
position
on VAT

Second stage
Analyze variations in
VAT provisions and
impact of each on

Country

Industry

Company

Determination of whether any VAT
or only a VAT in a specific form
would be best tax alternative

Resolution of a final stand on a
VAT and the various VAT
provisions

which tax alternative will disrupt the economy the least and will overall provide the least inequitable treatment of our citizenry?

Chapter 4 outlined in very general terms the effect of various tax alternatives on consumption, on savings and investment, on prices, on the distribution of the tax burden among both businesses and private citizens, on the U.S. balance of payments, on economic cycles, and on the administrative costs of both business and the government. This analysis was summarized in Exhibit 4–4 and need not be repeated here.

Clearly every tax alternative has its advantages and disadvantages. Those of the VAT can be summarized very briefly as follows:

1. Disadvantages of a VAT
   a) A VAT tends to be inflationary. Prices normally rise right away by the amount of the VAT, and this price increase usually stimulates demands for higher wages. However, the inflationary effect of a 3 percent VAT should

not be too great if the government took measures to constrain price increases. Furthermore, any tax can create certain inflationary pressures.

  b) A VAT has regressive characteristics. However, the heavy burden of the VAT on those with low and moderate incomes can be counterbalanced by appropriate changes in the income tax, welfare payments, and so forth. Most other tax alternatives also have elements of regressivity. Only the individual income tax is clearly progressive.

  c) A VAT would be more costly to administer than an increase in some existing tax. New tax machinery would have to be set up.

2. Advantages of a VAT

  a) The broad base of the VAT would give it great revenue-raising power at relatively low rates. This is a distinct advantage of a VAT over most tax alternatives.

  b) The VAT is generally neutral toward businesses of different types. Therefore, unlike the corporate income tax, business property taxes, and payroll taxes, it should not distort normal business decisions.

  c) The VAT would be a neutral factor in the U.S. balance of payments. Although the VAT would not help our balance of payments, it would not have the adverse effect of an increase in other business taxes, particularly an increase in the corporate income tax or payroll taxes.

  d) A VAT, in theory, might encourage savings by making consumption relatively more expensive. If savings were, in fact, encouraged by a VAT, this would promote investment. Except for the payroll tax, most other tax alternatives directly or indirectly discourage savings and/or investment.

The reader must weigh for himself the advantages and disadvantages of the VAT to determine whether this tax would be the "least bad" tax from the point of view of the nation.

Analyzing the impact of tax alternatives on an industry

In addition to being concerned about the impact of the various tax alternatives on the country as a whole, an industry must, of course, consider how the different tax alternatives will affect it individually. To determine this, an industry must make a six-step analysis:

Step one. The first step is a determination of the characteristics of the particular industry.

Step two. The next step is a consideration of the differential impact of the various tax alternatives on an industry with such characteristics. An example of the analytical technique that could be used is given in Exhibit 7–2 which uses the data developed in Chapter 5 (and Appendix B) to compare the effect of a VAT versus higher corporate income tax rates on an industry with the characteristics of the paper industry. A similar analysis could, of course, be made for other industries and for other tax alternatives.

EXHIBIT 7–2

Differential impact of a VAT versus higher corporate income tax rates on the paper industry

Industry characteristic	*Step 1* Characteristic of paper industry¹	*Step 2* Impact on paper industry because of this characteristic² VAT	CIT (higher rates)	*Preferable tax to paper industry*	*Step 3* Characteristic largely irrelevant because of another characteristic (in this context)	*Step 4* Characteristic of major importance (in this context)	*Preliminary weighting of tax preference*
1. Extent of incorporation	Largely incorporated	0	−	VAT	X		
2. Debt equity ratio	High debt equity ratio	0	+	CIT		X	CIT
3. Return on equity	Relatively low return on equity	0/−	+	CIT		X	CIT
4. Capital versus labor-intensive	Capital-intensive	0/+	−	VAT			
5. Amount of assets in land	Sizeable assets in land	0/+	0	VAT?			
6. Amount of assets in building	Sizeable assets in plant	−/0/+	0	No preference			
7. Industry-wide labor bargaining	No industry-wide bargaining	+	0	VAT			
8. Purchases from diversified sources	Purchases are *not* from diversified sources −	−		No preference			
9. Import cost component	Purchase of a fair number imports	0/+	+/0	CIT?			
10. Elasticity of demand	Inelastic demand	+	0/+	VAT	X		
11. Product substitutability (cross-elasticity)	Only limited cross-elasticity	0/−	+³	CIT			
12. Price competition in industry	Intense price competition	−/0	−/+	CIT		X	CIT
13. Diversified markets	Diversified markets	+	0/+	VAT?			
14. Producers of capital goods	Not producers of capital goods	−/+	+	CIT?			
15. Big exporters	Exports of only moderate importance	0/−/+	−/0	VAT			
16. Competing with imports	Not competing with imports	0/+	+/0	CIT?			

NOTES: 0 = tax's impact would be neutral
− = tax's impact would be unfavorable } in comparison with the impact on an industry with the opposite characteristic.
+ = tax's impact would be favorable
X = applicable
blank space = not applicable

¹The characteristics of the paper industry were determined from statistics in U.S. Bureau of the Census, *Statistical Abstract of the United States: 1971*, 92d ed. (Washington: U.S. Government Printing Office, 1971): and "The 500 Largest U.S. Industrial Corporations," *Fortune*, May 1972, pp. 188ff.
²Data based on Exhibits 5–1 and 5–2 in Chapter 5.
³Paper products have a limited cross-elasticity with plastic products. Since the plastic industry presently tends to be more profitable than the paper industry, the paper industry's competitors in plastics would be hurt more by higher corporate income taxes than the paper industry would.

As can be seen from the exhibit, certain characteristics of the paper industry would make it tend to favor the VAT, and other characteristics would make a higher corporate income tax preferable from the point of view of the industry. The industry must take further steps to weigh these different considerations.

Step three. To begin the weighting process, the industry must look at its own particular combination of characteristics to determine which ones are relevant in this context. For example, although the paper industry is largely incorporated, its profits have tended to be relatively low in recent years. Therefore, although the industry is subject to the corporate income tax, a higher tax on its profits might amount to fewer dollars than a new tax on its sales. In short, the fact that the industry has many corporations is of relatively little importance because of the industry's low profits. The demand for paper and paper products is relatively inelastic, but the supply has increased faster than the demand, and the supply cannot be readily reduced. Therefore, despite the fact that total demand for paper products is not likely to change with an increase in prices, the industry may not be free to raise its prices to shift a tax forward, even a VAT which is designed to be a tax on consumption rather than on business. The intense price competition in the industry eliminates any advantage derived from the relatively inelastic demand for paper products.

Step four. The next step in weighing the impact of different taxes is a determination of which characteristics are most important to the industry (after elimination of those characteristics found largely irrelevant — in this context — in step three). In the case of the paper industry, perhaps the most important characteristics are its high debt/equity ratio, its relatively low return on equity, its sizeable assets in land, and the intense price competition in the industry. However, one of these paper industry characteristics should not greatly affect the impact of these particular tax alternatives. An industry with large land holdings would be less concerned about a VAT versus the corporate income tax; the tax alternative with the biggest impact on a large landowner is the business property tax. The paper industry characteristics which would cause the greatest differential impact between a VAT and a higher corporate income tax would be its high debt/equity ratio, its relatively low return on equity, and the intense price competition in the industry. In each of these cases, higher corporate income tax rates would have a less adverse affect on the paper industry than the introduction of a VAT. An industry with low profits pays relatively little corporate income tax. An industry with intense price competition may not be able to shift the VAT forward fully to its customers as it should, in theory, be able to do. Industries with a high debt/equity ratio are given a competitive advantage by the corporate income tax since the interest due on debts is considered a tax-deductible business expense, while the profits earned by equity capital are subject to the tax.

Step five. The simplified analysis above, of course, does not take into consideration the fact that, to raise equal revenues, the alternatives are a 3 percent VAT or an increase of about 32 percent in corporate income tax rates. Before a final conclusion can be made about the differential impacts of the two tax alternatives on an industry like the paper industry, some effort should be made to quantify and further investigate these impacts.

a) How much corporate income tax is the paper industry presently paying? How much would its tax bill grow if the rates were raised to approximately 63 percent?

b) How many dollars would a 3 percent VAT on the paper industry's sales amount to? How much of this total would be the VAT on the paper industry's value added and how much on its purchases?

c) To what extent would the paper industry be able to shift to its customers the VAT on its sales? What has been the experience in this regard with paper and roughly analogous industries in Europe? When VAT rates have been increased in Europe, has the paper industry been able to shift the higher rate forward to its customers?

d) Would the paper industry's suppliers absorb the VAT or shift it forward to their customers in the paper industry? What has been the experience in this regard with suppliers to the paper industry in Europe? If the suppliers absorbed the VAT on their sales, then the paper industry would, of course, only be concerned about its ability to shift forward the VAT on its value added.

e) How would the paper industry's ability to shift the VAT forward compare with its ability to shift the corporate income tax forward? Can any evidence on this be gleaned from states which levy both a corporate income tax and some tax roughly comparable to a VAT (a retail or wholesale sales tax, an inventory tax, and so forth)?

f) On the basis of various shifting assumptions for the VAT paid on the paper industry's purchases, the VAT on its sales, and the corporate income tax paid on its profits, which tax would increase the paper industry's actual tax cost the most?

With another industry, with another set of characteristics, the questions to be investigated in greater detail would, of course, be somewhat different. A labor-intensive industry or one with strong unions would want to analyze the likely effect of a VAT on its wage bill. An industry with elastic demand for its products would be concerned about the effect of a VAT versus higher corporate income taxes on its sales at home and/or abroad. An industry with less intense price competition would not be concerned about its ability to shift the VAT forward to its customers. If the VAT were being compared with some tax alternative other than higher corporate income tax rates, again the questions to be studied would be somewhat different, depending both on the characteristics of the industry and the characteristics of the tax to which the VAT was being compared.

Step six. In analyzing the impact of any tax on an industry, some thought should also be given to how the revenues raised by the tax are likely to be spent. Are government expenditures likely to be the same with the various tax alternatives? If there might be any differences in the size or nature of government expenditures with the different tax alternatives, would this affect the particular industry?

In weighing all these factors, it should not be forgotten that there may be differences in the impact on various segments of the industry and on particular companies within the industry.

Analyzing the impact of tax alternatives on a company

The impact of any tax alternative on a given company will, of course, be colored by the impact of the alternative on the company's industry as a whole. However, a company with characteristics atypical of its industry might be affected quite differently from its competitors. To determine the impact of any tax change on a given company, an analysis must first be made of the tax's effect on the industry as a whole. Then a determination must be made of the particular company's characteristics and of the areas in which the company differs from the generality of its industry. Finally, using the data in Chapter 5 and Appendix B, an analysis can be made of the differential impact of the various tax alternatives on the particular company versus its competitors.

For example, while the analysis above indicated that the paper industry might find it at least to its short-term advantage if higher corporate income taxes rather than a VAT were levied, a highly profitable company within the industry would be in a better position with a VAT. A company with sizeable profits would certainly not like to face a 32 percent jump in its income tax rates. However, as in the industry analysis, the company should make some effort to quantify the impact of the various tax alternatives. Exactly how big would its tax bill be if the corporate income tax rate were raised to 63 percent? If the company were compelled to absorb all or part of the VAT, what would be the cost of a 3 percent VAT?

A company must also be concerned with the impact of the tax on its cash flow, working capital, and operating costs. As was indicated in Chapter 6, a VAT, in some cases, may not have a major effect on these aspects of a company's operations. However, the impact of a VAT depends on both the company's characteristics and the specific provisions of the VAT. It can be of considerable importance to a company which provisions are, in fact, written into a U.S. VAT.

Possible variations in the VAT provisions

Having looked at the likely impact of a VAT on the country as a whole, on his particular industry, and on his own company, the reader is perhaps ready to take an initial position on this new tax. Before making a final judgement, however, the reader should consider the possible variations in the VAT provisions and analyze the likely effect of the different variations on the nation, on his own industry, and on his company. Some variations may not make any great difference to the country as a whole, but may make a significant difference in the impact of the VAT on a particular company. Some variations may so change the effect of the tax as to cause the reader to alter his initial position on the VAT.

Following is a list of the VAT provisions about which the reader should be concerned. Beside each item is an indication of the pages in the preceding chapters where the item is discussed at greater length than it is here.

1. *Other tax changes which might be packaged with the VAT*
   a) Should individual income taxes be modified to compensate for the regressivity of the VAT? This would greatly diminish one of the major arguments against a VAT. (Chapter 3, p. 49; Chapter 4, pp. 73, 84–86.)
   b) Should revenues from the VAT be used to induce or compel a reduction in the use of residential property taxes to finance schools? Should the VAT be used as a vehicle for promoting changes in business property taxes? Will tying a VAT to changes in property taxes make the U.S. tax structure overall more equitable? How would such a tax package affect a particular industry or company? (Chapter 3, pp. 47–48, 50–52; Chapter 5, Exhibits 5-1, 5-8, 5-9.)
   c) Can the VAT be coordinated with state and local sales taxes? This would certainly simplify compliance problems for retailers. Should sales taxes be included in the VAT base? If so, this would tax more heavily those already subject to high sales taxes. (Chapter 3, pp. 52–53, 63.)
   d) Should excise taxes be included in the VAT base? If so, this would impose a heavier VAT burden on goods subject to excise taxes and would, in this sense, increase excise taxes. Would this be desirable or undesirable? (Chapter 3, pp. 52, 63.)

2. *Type of VAT (consumption, income, or gross product)*
   From the point of view of every industry and every company, it would be preferable to have a VAT of the consumption type, which gives full and immediate credit for the VAT paid on capital purchases. From the point of view of the economy, the consumption type VAT has the great advantage of eliminating any tax deterrent to capital investment. (Chapter 1, p. 6; Chapter 2, pp. 26–27; Chapter 3, pp. 63; Chapter 4, p. 90; Chapter 5, pp. 98, 101; Chapter 6, pp. 148, 156.

3. *VAT rate*
   a) The lower the VAT rate, the less the introduction of the tax will disrupt the economy. On the other hand, the lower the VAT rate the higher will be compliance and collection costs as a percentage of tax collections. Should the VAT rate be the 3 percent talked of in 1972? (Chapter 3, pp. 53, 62–65; Chapter 4, pp. 73–74; Chapter 6, pp. 155–56.)
   b) Should the president be given some leeway in changing VAT rates so the VAT could be used as a counter-cyclical tool? (Chapter 4, p. 90.)

4. *Number of VAT rates*
   Should there be a single VAT rate or should there be a dual VAT rate with a standard rate for most goods and a reduced rate for "necessities"? A single

rate is infinitely easier for the government to administer and for business to comply with. Dual rates would be one way of compensating for the regressivity of the VAT, but the VAT's regressivity can be compensated for much more effectively by adjustments in the individual income tax. Of course, industries producing goods likely to be classified as "necessities" might find it to their advantage to have a dual rate. If there is a dual rate, what goods should be eligible for the reduced rate? (Chapter 2, pp. 17–19, 38–39, 41–43; Chapter 3, pp. 53, 62–63; Chapter 4, pp. 82–86; Chapter 5, p. 97; Chapter 6, p. 156.)

5. *Zero-rating*

   a) Should anything beside exports be zero-rated, that is, exempt from the VAT both on sales and on purchases made to produce the goods? It is a great advantage to a company to have its product zero-rated, but zero-rating anything beside exports would distort the neutrality of the VAT and would complicate administration of the tax. (Chapter 2, pp. 19–21; Chapter 3, pp. 53–54, 56.)

   b) As a protective measure against waverings in the U.S. balance of trade, should the president be given some discretion in making adjustments in the zero-rating of exports? (Chapter 4, p. 89.)

6. *Exemptions*

   What goods and services should be exempted from the VAT but not zero-rated, that is, exempt from the VAT on sales but liable to the VAT on purchases made to produce the goods? Exemptions distort the neutrality of the VAT and complicate administration of the tax. They also are not always to the advantage of the exempt company. However, if exemptions are granted only to companies providing goods and services directly to consumers, exemptions would reduce the cost to the consumer of the exempted items. (Chapter 2, pp. 19–22; Chapter 3, pp. 53–56; Chapter 5, p. 97; Chapter 6, p. 156.)

   a) For social reasons, should the United States exempt from the VAT: educational services (Chapter 3, p. 58), medical services (Chapter 3, p. 58), and prescription medicines (Chapter 3, p. 58)?

   b) For administrative and technical reasons, should the United States follow the precedent of Europe and exempt from the VAT: financial services (Chapter 3, pp. 56–57) and legal services (Chapter 3, p. 57)?

   c) What should be the VAT provisions in regard to real estate? (Chapter 2, p. 21; Chapter 3, pp. 58–60; Chapter 5, pp. 99–100.) Should the sale and leasing of land be exempt? Should construction and repair work and the sale of new buildings be subject to the VAT? Should the sale of older buildings be exempt from the VAT? Should the leasing of residences be exempt? Should the leasing of business property be subject to the VAT?

   d) Should newspapers be exempt? (Chapter 2, p. 21; Chapter 3, p. 58.)

   e) What provisions should be made about cars and machinery traded in? (Chapter 2, p. 22; Chapter 3, p. 58.)

f) Should government purchases be exempt from the VAT? (Chapter 2, p. 21; Chapter 3, pp. 62, 65.)

g) Should agriculture be exempt or even zero-rated? (Chapter 2, pp. 23–24; Chapter 3, p. 60.)

h) Should retailers be included in the VAT? (Chapter 2, pp. 19, 40–43; Chapter 3, pp. 60–61.)

i) If any VAT exemptions are granted, should exempt firms be allowed the option of being included in the VAT? (Chapter 2, pp. 20, 22; Chapter 3, pp. 55–56.)

7. *Method of calculating the VAT*

Which method of calculation should be used: the subtraction/tax credit method; the subtraction/accounts method; or the addition method? The method used throughout Europe is the subtraction/tax credit method: A company multiplies its sales by the VAT rate and then subtracts from the resulting figure all the VAT paid on its purchases. (Chapter 1, pp. 4–6; Chapter 3, pp. 63, 65.)

8. *VAT base*

a) Should the VAT base be the price including or excluding sales taxes, excise taxes, import duties? (Chapter 3, p. 63.)

b) Should the VAT base be the actual cost to the customer, including shipping, installation, insurance, interest, and other such charges? (Chapter 3, pp. 63–65.)

9. *Breakage* (Chapter 6, pp. 158–59.)

a) Should a company's VAT liability be a statutory percentage of its sales or the tax actually collected?

b) Will the VAT collected on sales be dictated by a bracket schedule; and, if so, who will benefit from the breakage, it any?

c) How will the bracket schedule be constructed?

10. *Collection method*

Which VAT collection method should be used: the cash collection method (VAT liability on sales and VAT credits on purchases recognized only at the time of cash payment) or the invoice collection method (VAT liability on sales and credits on purchases recognized at the time of invoicing). The cash basis is generally advantageous to companies with credit sales, and the invoice basis is generally advantageous to companies with cash sales. Should companies be given the option of using either method? (Chapter 2, pp. 27–28; Chapter 3, pp. 65–66; Chapter 6, pp. 145–47.)

11. *Dating of VAT liability* (Chapter 2, p. 27; Chapter 3, p. 65; Chapter 6, p. 145.)

a) If the invoice method is used, should the effective date be the date the invoice is written or the date the goods or services are actually delivered?

b) Should special provisions be made for deliveries made over a period of time?

c) With the invoice method, should special provisions be made for payments made before delivery is effected? (In Europe the date of an invoice is generally regarded as the date of delivery.)

12. *Refund of VAT on sales never paid for*

The VAT law should make some provision for refunding to companies any VAT paid on invoices which the customer subsequently did not pay in full (for example, because a discount was later granted, because the goods were returned, because the customer went bankrupt). (Chapter 2, p. 27; Chapter 3, p. 66; Chapter 6, p. 160.)

13. *Refund of excess VAT credits*

Any company which paid more VAT on its purchases than it owed on its sales should be paid its VAT refund promptly by the government. Such companies should generally not have to wait until the end of the year or the quarter for their refund, nor should they be required to carry the credit forward into the next tax period unless the amount is a small one. (Chapter 2, p. 29; Chapter 3, p. 66; Chapter 6, pp. 148–49.)

14. *VAT credit on purchases*

Should businesses be given credit for the VAT paid on the purchase of gifts or entertainment for customers? (Chapter 3, p. 65.)

15. *VAT accounting period and payment period*

a) The VAT accounting period (the segment of time for which VAT liabilities and credits are calculated) is usually one month in the EEC countries, but it would help business' cash flow and reduce its compliance costs if the accounting period could be lengthened to two or even three months as it is in the Scandinavian countries and will be in the United Kingdom. However, companies entitled to VAT refunds (particularly exporters) would want the option of electing a one-month accounting period if the standard period were longer. (Chapter 2, pp. 28, 29; Chapter 3, p. 66; Chapter 6, pp. 147–48.)

b) A long VAT payment period (the time between the end of the accounting period and the time the tax is due) would also be to the advantage of business. In Europe the tax payment period ranges from 10 days to 1 month plus 20 days. Longer accounting periods and longer payment periods would slow down the flow of revenue to the government, but would compensate business in part for the cost of complying with the tax. (Chapter 2, p. 29; Chapter 3, p. 66; Chapter 6, pp. 147–48.)

c) If the VAT accounting period should be a short one, should a company be allowed just to estimate its VAT liability and to make a precise calculation only at the end of the quarter or the year? (Chapter 2, pp. 28, 29; Chapter 3, p. 66; Chapter 6, p. 156.)

d) Should importers be given a longer VAT payment period to compensate them for the special cash flow problems a VAT creates for them? (Chapter 5, pp. 100–101.)

16. *Special provisions for small businesses*

Presumably the VAT will make special provisions for small businesses to simplify administration of the tax, if for no other reason. (Chapter 2, pp. 24–25; Chapter 3, pp. 61–62.)

a) Should very small firms be exempt entirely from the VAT as they are in much of Europe?

b) Should the VAT liability be reduced for companies which are small but not small enough to qualify for full exemption?

c) Should small companies be given the option of calculating their VAT bills in some simplified fashion, such as a general estimate of their VAT liability based on past sales? Should this special option be designed to favor small businesses slightly to compensate them for the fact that their compliance costs may be more of a burden than those of larger companies? Or should the special option be designed to overtax small businesses slightly so as to encourage them to join the regular VAT system?

17. *The VAT and retail prices* (Chapter 3, p. 66; Chapter 6, p. 157.)

a) Should retailers be required to include the VAT in the sales price of each item on their shelves? Or can the VAT simply be added on at the time of sale?

b) If the VAT must be included in sales prices, should price tags indicate the VAT-exclusive price and the VAT as well as the total price including the VAT?

18. *VAT and the cost-of-living index*

Should the VAT be included in the cost-of-living index, as it is in Europe and as sales taxes currently are in the United States? If so, the VAT is certain to have an inflationary impact on wages. (Chapter 2, pp. 33–38; Chapter 4, pp. 72, 79.)

Would any of these variations in the VAT provisions cause the reader to change his initial position on the VAT? While one reader might be dubious about the VAT generally, his objections might be dissipated if certain provisions were written into the VAT. While another reader may consider the VAT the best tax alternative, he may feel that he could not support a VAT with certain characteristics. There are no simple answers to the dilemma of designing the least undesirable changes in the U.S. tax structure to meet the needs of a growing economy and a changing society.

appendix A

First and second directives of the EEC Council in regard to the VAT

FIRST DIRECTIVE OF THE COUNCIL
of 11 April 1967

with regard to the harmonization of the laws of the Member States relating to turnover taxes
(67/227/EEC)

> Unofficial translation prepared by the International Bureau of Fiscal Documentation based on the official Dutch and French texts.*

THE COUNCIL OF THE EUROPEAN ECONOMIC COMMUNITY

Having regard to the Treaty establishing the European Economic Community, and in particular Articles 99 and 100 thereof;

Having regard to the proposal of the Commission,

Having regard to the opinion of the Assembly,

Having regard to the opinion of the Economic and Social Committee,

Considering that the primary objective of the Treaty is to establish, within the framework of an economic union, a common market providing for healthy competition and having characteristics similar to those of an internal market;

Considering that the attainment of this objective presupposes the prior application, in the Member States, of laws relating to turnover taxes which neither distort conditions of competition nor impede the free circulation

---

* Published in the "Publikatieblad van de Europese Gemeenschappen" of 14 April 1967 (No. 71), at 1301/67; "Journal Officiel des Communautés Européennes" of 14 Avril 1967 (No. 71), at 1301/67.

of goods and services within the Common Market;

Considering that the laws now in force do not meet the above-mentioned requirements; and that it is therefore in the interest of the Common Market to harmonize the laws relating to turnover taxes with a view to the elimination, in so far as possible, of those factors which are capable of distorting conditions of competition, both on the national and Community levels, and to permitting the subsequent attainment of the objective of abolishing the levying of taxes at importation and the refunding of taxes at exportation with respect to trade between the Member States;

Considering that it is apparent from studies carried out, that such harmonization must result in the abolition of the systems of cumulative cascade taxes and in the adoption by all Member States of a common system of tax on value added;

Considering that a system of tax on value added will achieve the highest degree of simplicity and neutrality when the tax is levied in as general a manner as possible and when its scope of application includes all stages of production and distribution as well as the realm of the rendition of services; and that it is, accordingly, in the interest of the Common Market and of the Member States to adopt a common system the scope of which also extends to retail trade;

Considering, however, that the application of the tax to retail trade might give rise in some of the Member States to certain difficulties of a practical and political nature; and that, for this reason, Member States should have the option, subject to prior consulation, to apply the common system only up to and including the wholesale trade stage and to apply, where appropriate, an independent complementary tax at the retail trade stage or at the stage prior thereto;

Considering that it is necessary to proceed by stages, since the harmonization of turnover taxes will entail considerable modifications of the tax structures in the Member States and will have far-reaching consequences in the budgetary, economic and social spheres;

Considering that the replacement of the systems of cumulative cascade taxes in force in the majority of the Member States by the common system of tax on value added must, even if the rates and exemptions are not simultaneously harmonized, result in a neutral effect of the tax competition, in the sense that within each country similar goods will suffer the same tax burden irrespective of the number of stages in the production and distribution process, and that, in international trade, the amount of the tax borne by the goods will be known so that exact compensation for the tax can be effected; and that it is therefore desirable to provide, in the initial stage, for the adoption by all Member States of the common system of tax on value added without accompanying harmonization of rates and exemptions;

Considering that it is not possible at this juncture to determine the means by which and the period within which the harmonization of turnover taxes can lead to the attainment of the objective of abolishing the levying of taxes at importation and the refunding of taxes at exportation with respect to trade between the Member States; and that it is therefore preferable that the commencement of the second stage as well as the measures to be taken in respect thereof be determined at a later date on the basis of proposals made by the Commission to the Council,

HAS ADOPTED THE PRESENT DIRECTIVE:

Article 1

The Member States are to replace their present system of turnover taxes by the common system of tax on value added defined in Article 2.

In each Member State a law to effectuate this replacement is to be promulgated as rapidly as possible, so that it may enter into force at a date to be fixed by each Member State taking into account the state of its economy, but not later than 1 January 1970.

After the entry into force of this law, a Member State may not maintain or introduce any measure of standard-rate compensation for imports or exports in respect of turnover taxes with respect to trade between the Member States.

Article 2

The principle of the common system of tax on value added is to apply a general tax on consumption to goods and services directly proportional to the price of the goods and services, irrespective of the number of transactions during the production and dis-

tribution process preceding the stage at which the tax is imposed.

On each transaction, the tax on value added, calculated on the price of the good or service at the rate applicable to such good or service, is to be payable after deduction of the amount of the tax on value added which has directly affected the cost of the various components of the price.

The common system of tax on value added is to be applied up to and including the retail trade stage.

Nevertheless, until the abolition of the levying of taxes at importation and the refunding of taxes at exportation with respect to trade between the Member States, the latter are to have the option, subject to the consultation prescribed in Article 5, to apply this system only up to and including the wholesale trade stage, and where appropriate, to apply an independent complementary tax at the retail trade stage or at the stage prior thereto.

Article 3

The Council is to draw up, on a proposal of the Commission, a second directive concerning the structure and methods for the application of the common-system of tax on value added.

Article 4

In order to allow the Council to deliberate and, if possible, make its decisions before the end of the transitional period, the Commission is to submit to the Council, before the end of 1968, proposals specifying the means by which and the period within which the harmonization of turnover taxes can lead to the attainment of the objective of abolishing the levying of taxes at importation and the refunding of taxes at exportation with respect to trade between the Member States, while guaranteeing the neutrality of these taxes with respect to the origin of the goods and the rendition of services.

In this regard, account is to be taken, in particular, of the relationship between direct and indirect taxes, which differs between the Member States, of the consequences of a modification of the tax systems on the financial and budgetary policy of the Member States, as well as of the influence the tax systems exert on the conditions of competition and the social climate within the Community.

Article 5

In the event a Member State intends to utilize the option referred to in the last paragraph of Article 2, it is to approach the Commission in due time with a view to the application of Article 102 of the Treaty.

Article 6

The present directive is addressed to the Member States.

Done at Brussels, 11 April 1967

By the Council

The President

R. VAN ELSLNDE

SECOND DIRECTIVE OF THE COUNCIL
of 11 April 1967

with regard to the harmonization of the laws of the Member States relating to turnover taxes

Structure and methods for the application of the common system of tax on value added

(67/228/EEC)

Unofficial translation prepared by the International Bureau of Fiscal Documentation based on the official Dutch and French texts.*

THE COUNCIL OF THE EUROPEAN ECONOMIC COMMUNITY

Having regard to the Treaty establishing the European Economic Community, and particular Articles 99 and 100 thereof,

Having regard to the First Directive of the Council of 11 April 1967 with regard to the harmonization of the

---

* Published in the "Publikatieblad van de Europese Gemeenschappen" of 14 April 1967 (No. 71), at 1303/67; "Journal Officiel des Communautes Europeennes" of 14 April 1967 (No. 71), at 1303/67.

laws of the Member States relating to turnover taxes,

Having regard to the proposal of the Commission,

Having regard to the opinion of the Assembly,

Having regard to the opinion of the Economic and Social Committee,

Considering that the replacement of the turnover taxes in force in the Member States by a common system of tax on value added aims at the realization of the objectives defined in the First Directive;

Considering that until the abolition of the levying of taxes at importation and the refunding of taxes at exportation, it is possible to allow Member States substantial autonomy in the area of determining the rate or the different rates of the tax;

Considering that it is also possible to permit, on a transitional basis, certain differences in the methods for the application of the tax in the Member States; but that it is necessary, however, to provide for appropriate procedures so as, on the one hand, to guarantee neutrality of competition between the Member States and, on the other hand, to gradually restrict or eliminate the differences in question in order to result in a convergence of the national systems of tax on value added, so as to prepare for the implementation of the objective referred to in Article 4 of the First Directive;

Considering that in order to be able to apply the system in a simple and neutral manner and to maintain the normal rate of the tax within reasonable limits, it is necessary to limit special regimes and exception measures;

Considering that the system of tax on value added permits, where appropriate and for reasons of a social and economic nature, the effectuation of alleviations or increases in the tax burden on certain goods and services by means of a differentiation of rates, but that the introduction of nil rates gives rise to difficulties, it is therefore most desirable to strictly limit the cases of exemption and to institute alleviations considered necessary through the application of reduced rates at a sufficiently high level so as to normally allow the deduction of the tax paid in the preceding stage, a procedure which moreover leads, in general, to the same result as that which is now obtained by the application of exemptions under the cumulative cascade systems;

Considering that it has become possible to leave to the Member States themselves the determination of the rules concerning the numerous services whose cost does not influence the prices of goods and of the rules concerning the system to be applied to small enterprises, subject, as regards the latter, to the initiation of a prior consultation;

Considering that the need has become apparent for the providing of special regimes for the application of the tax on value added to the agricultural sector and to instruct the Commission to submit to the Council, as soon as possible, proposals to this effect;

Considering that it is necessary to provide for a relatively large number of special provisions covering interpretations, deviations and certain detailed application procedures and to draft a list of the services compulsorily subject to the common system, and that it is desirable that these provisions and this list should appear in the Annexes forming an integral part of the present directive;

HAS ADOPTED THE PRESENT DIRECTIVE:

Article 1

The Member States are to establish, according to a common system, a turnover tax herinafter referred to as "tax on value added."

The structure and methods for the application of this tax are to be established by the Member States in accordance with the provisions of the following articles and of Annexes. A and B.

Article 2

The following are to be subject to the tax on value added:

a) deliveries of goods and the rendering of services, effected for a consideration within the country by a taxable person;
b) importations of goods.

Article 3

The term "within the country" is to be understood as meaning the territory within which the State concerned applies the tax on value added; this territory must include, in principle, the whole of the national territory, including the territorial waters.

Article 4

"Taxable person" is to be understood as meaning any person who independently and regularly engages in transactions within the scope of the activities of a manufacturer, trader or a person who renders services, whether or not for profit.

Article 5

1. The term "delivery of a good" is to be understood as meaning the transfer of the power to dispose of a tangible asset as owner.
2. The following are also to be considered as a delivery within the meaning of paragraph 1:

   a) The actual handing over of a good pursuant to a contract which provides for the rental of a good for a certain period or for the installment sale of a good, in both cases subject to a clause to the effect that the ownership is to be acquired not later than the payment of the last installment;
   b) The transfer of the ownership of a good, against payment of an indemnity, pursuant to its expropriation by or in the name of a public authority;
   c) The transfer of a good effected pursuant to a purchase or sales commission contract;
   d) The delivery of a movable work made to order, that is to say, the handing over by a contractor to his principal of a movable good which he has manufactured from materials

and objects entrusted to him by the principal for this purpose, whether or not the contractor has supplied a part of the products used;

e) The delivery of an immovable work, including that comprising the incorporation of a movable good in an immovable good.

3. The following are to be assimilated to a delivery effected for a consideration:

a) The appropriation by a taxable person, in the scope of his enterprise, of a good which he sets apart for his private use or which he transfers gratuitously;

b) The use by a taxable person for the requirements of his enterprise of a good produced or extracted by him or by a third person on his behalf.

4. The place of a delivery is deemed to be located:

a) In the event a good is dispatched or transported either by the supplier, acquirer, or by a third person: at the place where the good is located at the moment of departure of the expedition or of transportation to the destination of the acquirer;

b) In the event a good is not dispatched or transported: at the the moment of the delivery.

5. The taxable event takes place at the moment the delivery is effected. However, with respect to deliveries involving payments on account prior to the delivery, it may be prescribed that the taxable event has previously taken place the moment of delivery of the invoice or, at the latest, at the moment of collection of the payment on account, to the extent of the amount invoiced or collected.

Article 6

1. The term "rendering of services" is to be understood as meaning any transaction which does not constitute a delivery of a good within the meaning of Article 5.

2. The rules prescribed in the present directive with respect to the taxation of the rendering of services are to be compulsorily applicable only to those services enumerated in Annex B.

3. The place of a rendering of services is deemed to be located, in principle, at the place where the service rendered, the right transferred or granted or the object rented is used or exploited.

4. The taxable event takes place at the moment the service is rendered. However, for services rendered of indeterminate lengths or exceeding a certain period or involving payments on account, it may be prescribed that the taxable event has previously taken place at the moment of delivery of the invoice or, at the latest, at the moment of collection of the payment on account, to the extent of the amount invoiced or collected.

Article 7

1. The term "importation of a good" is to be understood as meaning the entry of such good "within the country" within the meaning of Article 3.
2. On importation, the taxable event takes place at the time of this entry. The Member States have the option, however, to link the taxable event and claim to payment of the tax on value added, to the taxable event and claim to payment prescribed in respect of customs duties or other duties, taxes and levies at importation.

The same link may be established in respect of the taxable event and the claim to payment of the tax on value added for deliveries of imported goods subjected to a regime of suspension of customs duties or of other duties, taxes and levies at importation.

Article 8

The taxable base is to constitute:

a) For deliveries and services rendered, everything which constitutes the consideration for the delivery of the good or the rendering of the services, including all costs and taxes with the exception of the tax on value added itself;
b) For the operations referred to in Article 5(3)(a) and (b), the purchase price of the goods or of similar goods or, in the absence of a purchase price, the cost price;
c) For importations of goods, the value for customs purposes, increased by all the duties, taxes and levies which are due by reason of importation, with the exception of the tax on value added itself. The same base is applicable when the good is exempt from customs duties.

Each Member State is to have the option to increase the tax base for importations of goods by the incidental costs (packing, transportation, insurance, etc.) arising up to the place of destination, and which are not included in this base.

Article 9

1. The normal rate of the tax on value added is to be fixed by each Member State at a percentage of the taxable base which is to be the same for deliveries of goods and for services rendered.
2. Certain deliveries of goods and the rendering of certain services may, however, be subjected to increased rates or to reduced rates. Each reduced rate is to be fixed in such a manner that the amount of the tax on value added resulting from the application of this rate will normally permit the deduction of the entire tax on value added for which a deduction is authorized by Article 11.
3. The rate which must be applied at the importation of a good is to be that which is applied within the country with respect to a delivery of a similar good.

Article 10

1. The following are to be exempt from the tax on value added, sub-

ject to conditions to be determined by each Member State:

a) deliveries of goods dispatched or transported outside the territory within which the State concerned applies the tax on value added;

b) The rendering of services relating to goods referred to in (a) or to goods in transit.

2. Subject to the consultation prescribed in Article 16, the rendering of services relating to importations of goods may be exempted from the tax on value added.

3. Each Member State may, subject to the consultation prescribed in Article 16, determine those other exemptions which it considers necessary.

Article 11

1. In so far as the goods and services are used for the requirements of his undertaking, the taxable person is authorized to deduct from the tax for which he is liable:

a) the tax on value added for which he is invoiced in respect of the goods delivered to him and in respect of the services rendered to him;

b) the tax on value added paid in respect of imported goods;

c) the tax on value added which he has paid for the use of goods referred to in Article 5(3)(b).

2. The tax on value added borne by those goods and services which are used to effectuate nontaxable or exempt operations is not to be deductible.

The taxable person is, however, to be authorized to take a deduction if the deliveries of goods and the services rendered are effected outside of the territory or are exempt in accordance with Article 10(1) or (2).

As regards those goods and services which are used to effect both transactions carrying the right to a deduction and transactions which do not carry the right to a deduction, the deduction is to be allowed only for that portion of the tax on value added which is proportional to the amount assignable to the first mentioned transactions (pro rata rule).

3. The deduction is to be taken from the tax on value added due for the period in the course of which the deductible tax is invoiced in the case of paragraph 1(a) or paid in the case of paragraphs 1(b) and (c) (immediate deductions).

In the case of a partial deduction in accordance with paragraph 2, the amount of the deduction is to be provisionally determined according to the criteria established by each Member State and is to be adjusted after the end of the year when the ratio for the year of acquisition has been calculated.

As regards investment goods, the adjustment is to be effected in proportion to variations of the ratio occurring in the course of a five year period including the year in which the goods were acquired; the adjustment is to apply each year to only one fifth of the tax borne by the investment goods.

4. Certain goods and services may be excluded from the deduction system, in particular those which are likely to be exclusively or partially used for the private requirements of the taxable person or of his personnel.

Article 12

1. Every taxable person must maintain a sufficiently detailed book-keeping system so as to permit the application of the tax on value added and the control thereof by the tax administration.
2. Every taxable person must deliver an invoice in respect of the deliveries of goods to and the rendering of services for another taxable person.
3. Every taxable person must file a declaration each month indicating, in respect of transactions engaged in during the preceding month, all the information necessary for the computation of the tax and the deductions to be taken. Every taxable person must pay the amount of the tax on value added upon filing the declaration.

Article 13

If a Member State considers that, in exceptional cases, it would be advisable to adopt special measures so as to simplify collection of the tax or to prevent certain frauds, it is to inform the Commission and the other Member States.

Should there be objection from one or more States or from the Commission within one month, the request for a deviation is to be brought before the Council which is to rule on the issue, on a proposal of the Commission, within three months.

Should it appear from the conclusions of the Commission that it is only a question of a simplification of collection or of a measure designed to prevent fraud, the Council is to decide by a qualified majority on the deviation requested.

Should it appear, on the contrary, from the aforesaid conclusions that the proposed measure risks interfering with the very principles of the system set up by the present directive, and in particular, with the neutrality of competition between the Member States, the Council's decision is to be unanimous.

In either case, the Council is to decide according to the same procedure as to the length of application of such measures.

The State concerned may put the proposed measure into effect only after expiration of the period for entering an objection, or where an objection has been made, after the decision of the Council, if this be favorable.

These provisions are to cease to be applicable upon the abolition of the levying of taxes at importation and the refunding of taxes at exportation in respect of trade between the Member States.

Article 14

Each Member State is to have the option, subject to the consultation prescribed in Article 16, to apply to small enterprises, for which subjection to the normal system of the tax on value added would encounter difficulties, the particular system best adapted to its national requirements and possibilities.

Article 15

1. The Commission is to submit to the Council, as soon as possible, proposals for directives concerning the common methods for the application of the tax on value added to transactions relating to agricultural products.

2. Until the data fixed in the directives referred to in paragraph 1 for the effectuation of these common methods, each Member State has the option, subject to the consultation prescribed in Article 16, to apply to those engaged in agricultural activities, for whom subjection to the normal system of tax on value added would encounter difficulties, the particular system best adapted to its national requirements and possibilities.

Article 16

In those cases where a Member State is obliged, in accordance with the provisions of the present directive, to initiate consultations, it is to approach the Commission in due time with a view to the application of Article 102 of the Treaty.

Article 17

In view of the transition from the present system of turnover taxes to the common system of tax on value added, Member States are to have the option to:

—adopt transitional measures for the levying of the tax in advance;

—apply, during a certain transitional period, with respect to investment goods, the annual installment method of deductions (deductions pro rata temporis);

—exclude, entirely or partially, during a certain transitional period, investment goods from the deduction system provided for in Article 11;

and, subject to the consultation prescribed in Article 16:

—authorize, so as to grant a refund, total or partial, but general in scope, of the turnover tax levied up to the moment of the effectuation of the tax on value added, standard-rate deductions in respect of those investment goods not yet depreciated, as well as for inventories on hand at that time. The Member States have the option, however, to limit such deductions to goods exported during a period of one year from the effectuation of the tax on value added. In this event, such deductions can be applied only in respect of inventories which are on hand at the above-mentioned time and which are exported in an unaltered state;

—provide, until the abolition of the levying of taxes at importation and the refunding of taxes at exportation in respect of trade between the Member States, for well defined reasons of social interest and for the benefit of the ultimate consumers, reduced rates or even exemptions with possible reimbursement of taxes paid at an earlier stage, in so far as the aggregate incidence of such measures does not exceed that of the reliefs applied under the present system.

Article 18

The Commission is to present to the Council, after consulting with the Member States, for the first time on 1 January 1972 and every two years thereafter, a report on the functioning of the common system of tax on value added in the Member States.

Article 19

The Council, in the interest of the Common Market, is to adopt at the proper time, on a proposal of the Commission, the appropriate directives with a view to the completion of the common system of tax on value added and, in particular, the gradual restriction or elimination of those measures taken by the Member States in derogation of this system, in order to arrive at a convergence of the national systems of tax on value added, so as to prepare to give effect to the objective referred to in Article 4 of the First Directive.

Article 20

The Annexes form an integral part of the present directive.

Article 21

The present directive is addressed to the Member States.
Done at Brussels, 11 April 1967.

By the Council
The President
R. VAN ELSLANDE

ANNEX A

1. Ad Article 3

If a Member State intends to apply the tax on value added to a territory more limited in scope than its national territory, it is to initiate the consultation prescribed in Article 16.

2. Ad Article 4

The term "activities of a manufacturer, trader, or person who renders services" must be understood in a broad sense and encompasses all economic activities including, therefore, the extraction of minerals, agricultural activities and activities of the liberal professions.

If a Member State does not intend to impose tax on certain activities, it should do so by means of exemptions rather than by excluding those persons exercising such activities from the scope of the tax.

The Member States are to have the option to also consider anyone who carries out the transactions referred to in Article 4 on an occasional basis as a "taxable person."

The term "independently" is intended, in particular, to exclude from taxation those wage earners who are bound to their employer by an employment contract. This term also permits each Member State not to consider as separate, but as a single taxable person, those persons who, although independent from a juridical point of view, are, nevertheless, organically linked to one another by economic, financial and organizational bonds. A Member State that intends to adopt such a system is to initiate the consultation prescribed in Article 16.

The States, provinces, communes and other public law authorities are not, in principle, to be considered as taxable persons in respect of those activities which they exercise in their capacity as public authorities.

If, however, they exercise activities of a manufacturer, trader or person who renders services, they may be considered as taxable persons in respect of such activities.

3. Ad Article 5(1)

The term "tangible asset" is intended to include both movable and immovable tangible property.

Deliveries of electricity, gas, heat, refrigeration and similar commodities are to be considered as deliveries of goods.

In the event of a contribution to a company of a going-concern or a subdivision thereof, the Member States are to have the option to consider the recipient company as continuing the personality of the contributed enterprise.

4. Ad Article 5(2)(a)

For the purposes of the application of the present directive, the contract referred to in Article 5(2)(a) may not be split into part lease and part sale, but must be considered, from its conclusion, as a contract involving a taxable delivery.

5. Ad Article 5(2)(d) and (e)

Those Member States that, for specifically national reasons, would not be able to consider the transactions referred to in Article 5(2)(d) and (e) as deliveries should classify them under the category of services rendered while subjecting them to the rate which would be applicable if they were to remain classified as deliveries.

The following, *inter alia,* are to be considered as "immovable works":

—the construction of buildings, bridges, roads, harbors, etc., in performance of a construction contract;
—navying and the planting of gardens;
—installation work (e.g., of central heating);
—repairs to immovable property, other than current maintenance operations.

6. Ad Article 5(3)(a)

As regards the appropriation in an unaltered state of a good purchased by a taxable person, the Member States are to have the option to replace the imposition of tax by forbidding a deduction or by adjustment thereof if a deduction has already been effected.

However, appropriations effected for the making of gifts of insignificant value and of samples which, from a tax point of view, may be classified among general expenses must not be considered as taxable deliveries. Moreover, the provisions prescribed in Article 11(2) are not to be applied to such approprations.

7. Ad Article 5(3)(b)

This provision must only be applied to ensure equality of taxation between goods purchased and intended for the requirements of an enterprise which do not qualify for an immediate or complete deduction on the one hand, and goods produced or extracted by a taxable person, or on his behalf by a third person, which are to be used for the same purposes, on the other.

8. Ad Article 5(5)

The term "taxable event" means the point at which tax liability is created.

9. Ad Article 6(1)

The definition of a rendering of services set forth in this paragraph involves classification of the following, *inter alia,* as a rendering of services:

—the transfer of an intangible good;
—the discharge of an obligation to refrain from doing something;
—the rendering of a service pursuant to an expropriation made by, or in the name, of a public authority;
—the execution of a work bearing on a good, if such work is not con-

sidered as a delivery within the meaning of Article 5(2)(d) and (e) as, for example, current maintenance operations, the laundering of linen, etc.

This definition is not to be opposed to the taxation by the Member States of certain transactions effected by a taxable person as services "rendered to himself," when such a measure appears necessary to prevent distortions of competition.

10. Ad Article 6(2)

The Member States are to refrain, in so far as possible, from exempting the rendering of those services enumerated in Annex B.

11. Ad Article 6(3)

The Council, by unanimous decision on a proposal of the Commission, is to decree, before 1 January 1970, special provisions concerning certain types of services for which such rules may appear necessary in derogation from the provisions of Article 6(3). Until these provisions are decreed, each Member State has the option, with a view to simplifying collection of the tax, to deviate from the provisions of Article 6(3) while taking, however, the necessary measures to prevent double taxation or the nonimposition of tax.

12. Ad Article 8

Any Member State that applies the tax on value added only up to and, including the wholesale trade stage, may, in the case of goods sold at retail by a taxable person, reduce the taxable base by a certain percentage; the reduced base may not, however, be lower than the purchase or cost price increased, where appropriate, by the amount of the customs duties (including levies), duties and taxes charged on the goods, even if payment thereof has been suspended, with the exception of the tax on value added.

In the case of the importation of a good sold at retail, the same reduction must be applied to the tax base.

The Member States are free to define, according to their national point of view, the concept of "sale of goods at retail."

Subject to the consultation prescribed in Article 16, each Member State has the option to provide, so as to prevent fraud and in respect of restrictively designated goods and services, that in derogation of Article 8, the tax base may be not lower than a minimum base to be determined in its national law.

13. Ad Article 8(a)

The term "consideration" is to be understood as meaning everything which is received as a counterpart of the delivery of a good or of the rendering of a service, including incidental costs (packing, transportation, insurance, etc.), that is to say, not only the amount of the sums received, but also, for example, the value of the goods received in exchange, or in the case of expropriation by a public authority or in its name, the amount of compensation received.

Nevertheless, this provision is no

to be opposed to the exercise of the option, by each Member State that considers it necessary to achieve neutrality of competition to a wider extent, to exclude from the taxable base for deliveries, the indicental costs incurred from the place of delivery as defined in Article 5(4) and from taxing such costs as consideration for the rendering of services.

However, the costs paid in the name and for the account of the customer which are carried in the books of the supplier in suspense accounts are not to be incorporated in the taxable base.

Customs duties, and other taxes, duties, etc., paid on importation by customs agents and other customs intermediaries including forwarding agents, under their own name, may also be excluded from the taxable base corresponding to the rendition of the services they have furnished.

14. Ad Article 8(c)

In intracommunity trade, the Member States are to do their utmost to apply to importations of goods a tax base which corresponds, in so far as possible, to that applied for deliveries effected within the countries, this base comprising the same elements as those taken into account pursuant to Article 8(c).

At the latest by the time of the abolition of the levying of taxes at importation and the refunding of taxes at exportation with respect to trade between Member States and subject to the consultation prescribed in Article 16, each Member State has the option to apply to importations of goods originating from third countries a taxable base which corresponds, in so far as possible, to that used for deliveries effected within the country, this base comprising the same elements as those taken into account pursuant to Article 8(c).

15. Ad Article 9(2)

To the extent that use is made of the provisions of this paragraph for those transportation services referred to in Annex B, Point 5, they must be applied so that equality of treatment between the different means of transportation is ensured.

16. Ad Article 10(a)

The exemption prescribed in this provision refers to the delivery of a good which is directly exported, i.e., a delivery effected by the exporter. The Member States have the option, however, to extend the exemption to deliveries made at the preceding stage.

17. Ad Article 10(1)(b)

The Member States have the option, however, to refrain from granting this exemption if relief from the tax on value added which has burdened the rendition of these services is effected by way of a deduction for the person on whose behalf the services were rendered. Moreover, the Member States have the option, except with respect to the rendering of services pertaining to goods in transit, to limit such exemption to the rendering of services relating to goods the delivery of which inside the country is taxable.

18. Ad Article 10(2)

This provision pertains, in particular, to the rendition of services by international transportation enterprises at importation and to port services.

19. Ad Article 10(2) and (3)

To the extent that use is made of the provisions of these paragraphs in respect of those transportation services referred to in Annex B, Point 5, they must be applied so that equality of treatment between the different means of transportation is ensured.

20. Ad Article 11(1)(a)

In the cases referred to in Article 5(3), second sentence, and Article 6(4), second sentence, the deductions may be applied as soon as the invoice is received, even though the goods have not yet been delivered or the services have not yet been rendered.

21. Ad Article 11(2), second subparagraph

The Member States have the option, however, to limit the right of deduction to transactions relating to goods the delivery of which inside the country is taxable.

22. Ad Article 11(2), third subparagraph

The ratio is, in principle, to be determined with regard to the sum total of transactions effectuated by a taxable person (general ratio). A taxable person may obtain, exceptionally, however, administrative permission to determine special ratios for certain sectors of his activity.

23. Ad Article 11(3), first subparagraph

Subject to the consultation prescribed in Article 16, each Member State has the option, for reasons pertaining to the state of its economy, to exclude investment goods partially or wholly from the system of deductions, or to apply in respect of such goods, the annual installment method of deductions (deductions pro rata temporis) in lieu of the method of immediate deductions.

24. Ad Article 11(3), third subparagraph

The Member States have the option to fix certain tolerances in order to limit the number of deduction adjustments in the event of a variation of the annual ratio in comparison with the initial ratio which served as the basis for the deduction with respect to investment goods.

25. Ad Article 12(2)

The invoice must indicate, in a distinct manner, the price exclusive of tax and the corresponding tax at each different rate, as well as, where appropriate, the exemption.

Each Member State may provide, in special cases, for deviations for this provision as well as from the obligation prescribed in Article 12(2). Such deviations, however, must be strictly limited.

Notwithstanding the other measures to be taken by the Member States to ensure payment of the tax and to prevent fraud, all persons, whether or not taxable persons, who indicate the tax on value added on an invoice, are obliged to pay the amount thereof.

26. Ad Article 12(3)

Each Member State has the option, for practical reasons, to shorten the period prescribed in Article 12(3) or authorize certain taxable persons to file the declaration for each quarter, half year or year.

In the course of the first six months of each year, a taxable person is to file, where appropriate, a declaration concerning all the transactions entered into during the preceding year which is to include all the facts necessary for possible adjustments.

For importations of goods, each Member State is to establish the procedures for the declaration and the payment of tax which must result therefrom.

27. Ad Article 14

To the extent that use is made of the provisions of this Article in respect of those transportation services referred to in Annex B, Point 5, they must be applied so that equality of treatment between the different means of transportation is ensured.

28. Ad Article 17, fourth hyphen

The valuation of inventories may be carried out in particular by reference to transactions effectuated by the taxable persons in the course of preceding years.

ANNEX B

List of the services referred to in Article 6(2)

1. Transfers of patents, trademarks and other similar rights, as well as the granting of licenses with regard to these rights;
2. Activities, other than those included under Article 5(2)(d), relating to tangible movable property which are executed on behalf of a taxable person;
3. Services directed to preparing or coördinating the execution of construction projects, as for example, services provided by architects and firms supervising such works;
4. Commercial publicity services;
5. The transportation of goods and the storage of goods, as well as accessory services;
6. The rental of tangible movable goods to a taxable person;
7. The providing of personnel to a taxable person;
8. Services provided by consultants, engineers, planning offices and similar services, in the technical, economic or scientific fields;
9. The discharge of an obligation not to practice, in whole or in part, a professional activity or exercise a right specified in the present list;
10. Services of forwarding agents, brokers, commercial agents and other independent intermediaries, in so far as they relate to deliveries or importations of goods or the rendering of services enumerated in the present list.

appendix B

Differential impact of certain tax alternatives on industries with various characteristics

This analysis compares some aspects of the impact on different types of industries of the following tax alternatives: a VAT; an increase in corporate income tax rates; elimination of the 7 percent investment credit and a reduction in the depreciation allowances on the corporate income tax; an increase in the capital gains taxes paid by individuals; a surcharge on the individual income tax; reducing deductions allowed on the individual income tax; higher payroll taxes; higher business property taxes; and higher residential property taxes. The paragraphs are numbered to correspond with the list of industry characteristics in Exhibits 5–1 through 5–10 in Chapter 5 of the text.

1. *Highly incorporated versus largely unincorporated industries.* Most taxes (the VAT, payroll taxes, property taxes) do not distinguish between corporations and unincorporated firms. However, the corporate income tax hits only corporations, while unincorporated firms are taxed under the individual income tax. To the extent that there are differences in the provisions or the rates of the two income taxes, then corporations may have some tax advantage (or disadvantage) over unincorporated firms. The profits of corporations are subject to a second level of taxation as they are distributed to stockholders as dividends or reflected in higher stock prices which subject stockholders to capital gains taxes when the stock is sold.

2. *Industries with varying debt/equity ratios.* The VAT, property taxes, payroll taxes, and personal income taxes are generally neutral toward industries with varying debt/equity ratios. On the other hand, the corporate income tax and the income tax that is levied on unincorporated firms favor companies with a high debt/equity ratio, since interest payments on debts are a deductible business expense that reduces a company's tax liability, while the profits earned by equity capital are subject to these taxes. Increasing the capital gains taxes paid by individuals also indirectly hurts industries with high equity capital. It is primarily equity capital which enjoys capital gains, and it is therefore primarily stockholders rather than

bondholders who would be hurt by heavier taxation of capital gains. If capital gains were taxed more heavily, not only would investment in stocks become less attractive to potential investors, but current stockholders would have fewer funds after taxes to make new investments. Increases in corporate income taxes also make investment in high-equity industries less attractive, since profits before interest and taxes would have to be proportionately higher to make the investment worthwhile.

3. *Industries with a high return on equity (or sales).* Highly profitable industries would be hit most heavily by increases in either the corporate income tax or the income tax paid by unincorporated firms, since both these taxes are levied on a company's profits and a company with no profits pays no income taxes. A less-profitable company may, in certain situations, be *helped* by an increase in business income taxes. To the extent that business income taxes are shifted, the resultant increase in prices not only relieves the profitable companies from the burden of the tax, but also enables marginal companies, paying relatively little income tax, to raise their prices to cover their higher costs. A shifted corporate income tax provides a sheltering "price umbrella" over less-efficient companies. The higher the corporate income tax rate, the higher and broader is the umbrella. Of course, if business income taxes are not fully shifted, even a marginal company might be hurt by an increase in its income taxes: The dollar amount of the tax increase might be small for the marginal company, but *any* increase might put a severe burden on its limited profits.

Increases in capital gains taxes or higher individual income taxes would indirectly have adverse effects on companies with a high return on equity. Increasing such taxes on investment earnings would make private investment in profitable companies less attractive. Therefore, to raise new equity capital such companies would have to sell stock at a reduced price.

Most other taxes are not affected by the profitability of a company. For example, a company's payroll taxes depend on the size and pay scale of its labor force, not the size of its profits. A company's VAT bill depends on the size of its "value added," which is the sum not only of its profits but also of its wages, rent, interest, and other such expenses. Higher profits increase a company's value added, but so also do higher wages. In any case, any VAT paid by a company is generally passed on to customers and usually does not impose a tax burden on the company itself.

In whatever way tax revenues are increased in the United States, a profitable industry is in a better position to cope with any market changes produced directly or indirectly by the new tax. A profitable enterprise can more easily temporarily absorb the higher tax or higher wages; it is less likely to be destroyed by any drop in sales. It has the funds to develop new products or new markets, if necessary, to adjust to any changes in the economy induced by the new tax.

4. *Capital-intensive versus labor-intensive industries.* Any tax on profits (the corporate income tax or the income tax levied on unincorporated firms) hits capital-intensive industries more than labor-intensive industries; for, by definition, a capital-intensive enterprise needs higher profits to provide an adequate return on the larger

capital investment it must have for a given volume of business. Business property taxes also fall more heavily on capital-intensive industries, since these industries are likely to have more fixed assets subject to the tax. However, a company's property tax depends not only on the value of its assets, but also on its location: A company with small assets but located in the city may have a bigger property tax bill than a company with more taxable assets located in a suburban or rural area. Payroll taxes, unlike business income taxes and property taxes, impose a heavier burden on labor-intensive industries. The VAT and taxes on individuals (income taxes, residential property taxes) are generally neutral between capital-intensive and labor-intensive industries.

Some taxes which do not change a company's tax bill may indirectly affect its operating costs. For example, any tax which stimulates demands for higher wages has its biggest impact on companies in labor-intensive industries. Wage increases are most likely to be triggered by imposing a VAT or increasing residential property taxes, for residential property taxes are included and the VAT is likely to be included in the cost-of-living index to which many wages are tied. Individual income taxes and the part of payroll taxes paid by employees are not included in the cost-of-living index, but increases in these taxes are nevertheless likely to stimulate demands for higher wages. Any increase in a company's taxes (corporate income taxes, business property taxes, the part of payroll taxes paid by the employer) may be shifted to the consumer in the form of higher prices, and these higher prices will eventually arouse demands for higher wages. In the long run, then, *any* tax increase may lead to higher wages that would particularly affect labor-intensive industries, but the VAT and residential property taxes are likely to have the most immediate effect on wage demands.

Since capital goods are generally not produced in labor-intensive industries, wage increases might not cause such large price increases for capital goods as for other goods and services. Thus any tax change which triggers wage increases might give capital-intensive industries a dual advantage: The cost of their capital purchases might not rise as rapidly as other costs, and higher wage bills would have less impact on them than on labor-intensive industries. On the other hand, capital-intensive industries would be hit twice by any increase in the corporate income tax: Not only would their tax bill be enlarged, but, to the extent that this tax is shifted, the cost of capital goods would rise sharply, since these goods are generally produced in companies particularly affected by such a tax increase.

A consumption type VAT is sometimes regarded as giving an advantage to capital-intensive industries in that a credit is given for any VAT paid on capital purchases. However, this VAT provision does not, in fact, reduce the cost of capital goods; it simply eliminates any tax deterrent to capital investment.

5. *Industries with sizeable assets in land.* Obviously industries owning a great deal of land would be particularly affected by any increase in business property taxes. However, since property taxes vary so much from district to district, the size of a company's property tax bill may depend as much on the location as on

the value of property it owns. Increases in residential property taxes would hurt the housing industry but would not directly affect most businesses; however, any differences between districts in the rate at which residential property taxes increased might depress land values in some areas while boosting them in others.

Most other taxes are largely neutral between industries with large landholdings and those with other types of assets, but a few of the possible tax changes would have some impact on landowners. Increasing capital gains taxes would make investment in land less attractive since any profits derived from rising land values would be more heavily taxed than at present. If deductions for property taxes and mortgage interest were eliminated from the personal income tax, consumers would be less interested in buying land, and in some cases land values might fall even in nonresidential areas. On the other hand, simply increasing the rates of the individual income tax should not affect land values, nor should increases in payroll taxes or corporate income taxes. The VAT is usually not levied on the sale and leasing of land; but it also is, in effect, not levied on the sale and leasing of other types of assets (since a nonexempt company receives credit for any VAT paid on such transactions).

6. *Industries with sizeable assets in buildings.* The various tax changes would have much the same impact on industries owning many buildings as those with large land holdings. Increases in business property taxes would hurt both types of industries, and higher residential property taxes, if rising at different rates in different districts, might depress both land and building values in some areas and raise them in others. Higher residential property taxes would, of course, hurt both the housing industry and owners of rental housing. Increases in capital gains taxes would make investment in both land and buildings less attractive, but eliminating the individual income tax deductions for property taxes and mortgage interest is more likely to affect land values than building values in nonresidential areas. Such a change in the individual income tax would, of course, have a detrimental effect on the housing industry. Raising the rates of the individual income tax, the corporate income tax, or payroll taxes would not impose a heavier tax burden on industries owning many buildings than on industries with other types of assets.

Because buildings are constructed by labor-intensive companies, any tax change that triggered wage increases would have a particularly large impact on construction costs. The value of existing buildings as well as the cost of constructing new ones would rise.

The impact of a VAT on building owners would depend on the provisions ultimately written into the tax. If the VAT were imposed on the sale of newly constructed buildings but not on older buildings, older buildings would have a price advantage for two reasons: They would have no VAT included in their construction costs, and they would have been built before any VAT-triggered wage increases. This effect would be compounded if the VAT were not levied on the rental of industrial and commercial buildings: The VAT levied on the construction of such buildings would necessitate higher rents, but, without a VAT officially levied on business rentals, the tenants would receive no credit on their tax bill for the VAT cost hidden in the rent. Of course, with the passage of time, market forces would eliminate the price and rental differentials between pre- and post-VAT buildings, and owners of pre-VAT buildings would enjoy a windfall as their property rose in value.

7. *Industries with industry-wide labor bargaining or strong unions.* Any tax change that stimulates demands for higher wages may have its biggest impact on industries with industry-wide labor bargaining. Such industries are usually compelled to grant wage increases faster than industries whose labor unions have less muscle. Many capital-intensive industries, such as automobiles and steel, have strong unions; they, therefore, may be hurt more by wage increases than labor-intensive industries with a comparatively larger labor force but with weaker labor unions. Since the VAT will probably be included and residential property taxes are included in the cost-of-living index, they are the taxes which would immediately affect industries with escalator clauses in their wage contracts and would quickly trigger wage demands in other industries with industry-wide labor bargaining. However, other taxes paid by individuals (for example, the income tax, payroll taxes) are also likely to arouse union demands for higher wages even though these taxes are not included in the cost-of-living index.

8. *Industries making purchases from diversified sources.* If a tax change causes differential price increases, then industries with alternative sources of supply might be able to make substitute purchases to take advantage of the differences in the price hikes. This would be of particular importance with taxes that impose a heavier burden on some types of industries than on others: the corporate income tax, the income tax on unincorporated firms, business property taxes, and payroll taxes. Having diversified sources would be of less advantage with taxes that are relatively neutral toward various types of companies: the VAT and the individual income tax. Even with these taxes, however, differential price increases might occur, largely because of the wage demands such taxes may stimulate. Higher residential property taxes might perhaps trigger varying price increases, in part because such taxes may affect land values even in nonresidential areas, but mostly because the rates of these taxes vary so much from district to district and may, therefore, have a differential impact on the economy, wages, and the availability of labor in the various districts.

9. *Industries with a high import cost component.* Any tax change that caused domestic prices to rise would make imports comparatively cheaper than domestic goods. This would give a relative advantage to industries which were heavy purchasers of imports. Since *any* tax increase may lead ultimately to higher prices, any change in the present U.S. tax structure could give a competitive advantage to heavy purchasers of imports—assuming, of course, that the countries providing the imports were not suffering a similar inflation.

Initially, however, a VAT would be neutral in impact between industries purchasing domestic goods and those purchasing imports, for an equal VAT would be levied on both types of goods. Other taxes levied on individuals rather than businesses (the individual income tax, residential property taxes, and that part of the payroll tax levied on employees) would not affect prices immediately, and even business taxes (the corporate income tax, the income tax levied on unincorporated firms, and business property taxes) would increase prices only over a period of time, for, even if these taxes are fully shifted, the shifting is likely to be gradual and uneven. Higher payroll taxes would probably cause the most immediate price differentials between domestic and imported goods, for it seems likely that these taxes are shifted as rapidly as wage increases are. But all of these various tax changes may, in time, induce price increases or wage increases, either of which may trigger an inflationary spiral and therefore make imports comparatively cheaper than domestic goods.

10. *Industries with high elasticity in the demand for their product.* Some products whose prices rise because of a tax change may suffer reduced sales, while the sales of other products, enjoying relatively inelastic demand, would be affected less by such price increases. Since the VAT is usually shifted forward at once, it is the tax which causes the most immediate price increases. In the short run, then, the VAT is perhaps the tax which would dampen most the sales of products with elastic demand. This effect would be compounded by the fact that a VAT tends to impose a greater burden on lower-income groups who generally spend a higher proportion of their income. Payroll taxes probably are shifted forward quite rapidly, too, and would therefore soon discourage the sales of products with elastic demand. Other business taxes (the corporate income tax, the income tax paid by unincorporated firms, business property taxes) may be shifted to the consumer and thus cause prices to rise, but any shifting is likely to be gradual and uneven.

Taxes on individuals (income taxes, residential property taxes, the part of payroll taxes paid by employees) affect sales in a different way: They reduce consumers' disposable income and therefore shrink consumer purchases, particularly for products with elastic demand. The nature of the tax increase may affect the impact on consumer spending: An increase which particularly hit high-income groups (for example, taxing capital gains fully or reducing certain of the deductions allowed on the income tax) might hurt consumer demand less than increases which affected all income groups (levying a surcharge on the income tax, raising payroll taxes, or raising residential property taxes). On the other hand, increases which affected primarily upper-income groups might particularly hurt sales of "luxuries." Increasing residential property taxes or eliminating the income tax deductions for mortgage interest and property taxes would have its biggest impact on housing sales, but other changes in the taxes paid by individuals would have a more generalized effect on sales.

Increasing most taxes on individuals, particularly the income tax and payroll taxes, reduces disposable income as soon as the tax increase goes into effect. Thus, like a VAT, such tax increases are likely to dampen consumer sales quite rapidly. On the other hand, direct taxes levied on business do not immediately affect disposable income: If shifted in the form of higher prices, they reduce *real* income, but the effect of business taxes on prices and sales is likely to be more subtle and indirect.

One change in business' direct taxes, however, would probably have an immediate effect on sales of capital goods: Elimination of 7 percent investment credit or reduction of depreciation allowances would remove some of business' incentive to make capital purchases. Taxing fully the capital gains of individuals might also diminish sales of capital goods, for such a tax change would reduce the funds available from investors (and the incentive to invest).

Although all these tax changes may dampen the sales of certain goods, they may boost the sales of other goods because of the rise in government spending made possible by the tax change.

11. *Industries with high product substitutability (high cross-elasticity).* Tax changes may affect customers' purchasing habits in either of two ways. Customers, unhappy about either higher prices or reduced disposable income caused by a tax change, may try to economize by buying cheaper products, where substitution is feasible. This can happen even if the price increases are general throughout the economy, as they would be with a VAT.

Secondly, if a tax change leads to differential price increases, it may encourage customers to switch from products hard hit by the tax change to products less affected by the tax. The corporate income tax, the income tax paid by unincorporated firms, business property taxes, and payroll taxes all impose a heavier tax burden on some types of industries than others, and therefore tend to cause differential price increases if the taxes are shifted forward. If residential property taxes increase at different rates in different areas, wages may rise unevenly as workers try to recoup their higher tax payments by demanding wage increases. In some cases this may lead to differential price increases in competing products. Such differential price increases are likely to affect purchasing patterns and therefore the sales of certain goods.

Any tax change which reduced the incentive of business to invest, or the funds available for investment, might make it more difficult for a company to improve its product vis-à-vis possible substitute products. Of course, if the industries producing the alternative products were equally affected by the tax change, there would be no change in the competitive positions of the various products. Any direct tax on business, unless fully shifted, would reduce profits and, presumably, the retained earnings available for investment. However, of all the possible changes in the direct taxes on business, the one which would most discourage investment in product improvement would be the elimination of the investment credit and the reduction in depreciation allowances.

12. *Industries with intense price competition.* Industries with intense price competition (because of such factors as excess capacity in relation to demand) would be particularly affected by the VAT, because such industries might have difficulty shifting this tax to their customers as, in theory, they should. Industries

with intense price competition thus might end up with a tax cost which other businesses did not have. Such industries would also have greater difficulty shifting forward those taxes that are designed to be taxes on business (such as the corporate income tax, payroll taxes, and business property taxes) but that are probably shifted forward, at least in part, by many businesses. Increasing taxes directly or indirectly imposed on individuals would reduce consumer demand and might, therefore, depress prices in an industry already suffering from greater than usual price competition. Of course, if the tax-induced drop in consumer demand is fully compensated for by higher government spending, the demand for certain products—even those produced in industries with intense price competition—might be unchanged or even rise.

One tax change would be to the advantage of an industry with such price competition that it operated at a loss or with negligible profits: a higher corporate income tax. A loss industry would not be affected immediately by an increase in this tax and, if the tax were shifted, would not need to raise its prices as much as high-profit industries.

A tax change which had a differential impact on various types of companies might make it more difficult for one type of company to compete with other types of companies in the same industry. For example, higher payroll taxes would make it more difficult for small, labor-intensive companies to compete with the big, capital-intensive companies in the same industry. Higher corporate taxes, on the other hand, would give a competitive advantage to labor-intensive, unincorporated companies. Higher property taxes on either business or residences would hurt companies in areas where these taxes rose more steeply than in other areas. The VAT and the private individual's income tax, which are comparatively neutral toward business, would be less likely to affect the relative competitive position of companies in the same industry.[1] However, even these two taxes tend to push wages up, and this may hurt one company more than another.

13. *Industries with diversified markets.* If a tax change causes sales of some products to fall, either because of price increases or a decline in disposable income, companies with diversified markets may be better able to compensate for any shrinking sales by promoting sales of other types or in other areas which are less affected by the tax change or which are benefiting from higher government expenditures. Having diversified markets is an advantage to a company no matter what change is made in the U.S. tax structure. For this reason, any tax is likely to stimulate horizontal integration of companies.

14. *Producers of capital goods.* Increases in most business taxes would discourage investment in capital goods. If the taxes were not fully shifted, companies would have smaller profits and presumably smaller retained earnings to invest in capital equipment. Fewer capital investments would be worthwhile if taxes reduced net profits, for, to be attractive, pretax returns on an investment would have to be

---

[1] It should be recalled, however, that unincorporated firms are taxed through individual income tax, and any increase in this tax penalizes such firms vis-à-vis corporations.

greater. Higher tax rates on corporate profits certainly discourage capital invest-ment. The reduction in the incentive to invest would be even greater if the corporate income tax were modified to eliminate the 7 percent investment credit and the new depreciation allowances. Where business property taxes are levied on capital assets, raising these taxes would also discourage the purchase of capital goods.

On the other hand, any tax increase that pushed up labor costs might prompt companies to invest in labor-saving equipment and thus promote the sale of capital goods. Increases in payroll taxes immediately raise a company's labor costs and thus provide a strong incentive for capital investment. Increasing almost any tax paid directly or indirectly by individuals might, in time, lead to demands for higher wages and thus create pressure to cut labor costs by purchasing capital goods.

In general, then, increasing business taxes other than the payroll tax would dis-courage capital investment, while levying higher taxes on individuals either directly (income tax) or indirectly (VAT) might eventually promote investment in labor-saving equipment. A consumption type VAT, with its provision for credits for any VAT paid on capital purchases, ensures that there is no tax deterrent to capital investment and might, in fact, have the psychological effect of encouraging the purchase of capital goods.

One tax imposed on individuals, however, would discourage capital investment if it were increased: the capital gains tax. Increasing this tax would have little effect on wage demands but would decrease both the personal funds available for invest-ment and the incentive for investments made with the expectation of capital gains. This reduction in investment funds would in turn tend to reduce purchases of capital goods.

Even those taxes on individuals which encourage investment in labor-saving equipment would discourage business expansion and the purchase of capital goods if the tax-induced drop in consumer demand were not fully compensated for by higher government spending. In those situations where a tax change did not affect total sales of capital goods, the nature and location of capital purchases might change, nevertheless, because of the shift from private to public spending and changes in market forces fostered by the tax.

15. *Industries with large exports.* Most tax changes which lead directly or indirectly to higher prices will make it harder for American companies to sell their goods abroad. Initially a VAT would not affect the selling prices of export goods, since this tax is fully rebated on such goods. However, the prices of all other goods would generally rise by at least the amount of the VAT, and this in turn would stimu-late demands for higher wages. Higher wages would increase the cost of producing export goods, and eventually the price of export goods would probably rise despite the VAT rebate given such goods. Increasing any other tax paid by individuals would have much the same effect: Initially, export prices would not change, but, if the tax increase led to demands for higher wages, export prices would eventually rise.

Increasing any business tax would have a more direct effect on export prices:

To the extent that the tax were shifted, export prices would rise, unless, of course, a company elected to shift the higher tax solely onto its product sold within the country. Since at present the big exporters in this country are generally affected more by the corporate income tax than other business taxes, a rise in the corporate income tax would be more likely to affect export prices (and sales) than increases in payroll taxes or business property taxes.

If any of these higher business taxes were not shifted fully, companies would have smaller retained earnings to invest in either product improvement or cost reduction. As a consequence, U.S. goods might eventually become less competitive on the international market, and sales might fall even if export prices did not change. Increasing one tax paid by individuals might have a similar effect: Higher capital gains taxes might reduce funds available for business investment in product improvement.

16. *Industries competing with imports.* The various tax changes would affect industries competing with imports in much the same way as they would affect industries with large exports. Any tax change that increased prices would make U.S. goods less able to compete with products of other countries. Initially any tax paid directly or indirectly by individuals would not impede the ability of U.S. companies to compete with imports. An equal VAT would be levied on both domestic goods and imports. Increases in the individual income tax or residential property taxes, in the short term, would change the prices of neither domestic goods nor imports. However, all of these taxes might, in time, lead to higher wages, and put domestic goods at a competitive disadvantage vis-à-vis imports.

Increases in the taxes paid directly by business would have a more immediate impact on industries competing with imports: If such taxes were shifted, the prices of domestic goods would rise faster than import prices. If these taxes were not fully shifted, companies would have lower retained earnings to invest in improvements to make their products more salable. Higher capital gains taxes on individuals also would be likely to reduce the private funds available for investment by business in product improvement.

appendix C

Selected bibliography

VALUE ADDED TAXATION

Aaron, Henry. "The Differential Price Effects of a Value Added Tax." *National Tax Journal,* June 1968, pp. 162–75.

Advisory Commission on Intergovernmental Relations. "Essential Ingredients of a Plan to Substitute a Federal Value-Added Tax for Residential School Property Taxes." Washington, D.C., February 9, 1972.

Bacon, Donald W. "Administrative and Compliance Procedures Under a Value Added Tax." Paper presented at the Tax Institute of America Symposium, Raleigh, N.C., November 16, 1972.

*Bauer, David. "A U.S. Value-Added Tax?" *Conference Board Record,* April 1971, pp. 29–32.

Berglas, Eitan. "The Effect of the Public Sector on the Base of the Value Added Tax." *National Tax Journal,* December 1971, pp. 459–64.

Bogan, Eugene. "A Federal Tax on Value Added — What's Wrong with It? Plenty!" *Taxes — The Tax Magazine,* October 1971, pp. 600–619.

Cambridge Research Institute. *The Value-Added Tax in the United States — It's Implications for Retailers.* Cambridge, 1970.

Commerce and Industry Association of New York, Inc. *Value Added Tax: A Business View,* New York, 1970.

Due, John F. "The Value-Added Tax." *Western Economic Journal,* Spring 1965, pp. 165–71.

Ebel, Robert D. *The Michigan Business Activities Tax.* East Lansing: Michigan State University, 1972.

Ebel, Robert D.; Papke, James A.; and Krannert, Herman C. "A Closer Look at the Value-Added Tax: Propositions and Implications." *1967 Proceedings of the Sixtieth Annual Conference on Taxation.* Sacramento: National Tax Association, 1967, pp. 155–70.

Fowlkes, Frank. "Administration Leans to Value-Added Tax to Help Solve National Fiscal Crises." *National Journal,* February 5, 1972, pp. 210–11.

*Harriss, C. Lowell. "Value-Added Taxation." *Columbia Journal of World Business,* July 1971, pp. 78–86.

---

* Article or book particularly useful for this study.

Insley, Gordon. "The Value Added Tax and Financial Institutions." Paper presented at the Tax Institute of America Symposium, Raleigh, N.C., November 16, 1972.

*Johnson, Harry, and Krauss, Mel. "Border Taxes, Border Tax Adjustments, Comparative Advantages, and the Balance of Payments." *Canadian Journal of Economics,* November 1970, pp. 595–602.

Jones, Sidney L. "The Value Added Tax." *Michigan Business Review,* July 1972, pp. 8–13.

Krauss, Mel, and Bird, Richard M. "The Value Added Tax: Critique of a Review." *Journal of Economic Literature,* December 1971, pp. 1167–73.

*Lindholm, Richard W. "Integrating a Federal Value Added Tax with State and Local Sales Levies." *National Tax Journal,* September 1971, pp. 403–11.

*_____. "Taxing Retailing and Service with the Value Added Tax." *Conference Board Record,* February 1972, pp. 17–20.

_____. "Toward a New Philosophy of Taxation." *The Morgan Guaranty Survey,* January 1972, pp. 3–8.

_____. "The Value Added Tax: Rejoinder to a Critique." *Journal of Economic Literature,* December 1971, pp. 1173–79.

_____. "The Value Added Tax: A Short Review of the Literature." *Journal of Economic Literature,* December 1970, pp. 1178–89.

*_____. "Value Added Tax vs. Corporation Income Tax." *Business Economics,* January 1970, pp. 62–65.

Maital, Shlomo, and Shlomo, Krevinsky. "Shifting Parameters and the Value Added Tax: A Note." *National Tax Journal,* June 1970, pp. 221–22.

Matthiasson, Björn. "The Value-Added Tax." *Finance and Development,* March 1970, pp. 40–46.

McClure, Charles E., Jr. "Taxes and the Balance of Payments: Another Alternative Analysis." *National Tax Journal,* March 1968, pp. 57–69.

_____. "The TVA and Fiscal Federalism." Mimeographed paper.

Missorten, Walter. "Some Problems in Implementing a Tax on Value Added." *National Tax Journal,* December 1968, pp. 396–411.

Musgrave, Richard A. "Problems of the Value-Added Tax." *National Tax Journal,* September 1972, pp. 425–30.

Nixon, President Richard. "State of the Union Message." Presented to members of the Second Session of the 92d Congress, January 20, 1972.

Nolan, John S. "Advantages of Value Added or Other Consumption Tax at the Federal Level." Remarks before the National Tax Association Seminar, Boston, Mass., April 13, 1972.

Oakland, William H. "The Theory of the Value-Added Tax: I. A. Comparison of Tax Bases." *National Tax Journal,* June 1967, pp. 119–36.

_____. "The Theory of the Value-Added Tax: II. Incidence Effects." *National Tax Journal,* September 1967, pp. 270–81.

Sanden, B. Kenneth. "The Value-Added Tax—Its Advantages and Disadvantages." *Tax Policy.* Tax Institute of America, Princeton, N.J., May–June 1972.

_____. "Value Added Tax: Substitute or New Source of Revenue?" *Tax Executive,* April 1972, pp. 168–74.

Shoup, Carl S. "Consumption Tax, and Wages Type and Consumption Type of Value-Added Tax." *National Tax Journal,* June 1968, pp. 153–61.

_____. "Theory and Background of the Value-Added Tax." *1955 Proceedings of the Forty-Eighth Annual Conference on Taxation.* Sacramento: National Tax Association, 1955, pp. 6–19.

*Smith, Dan Throop. "Value-Added Tax: The Case For." *Harvard Business Review,* November–December 1970, pp. 77–85.

*_____. "When – If – We Have the VAT." *Harvard Business Review,* January–February 1973.

Statham, Robert R. "The Value-Added Tax." Staff report to the Taxation Committee of the Chamber of Commerce of the United States, Washington, D.C., January 24, 1972.

Stoddard, William I. "Effect of a VAT on Service Industries." Paper presented to the Tax Institute of America Symposium, Raleigh, N.C., November 16, 1972.

*Sullivan, Clara K. *The Tax on Value Added.* New York: Columbia University Press, 1965.

Surrey, Stanley S. "A Value-Added Tax for the United States." Remarks to the National Association of Manufacturers, New York, December 6, 1968.

*_____. "Value-Added Tax: the Case Against." *Harvard Business Review,* November–December 1970, pp. 86–94.

"Tax Tag for Value Added." *Industry Week,* April 26, 1971, pp. 27–30.

Taxation with Representation. "Testimony prepared for the Executive Office of the President and the Department of the Treasury regarding the Value Added Tax." Arlington, Va., 1972.

Taxation with Representation. "The Value Added Tax: A Preliminary Analysis." Arlington, Va., 1972.

Ture, Norman B. "A Federal Value-Added Tax: Some Possibilities." Speech to the Taxation Committee, National Association of Manufacturers, New York, November 17, 1970.

*_____. "Economic Aspects of a United States VAT." Paper presented at the Tax Institute of America Symposium, Raleigh, N.C., November 15, 1972.

_____. "The Value Added Tax: The Basic Step Toward Tax Reform." Remarks to the 59th Annual Meeting of the Chamber of Commerce of the United States, Washington, D.C., April 27, 1971.

_____. "The Value Added Tax." Discussion presented to the Joint Economic Committee of the United States Congress, March 22, 1972.

Union Carbide Corporation. Statement to the Committee on Ways and Means, U.S. House of Representatives, June 27, 1968.

Wallich, Henry C. "The Brewing Interest in VAT." *Fortune,* April 1971, pp. 94ff.

Weinrobe, Maurice D. "Corporate Taxes and the United States Balance of Trade." *National Tax Journal,* March 1971, pp. 79–85.

VALUE ADDED TAXATION IN EUROPE

"Adoption of the First Two Directives on the Harmonization of Turnover Taxes Introducing a Common Value-Added System." *European Taxation,* February 1967, pp. 44–45.

"Belgium: Prices Go VAT." *The Economist,* January 2, 1971, p. 54.

*Chancellor of the Exchequer. *The Value Added Tax.* Green paper presented to Parliament, March 1971. London: Her Majesty's Stationery Office, 1971.

"Changing to TVA." *The OECD Observer,* February 1970, pp. 13–18.

Cohen, Hon. Edwin S. "Foreign Experience with a Value Added Tax."

National Tax Journal, September 1971, pp. 399–402.

Commission des Communautés Européennes. *Conséquences budgétaires, économiques et sociales de l'harmonisation des taux de la TVA dans la CEE.* Études No. 16. Brussels, 1970.

Commission of the European Communities. "Memorandum Concerning Border Tax Adjustments." Brussels, April 2, 1969.

"The Common System of Tax on Value-Added." *European Taxation,* July–August 1967, pp. 147–208.

Confederation of British Industry. "Budget Representations 1972."

———. "Report of the CBI Value Added Tax Working Party." September 1970.

European Communities. "The Value Added Tax in the European Community." Community Topics No. 36, July 1970.

European Free Trade Association. "General Considerations on Value Added Tax." Annex to EFTA 62/69, January 28, 1970.

Forte, Francesco. "On the Feasibility of a Truly General Value-Added Tax: Some Reflections on the French Experience." *National Tax Journal,* December 1966, pp. 337–61.

"France: Simplification of the TVA and Reduction of Certain Rates." *European Taxation,* January 1970, pp. I/26–I/30.

*International Bureau of Fiscal Documentation. *Value Added Taxation in Europe.* Amsterdam, The Netherlands, 1971.

Lindholm, Richard. "The Sophisticated Swedish Tax Policy." *California Management Review,* Fall 1972, pp. 75–58.

*"Luxembourg: Bill for the Introduction of a Turnover Tax on Value Added." *European Taxation,* June 1969, pp. 119–26.

*National Economic Development Office. *Value Added Tax.* London: Her Majesty's Stationery Office, 1971.

*"Netherlands: 1968 Bill to Introduce a Turnover Tax on Value Added." *European Taxation,* February 1968, pp. 30–46.

*Norr, Martin, and Hornhammer, Nils G. "The Value-Added Tax in Sweden." *Columbia Law Review,* March 1970, pp. 379–422.

*"Norway: Bill for the Introduction of a Turnover Tax on Value Added." *European Taxation,* June 1969, pp. 127–33.

Organization for Economic Cooperation and Development. *Border Tax Adjustments and Tax Structures in OECD Member Countries.* Paris, 1968.

*Organization for Economic Cooperation and Development, Fiscal Committee. "Report on the Taxation of Farmers and Small Traders under Value Added Tax Systems." Paris, March 29, 1971.

Organization for Economic Cooperation and Development. "Some Problems Concerning Value-Added Taxation." February 1970.

Price Waterhouse & Co. "The Value Added Tax in the United Kingdom." London, April 1972.

Rybczynski, T. M., ed. *The Value-Added Tax. The U.K. Postion and the European Experience.* Papers read at Business Economists' Group Conference Sponsored by the United Cominions Trust Ltd. Oxford: Basil Blackwell, 1969.

Sanden, B. Kenneth. "The Value-Added Tax—What It Is, How It Works—Experience in Foreign Countries." Paper delivered to Tax Institute of America Symposium, Raleigh, N.C., November 15, 1972.

*Shoup, Carl S. "Experience with the Value-Added Tax in Denmark and Prospects for Sweden." *Finanzarchiv,* March 1969, pp. 236–52.

"The Swedish Value Added Tax." *European Free Trade Association Bulletin,* June 1970, pp. 17–18.

*Tait, Alan A. *Value Added Tax,* London: McGraw-Hill, 1972.

Tax Foundation, Inc. "Tax Harmonization in Europe and U.S. Business." New York, August 1968.

*"The Turnover Tax on Value Added in Europe." *European Taxation,* November–December 1968, pp. 239–310.

"VAT is Coming." *The Economist,* September 4, 1971, pp. 54–55.

"VAT Went Right." *The Economist,* March 25, 1972, pp. 88–91.

THE U.S. TAX STRUCTURE

Bateman, J. Fred. "Taxes: Who Benefits and Who Pays?" *Business Horizons.* Indiana University Graduate School of Business, February 1972, pp. 51–62.

Cantor, Arnold. "Tax Justice: A Giant Step Backward." *The American Federationist,* January 1972, pp. 1–7.

*"The Coming Change in the Property Tax." *Business Week,* February 12, 1972, pp. 50–56.

First National City Bank. "Tax Reform, or Slamming a Revolving Door" and "Doesn't Anybody Love Property Taxes?" *Monthly Economic Letter,* May 1972, pp. 9–15.

Herriot, Roger A., and Miller, Herman P. "Tax Changes Among Income Groups – 1962–68." *Business Horizons.* Indiana University Graduate School of Business, February 1972, pp. 41–50.

Johnston, Kenneth S. *Corporations' Federal Income Tax Compliance Costs,* Bureau of Business Research Monograph No. 110. Columbus: Ohio State University, College of Commerce and Administration, 1943.

Morgan, Daniel C., Jr. *Retail Sales Tax: an Appraisal of New Issues.* Madison and Milwaukee: University of Wisconsin Press, 1964.

Musgrave, Richard A. *The Theory of Public Finance: a Study in Public Economy.* New York: McGraw-Hill, 1959.

New York State Commission on the Quality, Cost, and Financing of Elementary and Secondary Education. *Report,* New York, 1972.

Pechman, Joseph A. *Federal Tax Policy.* Washington, D.C.: The Brookings Institution, 1971.

*The President's Task Force on Business Taxation. *Business Taxation,* Washington, D.C.: U.S. Government Printing Office, September 1970.

The Role of Direct and Indirect Taxes in the Federal Revenue System. A conference report of the National Bureau of Economic Research and The Brookings Institution. Princeton: Princeton University Press, 1964.

*Schultze, Charles; Fried, Edward; Rivlin, Alice; and Teeters, Nancy. *Setting National Priorities: The 1973 Budget.* Washington, D.C., The Brookings Institute, 1972.

Shoup, Carl S. *Public Finance.* Chicago: Aldine Publishing, 1969.

Smith, Dan Throop. *Federal Tax Reform: the Issues and a Program.* New York: McGraw-Hill, 1961.

———. "High Progressive Tax Rates: Inequity and Immorality?" *University of Florida Law Review,* Spring 1968, pp. 451–63.

Smith, George Kline. *A Study of Tax Policy and Capital Formation.* New York: National Association of Manufacturers, 1969.

Tax Foundation, Inc. Project Note No. 48. *Retail Sales and Individual In-*

come *Taxes in State Tax Structures.* New York: Tax Foundation, Inc., 1962.

Tax Institute of America. *Alternatives to Present Federal Taxes.* Princeton: Tax Institute of America, 1964.

Weinstein, Bernard, and Mintz, Steven. "Some New Federal Revenue Sources for Education." *Planning and Changing,* July 1972, pp. 28–36.

*Yocum, James C. *Retailers' Costs of Sales Tax Collection in Ohio.* Bureau of Business Research Monograph No. 100. Columbus: Ohio State University, College of Commerce and Administration, 1961.

Young, John H. "Tax Reform—The Next Stage." *Tax Law Review,* Winter 1972, pp. 247–300.